FOR DUMMIES

BESTSELLING
BOOK SERIES

The iMac™ For Dummies,® 2nd Edition

Cheat Sheet

D1363859

What've You Got There?

To find out how much memory your iMac has and what system-software version, choose About This Computer from the menu (see Chapter 1). Write the answers down here.

Your iMac OS version _____

Built-in memory: _____

Surviving the First Half Hour

You may need this information only at the very beginning of your iMac career — but you'll *really* need it.

Turning on the iMac

Press the On/Off button. It's the round button at the upper-right corner of your keyboard (see Chapter 1).

Turning off the iMac

1. Save your work onto the hard drive by choosing Save from the File menu.
2. Press the round On/Off button on your keyboard.
3. In the dialog box that appears, click Shut Down.

Troubleshooting Keystrokes

The iMac is frozen, but the cursor moves: Press ⌘-Option-Esc and then click the Force Quit button. Save your work in each program; then restart the iMac. (Works about half the time. Other times, read on.)

The iMac has completely frozen: Restart by pressing the On button for six seconds. If that doesn't work, press the Restart button nestled on the iMac's right-side panel. On new iMacs, the Restart button is a tiny button bearing a left-pointing triangle. On older models, insert a straightened paper clip into the tiny, triangle-marked hole. If none of these steps work, unplug the iMac. Plug it back in and turn it on.

All icons appear blank: As the iMac starts up, hold down ⌘-Option. When asked to rebuild the desktop, click OK.

A weird problem keeps recurring: As the iMac starts up, press Shift until you see "Extensions Off." Only basic functions work now (no faxing, no Internet), but the iMac runs clean and pure. See Chapter 16 to finish the troubleshooting; this trick at least gets you into your iMac.

You're panicking: Call Apple's hotline: 800-500-7078.

...you create is represented by an icon and is usually stored inside an electronic folder, which looks like a file folder on your screen. Everyone sometimes misplaces a file. Here's what to do.

1. Choose Sherlock from the menu.
2. Type a few letters of the missing file's name.

   You don't have to type the whole name — only enough to distinguish it. Capitalization doesn't matter.

3. Press the Return key or click the Find button.

   The iMac roots through your files. When it shows you a list of all icons that match, click one (to see where it is) or double-click (to open it).

Renaming a file

1. Click an icon (once) and press Return.
2. Type a new name; then press Return.

A file's name can be up to 31 letters long. If you make a mistake, backspace by pressing the Delete key.

To insert a CD-ROM

Hold the CD by its edges (or the hole), label side up.

New iMacs: Insert one edge of the disc into the front-panel slot until the iMac slurps it inside.

Older iMacs: Does your iMac's front panel have a pushbutton just under the word "iMac"? Press this button to make the tray pop out an inch or so. Pull the tray out all the way. Gently snap the CD-ROM into the tray; push the tray shut.

Regardless of your iMac model, the CD icon now shows up on the screen.

Ejecting a CD or other disk ‹

Drag the disk's icon onto the Trash can. Or click the disk icon (once) and choose Eject Disk from the Special menu.

Copying a file onto a disk

You can't drag icons onto a CD. If you've bought a floppy drive, Zip drive, or other disk drive for your iMac, however, just drag any file's icon (below, left) onto the disk's icon (below, right) and let go.

For Dummies®: Bestselling Book Series for Beginners

The iMac™ For Dummies, 2nd Edition

BESTSELLING BOOK SERIES

What All These Little Controls Do

They call this box a *dialog box* because the iMac is asking questions it needs answered. Here are the elements of a typical dialog box.

Radio buttons

Named after the pushbuttons on a car radio, where only one can be pushed in at a time. Likewise, only one iMac radio button can be selected at a time.

Check boxes

Used to indicate whether an option is on or off. Click once to place the X in the box; click again to remove the X (and turn off the option).

Text fields

You're supposed to type into these blanks. To move from one blank to another, either click with the mouse or press the Tab key.

Pop-up menus

When you see this, you're seeing a *pop-up menu.* Point to the text, hold down the mouse button, and make a selection from the minimenu that drops down.

Buttons

Every dialog box has a clearly marked button or two (usually OK and Cancel) that make the box go away — your escape route.

Click OK (or Print, or Proceed, or whatever the button says) to proceed with the command you originally chose from the menu. Click Cancel if you want to back out of the dialog box, as though you'd never issued the command.

See the thick black outline around the Print button above? You don't have to use the mouse to click that button; you can press either the Return or Enter key on your keyboard instead.

Working with Several Programs

The iMac lets you run more than one program at once. If you keep launching programs, eventually you'll be told you're out of memory. Until then, here are some pointers.

Determining what programs are running

Put the cursor on the icon in the upper-right of your screen; hold down the mouse button. The *Application menu* drops down, listing all the programs you've launched. The frontmost one, the one you're working in now, is indicated by a check mark and is also named in the menu bar.

Quitting programs to free up memory

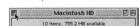

1. Use your Application menu, as illustrated above, to choose the program's name.
2. From the File menu, choose Quit.

Working with iMac Windows
Opening or closing a window

Every window was once an *icon* that you double-clicked to see what was inside.

1. Double-click any icon to open its window.
2. To get rid of a window, click the *close box* in the upper-left corner.

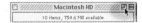

Bringing concealed icons into view

When a window is too small to show you everything within it, you'll see gray *scroll bars* along the bottom or right side.

1. Point to one of the small arrows on the scroll bar and press the mouse button continuously (below, left). Your view of the window slides in the direction of the arrow, showing you what's hidden beyond the edges (below, right).

2. To make the window as large as necessary to view all the icons, click the *zoom box.*

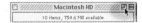

For Dummies®: Bestselling Book Series for Beginners

TM

References for the Rest of Us!®

BESTSELLING BOOK SERIES

Are you intimidated and confused by computers? Do you find that traditional manuals are overloaded with technical details you'll never use? Do your friends and family always call you to fix simple problems on their PCs? Then the ...*For Dummies*® computer book series from IDG Books Worldwide is for you.

...*For Dummies* books are written for those frustrated computer users who know they aren't really dumb but find that PC hardware, software, and indeed the unique vocabulary of computing make them feel helpless. ...*For Dummies* books use a lighthearted approach, a down-to-earth style, and even cartoons and humorous icons to dispel computer novices' fears and build their confidence. Lighthearted but not lightweight, these books are a perfect survival guide for anyone forced to use a computer.

> "I like my copy so much I told friends; now they bought copies."
> — Irene C., Orwell, Ohio

> "Quick, concise, nontechnical, and humorous."
> — Jay A., Elburn, Illinois

> "Thanks, I needed this book. Now I can sleep at night."
> — Robin F., British Columbia, Canada

Already, millions of satisfied readers agree. They have made ...*For Dummies* books the #1 introductory level computer book series and have written asking for more. So, if you're looking for the most fun and easy way to learn about computers, look to ...*For Dummies* books to give you a helping hand.

IDG
BOOKS
WORLDWIDE

The iMac™

FOR

DUMMIES®

2ND EDITION

The iMac™ FOR DUMMIES®
2ND EDITION

by David Pogue

IDG Books Worldwide, Inc.
An International Data Group Company

Foster City, CA ◆ Chicago, IL ◆ Indianapolis, IN ◆ New York, NY

The iMac™ For Dummies®, 2nd Edition

Published by
IDG Books Worldwide, Inc.
An International Data Group Company
919 E. Hillsdale Blvd.
Suite 400
Foster City, CA 94404
www.idgbooks.com (IDG Books Worldwide Web site)
www.dummies.com (Dummies Press Web site)

Library of Congress Catalog Card No.: 99-66470

ISBN: 0-7645-0648-X

Printed in the United States of America

10 9 8 7 6 5 4 3

2B/RX/RS/ZZ/IN

Distributed in the United States by IDG Books Worldwide, Inc.

Distributed by CDG Books Canada Inc. for Canada; by Transworld Publishers Limited in the United Kingdom; by IDG Norge Books for Norway; by IDG Sweden Books for Sweden; by IDG Books Australia Publishing Corporation Pty. Ltd. for Australia and New Zealand; by TransQuest Publishers Pte Ltd. for Singapore, Malaysia, Thailand, Indonesia, and Hong Kong; by Gotop Information Inc. for Taiwan; by ICG Muse, Inc. for Japan; by Intersoft for South Africa; by Eyrolles for France; by International Thomson Publishing for Germany, Austria and Switzerland; by Distribuidora Cuspide for Argentina; by LR International for Brazil; by Galileo Libros for Chile; by Ediciones ZETA S.C.R. Ltda. for Peru; by WS Computer Publishing Corporation, Inc., for the Philippines; by Contemporanea de Ediciones for Venezuela; by Express Computer Distributors for the Caribbean and West Indies; by Micronesia Media Distributor, Inc. for Micronesia; by Chips Computadoras S.A. de C.V. for Mexico; by Editorial Norma de Panama S.A. for Panama; by American Bookshops for Finland.

For general information on IDG Books Worldwide's books in the U.S., please call our Consumer Customer Service department at 800-762-2974. For reseller information, including discounts and premium sales, please call our Reseller Customer Service department at 800-434-3422.

For information on where to purchase IDG Books Worldwide's books outside the U.S., please contact our International Sales department at 317-596-5530 or fax 317-596-5692.

For consumer information on foreign language translations, please contact our Customer Service department at 1-800-434-3422, fax 317-596-5692, or e-mail rights@idgbooks.com.

For information on licensing foreign or domestic rights, please phone +1-650-655-3109.

For sales inquiries and special prices for bulk quantities, please contact our Sales department at 650-655-3200 or write to the address above.

For information on using IDG Books Worldwide's books in the classroom or for ordering examination copies, please contact our Educational Sales department at 800-434-2086 or fax 317-596-5499.

For press review copies, author interviews, or other publicity information, please contact our Public Relations department at 650-655-3000 or fax 650-655-3299.

For authorization to photocopy items for corporate, personal, or educational use, please contact Copyright Clearance Center, 222 Rosewood Drive, Danvers, MA 01923, or fax 978-750-4470.

is a registered trademark under exclusive license to IDG Books Worldwide, Inc. from International Data Group, Inc.

About the Author

Ohio-bred **David Pogue** never touched a computer — nor wanted to — until Apple Computer suckered him into it by selling Macs half-price at Yale, from which he graduated *summa cum laude* in 1985. Since then, Pogue has merged his two loves — the musical theatre and Macs — in every way he could dream up: by spending ten years in New York as a Broadway theatre conductor; writing manuals for music programs like Finale; and becoming the Mac guru to every Broadway and Hollywood creative-type he could get his hands on — Mia Farrow, Carly Simon, Mike Nichols, Stephen Sondheim, Gary Oldman, Harry Connick, Jr., and others.

In his other life, Pogue writes the award-winning, back-page column, "The Desktop Critic," for *Macworld* magazine. His résumé also boasts some *real* accomplishments, like winning the Ohio spelling bee in seventh grade, being the only nonlawyer in three generations, and getting a Viewer Mail letter read on David Letterman.

With his madly adored wife Jennifer, son Kelly, daughter Tia, and Bullwinkle the Wonderdog, he lives in Connecticut, where he does magic tricks and plays the piano. The family photos lurk on the World Wide Web at *www. davidpogue.com.*

Also by David Pogue:

Macs For Dummies
MORE Macs For Dummies
The iBook For Dummies
Macworld Mac Secrets (with Joseph Schorr)
Magic For Dummies
Classical Music For Dummies (with Scott Speck)
Opera For Dummies (with Scott Speck)
PalmPilot: The Ultimate Guide
Hard Drive (a novel)
The Microsloth Joke Book
The Great Macintosh Easter Egg Hunt
Tales from the Tech Line
The Weird Wide Web (with Erfert Fenton)

ABOUT IDG BOOKS WORLDWIDE

Welcome to the world of IDG Books Worldwide.

IDG Books Worldwide, Inc., is a subsidiary of International Data Group, the world's largest publisher of computer-related information and the leading global provider of information services on information technology. IDG was founded more than 30 years ago by Patrick J. McGovern and now employs more than 9,000 people worldwide. IDG publishes more than 290 computer publications in over 75 countries. More than 90 million people read one or more IDG publications each month.

Launched in 1990, IDG Books Worldwide is today the #1 publisher of best-selling computer books in the United States. We are proud to have received eight awards from the Computer Press Association in recognition of editorial excellence and three from Computer Currents' First Annual Readers' Choice Awards. Our best-selling *...For Dummies®* series has more than 50 million copies in print with translations in 31 languages. IDG Books Worldwide, through a joint venture with IDG's Hi-Tech Beijing, became the first U.S. publisher to publish a computer book in the People's Republic of China. In record time, IDG Books Worldwide has become the first choice for millions of readers around the world who want to learn how to better manage their businesses.

Our mission is simple: Every one of our books is designed to bring extra value and skill-building instructions to the reader. Our books are written by experts who understand and care about our readers. The knowledge base of our editorial staff comes from years of experience in publishing, education, and journalism — experience we use to produce books to carry us into the new millennium. In short, we care about books, so we attract the best people. We devote special attention to details such as audience, interior design, use of icons, and illustrations. And because we use an efficient process of authoring, editing, and desktop publishing our books electronically, we can spend more time ensuring superior content and less time on the technicalities of making books.

You can count on our commitment to deliver high-quality books at competitive prices on topics you want to read about. At IDG Books Worldwide, we continue in the IDG tradition of delivering quality for more than 30 years. You'll find no better book on a subject than one from IDG Books Worldwide.

John Kilcullen
Chairman and CEO
IDG Books Worldwide, Inc.

Steven Berkowitz
President and Publisher
IDG Books Worldwide, Inc.

Eighth Annual Computer Press Awards ≥ 1992

Ninth Annual Computer Press Awards ≥ 1993

Tenth Annual Computer Press Awards ≥ 1994

Eleventh Annual Computer Press Awards ≥ 1995

IDG is the world's leading IT media, research and exposition company. Founded in 1964, IDG had 1997 revenues of $2.05 billion and has more than 9,000 employees worldwide. IDG offers the widest range of media options that reach IT buyers in 75 countries representing 95% of worldwide IT spending. IDG's diverse product and services portfolio spans six key areas including print publishing, online publishing, expositions and conferences, market research, education and training, and global marketing services. More than 90 million people read one or more of IDG's 290 magazines and newspapers, including IDG's leading global brands — Computerworld, PC World, Network World, Macworld and the Channel World family of publications. IDG Books Worldwide is one of the fastest-growing computer book publishers in the world, with more than 700 titles in 36 languages. The "...For Dummies®" series alone has more than 50 million copies in print. IDG offers online users the largest network of technology-specific Web sites around the world through IDG.net (http://www.idg.net), which comprises more than 225 targeted Web sites in 55 countries worldwide. International Data Corporation (IDC) is the world's largest provider of information technology data, analysis and consulting, with research centers in over 41 countries and more than 400 research analysts worldwide. IDG World Expo is a leading producer of more than 168 globally branded conferences and expositions in 35 countries including E3 (Electronic Entertainment Expo), Macworld Expo, ComNet, Windows World Expo, ICE (Internet Commerce Expo), Agenda, DEMO, and Spotlight. IDG's training subsidiary, ExecuTrain, is the world's largest computer training company, with more than 230 locations worldwide and 785 training courses. IDG Marketing Services helps industry-leading IT companies build international brand recognition by developing global integrated marketing programs via IDG's print, online and exposition products worldwide. Further information about the company can be found at www.idg.com.   1/24/99

Author's Acknowledgments

This book was made possible by the enthusiasm and support of IDG Books Worldwide's John Kilcullen; Project Editor Mary Goodwin; Acquisitions Manager Mike Roney; and everyone else in the sprawling universe of IDG Books voicemail.

Thanks, too, to technical editor Tim Warner. And a tip 'o' the mouse to Apple's cofounder Steve Jobs and his chief designer Jonathan Ive. Their vision and refusal to compromise produced the glorious, smash-hit, see-through computer called the iMac.

Above all, my gratitude and love go to the lovely Jennifer, Kelly, and Tia, who stood by me (or crawled by me, as the case may be) during the writing of this book.

The David Pogue Pledge

As in all my Macintosh books, I make the following guarantee:

1. I will reply to every reader e-mail. My address is *david@pogueman.com*. (I'll respond cheerfully to messages that pertain to the material *in this book*. If you ask me for technical help on other topics, I'm afraid I can only refer you to the list of self-help sources in Chapter 17.)

2. I will not use trendoid terms in my writing: *the user* when I mean you; *price point* when I mean price; *performance* when I mean speed; and so on.

3. I will never put an apostrophe in the possessive word *its*.

4. I will post, on my Web page (*www.davidpogue.com*), any corrections and updates to this book that may surface.

Publisher's Acknowledgments

We're proud of this book; please register your comments through our IDG Books Worldwide Online Registration Form located at http://my2cents.dummies.com.

Some of the people who helped bring this book to market include the following:

Acquisitions, Editorial, and Media Development

Project Editor: Mary Goodwin

Acquisitions Editor: Mike Roney

Technical Editor: Tim Warner

Editorial Manager: Leah Cameron

Editorial Assistant: Constance Carlisle

Production

Project Coordinator: E. Shawn Aylsworth

Layout and Graphics: Angela F. Hunckler, Tracy Oliver, Brent Savage, Brian Torwelle, Maggie Ubertini, Dan Whetstine

Proofreaders: Laura Albert, Corey Bowen, Rachel Garvey, John Greenough, Charles Spencer

Indexer: Sharon Hilgenberg

Special Help
Amanda Foxworth

General and Administrative

IDG Books Worldwide, Inc.: John Kilcullen, CEO; Steven Berkowitz, President and Publisher

IDG Books Technology Publishing Group: Richard Swadley, Senior Vice President and Publisher; Walter Bruce III, Vice President and Associate Publisher; Joseph Wikert, Associate Publisher; Mary Bednarek, Branded Product Development Director; Mary Corder, Editorial Director; Barry Pruett, Publishing Manager; Michelle Baxter, Publishing Manager

IDG Books Consumer Publishing Group: Roland Elgey, Senior Vice President and Publisher; Kathleen A. Welton, Vice President and Publisher; Kevin Thornton, Acquisitions Manager; Kristin A. Cocks, Editorial Director

IDG Books Internet Publishing Group: Brenda McLaughlin, Senior Vice President and Publisher; Diane Graves Steele, Vice President and Associate Publisher; Sofia Marchant, Online Marketing Manager

IDG Books Production for Dummies Press: Debbie Stailey, Associate Director of Production; Cindy L. Phipps, Manager of Project Coordination, Production Proofreading, and Indexing; Tony Augsburger, Manager of Prepress, Reprints, and Systems; Laura Carpenter, Production Control Manager; Shelley Lea, Supervisor of Graphics and Design; Debbie J. Gates, Production Systems Specialist; Robert Springer, Supervisor of Proofreading; Kathie Schutte, Production Supervisor

Dummies Packaging and Book Design: Patty Page, Manager, Promotions Marketing

◆

The publisher would like to give special thanks to Patrick J. McGovern, without whom this book would not have been possible.

◆

Contents at a Glance

Cartoons at a Glance

By Rich Tennant

page 343

page 305

page 153

page 5

page 105

page 265

page 363

Fax: 978-546-7747
E-mail: richtennant@the5thwave.com
World Wide Web: www.the5thwave.com

Table of Contents

Introduction

<img>...</img>

*I*f you bought an iMac, you're unbelievably smart (or lucky). You've neatly eliminated most of the hassle, frustration, and annoyance that normally comes with buying a computer. You've saved an incredible amount of money, while still getting a fast, state-of-the-art machine; and you've significantly enhanced your office décor. (Especially if your wallpaper is Grape, Lime, Tangerine, Blueberry, Strawberry, Graphite, or Original Blue-Green.)

That's not just PR baloney, either; the iMac truly is a dramatically different machine. For example, on an iMac, cables emerge from the *side* of the computer, where you can get at them. Why did it take 20 years for the computer industry to realize that the *back* of a computer is the *least* convenient spot for connections?

The iMac also has everything you need built in: a modem (so you can use the Internet and e-mail), a CD-ROM (so you can easily install new programs), and a glorious color screen (so you don't have to set up your own). Selling a complete computer in one handy bundle isn't a new idea — but rarely has it all worked together so smoothly. And, of course, never before has all of this good stuff come in a futuristic-looking case that you can move from room to room without calling a bunch of friends over to help.

In short, the iMac is the gadget that comes closest to fulfilling the vision of Apple founder Steve Jobs: to make a personal computer that's simply another appliance. You don't have to buy memory upgrades for your TV, do you? You don't have to hire a consultant to install your toaster oven, right? So why should computers be any more complicated?

Who Needs an iMac Book?

If the iMac is so simple, then who needs a book about it?

Well, despite all the free goodies you get with the iMac, a *manual* isn't among them. You need somewhere to turn when things go wrong, when you'd like to know what the add-on software does, or when you want to stumble onto the Internet for the first time.

By the way, of *course* you're not a dummy. Two pieces of evidence tell me so: for one thing, you're learning the iMac, and for another, you're reading this book! But I've taught hundreds of people how to use their Macs, and an awful lot of them start out saying they *feel* like dummies when it comes to computers. Society surrounds us with fast-talking teenagers who grew up learning English from their Nintendo sets; no wonder the rest of us sometimes feel left out.

But you're no more a dummy for not knowing the iMac than you were before you knew how to drive. Learning a Macintosh is like learning to drive: After a lesson or two, you can go anywhere your heart desires.

So when we say *Dummies,* we're saying it with an affectionate wink. Still, if the cover bothers you even a little — I'll admit it, you wouldn't be the first — please rip it right off. The inner cover, we hope, will make you proud to have the book out on your desk.

How to Use This Book (Other Than as a Mouse Pad)

If you're starting from the very, *very* beginning, read this book from the end — start with Appendix A, where you can find an idiot-proof guide to setting up your computer.

Otherwise, start with the very basics in Chapter 1; turn to Chapter 15 in times of trouble; and consult the other chapters as the spirit moves you.

The book winds down with Appendix B, which contains contact info for a number of important Mac companies and publications, and Appendix C, a sampler of cool add-on products that fit the iMac's special USB connectors.

Macintosh conventions

Macintosh conventions? Sure. They're called Macworld Expos, and there's one in Boston and one in San Francisco each year.

Conventions in this book

Oh, *that* kind of convention.

So that we'll be eligible for some of the more prestigious book-design awards, I've marked some topics with these icons:

Nerdy stuff that's okay to skip but will fascinate the kind of people who read Tom Clancy novels.

The Macintosh is the greatest computer on earth, but it's still a computer. Now and then it does unexplainable stuff, which I'll explain.

A shortcut so you can show off.

Denotes an actual You-Try-It Experience. Hold the book open with a nearby cinder block, put your hands on the computer, and do as I say.

A few new, cool things about Mac OS 9 and later. (See Chapter 1 to find out what Mac OS 9 is.)

Apple and obsolescence

One more thing before you delve in: Apple is the gigantic Silicon Valley computer company that started out as a couple of grungy teenagers in a garage. Each time Apple introduces a new iMac model, it's faster, more powerful, and less expensive than the model *you* already bought. People love Apple for coming up with such great products — but they also feel cheated at having paid so much for a suddenly outdated machine.

Feel whatever you want, of course. But if you're going to buy a computer, accept the fact that your investment is going to devalue faster than real estate in Chernobyl.

Here's a promise: No matter how carefully you shop or how good a deal you got on your iMac today, it will be replaced by a less expensive or souped-up version within a year. (It'll still *work* just fine, and be more or less up-to-date, for about five years.)

With that quick and inevitable computer death looming, how can people psych themselves into spending $1,000 or $1,200 for a computer? Simple: They believe that in those few short years, the computer will speed them up enough, and enhance their productivity enough, to cover the costs easily.

That's the theory, anyway.

Part I
For the Absolute Computer Virgin

The 5th Wave   By Rich Tennant

"It's been two days, Larry. It's time to stop enjoying the new-computer smell and take the iMac out of the box."

In this part . . .

There are three ways to learn how to use a new computer. You can consult the manual; unfortunately, your iMac didn't come with one. You can take a course (like you've got time for that?). Or you can read a book like this one.

In these opening chapters, you'll learn, as kindly and gently as possible, how to get up and running on your iMac — and nothing else.

Chapter 1

How to Turn On Your iMac (and What to Do Next)

In This Chapter

▶ How to turn the iMac on (and off)

▶ Confronting weird new words such as *mouse, menu,* and *system*

▶ Doing windows

▶ Mindlessly opening and closing folders

*I*f you haven't hooked up your iMac yet, go now to the mercifully brief Appendix A, which gently guides you through the ten-second experience of plugging everything in.

Box Open. Now What?

At this moment, then, you should have a ready-to-roll iMac on your desk, in all its transparent fruit–colored plastic glory, and a look of fevered anticipation on your face.

Switching on the iMac

In this very first lesson, you'll be asked to locate the On button. It's in the upper-right corner of your keyboard. It's round, and it bears the universal symbol for iMac On-Turning.

Try pressing this button now. If the iMac responds in some way — a sound plays, the screen lights up, missiles are launched from the Arizona desert — then your machine is working. Skip ahead to the following section, "The startup slide show."

If pressing that key didn't do anything, try pressing the identical-looking button on the face of the machine itself. If that works, your keyboard may not be plugged into the right side of the iMac. And if even the front-panel button doesn't work, your iMac isn't plugged into a working power outlet. I'll wait here while you get that problem sorted out.

The startup slide show

If your On-button experiment was successful, you hear a chord, and after a few seconds, an image appears on the screen. Now you get to witness the Macintosh Startup Slide Show, revered by millions. First, you see a quick glimpse of the smiling Macintosh. It looks like this:

(In the rare event that your smiling Macintosh looks like this —

— your iMac is upside-down.)

Next slide: You see the famous Mac OS logo, looking like Picasso's portrait of a schizophrenic:

During this time, the bottom of your screen fills with little inch-tall pictures. In Macintosh lingo, the term for "little inch-tall pictures" is *icons.* These particular icons represent the different features of your Mac, each turning itself on and preparing for action: One represents your CD-ROM drive, another's for dialing the Internet, and so on. Much, much, much more information about these startup-item doodads is in Chapter 12.

At last, the colored full-screen pattern, called the *desktop,* appears. Congratulations! You've arrived.

If you saw anything else during the startup process — such as a blinking question-mark icon, a strange error message, or thick black smoke — you've just met your first computer problem. Proceed directly to Chapter 15. This problem and many others are explained — and solved — for you there.

Your First Moments Alone Together

As any gadget lover can tell you, the most exciting period of appliance ownership comes at the very beginning. You're gonna love this stuff.

The Setup Assistant — and your iMac edition

The first time you turn on your iMac, you're treated to a special slide-show interview called the *Mac OS Setup Assistant.* How much you enjoy this experience depends on which kind of iMac you bought.

The modern, CD slot-loading iMac

These days, iMacs are smoother, faster, and classier than they used to be — not to mention less expensive. You can identify one of these smoother, faster, classier machines with a glance at the front panel. Instead of a pull-out *drawer* for inserting CD discs, modern iMacs have a *slot,* like the ones on the dashboards of expensive cars. Modern iMacs have a million other enhancements (see the end of this chapter), but the CD slot is the quickest visual indication. That's why Apple calls today's iMac line the *CD slot-loading* models. That's how I'll refer to them in this book, too.

But I digress. The first time you turn on a CD slot-loading iMac, the entire screen is filled with a movie. Lights! Music! Animation! Motion sickness! During this show, you'll be invited to set up an Internet account (assuming you've hooked up a phone wire to your iMac, as described in Appendix A). You're asked for your name, address, credit-card number, and whether or not you want to get junk mail. The iMac dials a couple of times, and your Internet account is created automatically, like this:

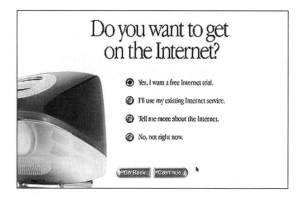

 If now isn't the time to set up an Internet account, it's easy to decline. You'll find much, much more about the Internet and creating an account in Chapter 6 of this book.

The classic, CD tray-loading iMac

All iMac models sold before October 1999 have a plastic door on the right side of the machine. You open this door to get at the connectors. These traditional iMacs also have a drawer or tray, for inserting CD discs, that pops out of the front panel. Now you know why Apple calls these traditional iMacs *CD tray-loading* models. That's how I'll refer to these iMacs in this book.

When you first turn on *these* models, there's no music — just an interview. On one screen after another, your iMac asks about your current time zone, what printer you have, and so on.

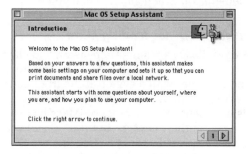

Many of the questions it asks probably don't apply to you. For example, several of the Assistant's screens have to do with the office network you're connected to — and you probably aren't connected to one.

Therefore, the quickest way to get rid of this intrusive little program is to press ⌘-Q — that is, while pressing the ⌘ key (just to the left of the space bar on the keyboard), type the letter Q. Then release both keys.

Moving the mouse

The *mouse* is the round, plastic, yo-yo-like thing on the desk beside your keyboard. Having trouble visualizing it as a rodent? Think of the cord as its tail and (if it helps you) draw little eyeballs on the sloping side facing you.

To use the mouse, keep it turned so that the cord points away from you. If you aspire to become a touch-mouser, someone who's able to keep the mouse oriented correctly without looking, notice the subtle groove on the mouse button. That's for your index finger to use as a landmark.

Now then, roll the mouse across the desk (or mouse pad). See how the arrow pointer moves across the screen? For the rest of your life, you'll hear that pointer called the *cursor.* And for the rest of your life, you'll hear moving the mouse called *moving the mouse.*

Try lifting the mouse off the desk and waving it around in midair like a remote control. Nothing happens, right? The mouse controls the cursor only when it's on a flat surface. (The two-toned ball on the bottom of the mouse detects movement when you roll it around.) That's a useful feature — you can pick up the mouse when you run out of desk space, but the cursor will stay in place on the screen. Only when you set the mouse down and begin to roll it again will the cursor continue moving.

What's on the menu?

Let's try some real computing here. Move the cursor up to the light-gray strip at the top of the screen. It's called the *menu bar,* named after a delightful little pub in Silicon Valley. Touch the arrow on the word *Special.* (The *tip* of the iMac's arrow is the part you need to worry about. Same thing with real-life arrows, come to think of it.)

Pointing to something on the screen in this way has a technical term: *pointing.* (Think you're going to be able to handle this?)

Now put your index finger on the button on the mouse and briefly, quickly, press the button down (and then release it). If all went well, you should see a list of commands drop down from the word *Special,* as shown here:

Congratulations — you've learned how to *click the mouse* (by pressing the button), and you've also learned to *pull down a menu* (the list of commands). Try clicking anywhere on the colored backdrop of your screen (or just waiting 15 seconds); the menu disappears.

The big turn-off

Before we get into 3-D color graphs, space-vehicle trajectories, and DNA analysis, I guess I should tell you how to turn the iMac *off.*

In a pinch, sure, you can just yank the power cord out of the wall. But regularly turning off the iMac by chopping off its power can eventually confuse the poor thing and lead to technical problems. Instead, you're supposed to turn off your iMac using one of these two delightful methods:

✔ **The keyboard way:** Press the power button (the same one you used to turn the iMac on) for a couple of seconds. This box appears:

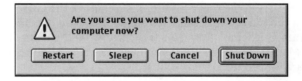

If you've had enough for one session, use the mouse to click the Shut Down button. (The computer turns itself off.) If you're ready to read on, though, confident that you now know how to turn this thing off, click the Cancel button instead.

✔ **The mouse way:** Click the word *Special* (hereafter known as the *Special menu*) again. When the list of commands appears, roll the mouse downward so that each successive command turns dark. When each menu command turns dark, it's said to be *highlighted.*

(The only commands that don't get highlighted are the ones that are dimmed, or *grayed out.* They're dimmed because they don't make any sense at the moment. For example, if no disc is in the CD-ROM drive, choosing Eject Disk wouldn't make any sense. So the Mac makes that command gray, which means it's unavailable to you.)

All about sleep

Believe it or not, many iMac owners never turn the machine off. Instead, whenever they're not using it, they let the iMac *sleep*. When the iMac is asleep, the screen is dark, the components inside stop whirring, all activity stops, and electricity consumption slows to a trickle. When you press a key later, the computer brightens right up. Whatever was on the screen is still there, instantly ready for you to begin working again.

When you first buy an iMac, it's set to sleep automatically about 30 minutes after you've stopped using it. You can adjust this timing using the Energy Saver control panel (see Chapter 12); but you can also make the machine sleep instantly, on your command, which is useful when you're browsing the Pokémon Web site at work and the boss walks by.

To do so, press the power button on the keyboard. When the "Are you sure you want to shut down?" box appears, click Sleep (or press the S key on the keyboard). The iMac blinks right off to sleep.

While it's dozing, the front-panel power button blinks to let you know that the machine isn't entirely off. In fact, if you have a CD slot-loading model, that front power button doesn't just blink — it *breathes,* slowly throbbing like the living thing it is.

Roll the mouse all the way down to the words *Shut Down* so that they're highlighted.

If you do, in fact, want to turn the iMac off for now, release the mouse button. The Mac turns itself off completely. If you'd rather proceed with this chapter's teachings, don't let go of the button yet. Instead, slide the cursor off the menu in any direction and then click the mouse button. The menu snaps back up like a window shade and nothing else happens. (A menu command only gets activated when you release the mouse while the cursor's on a command.)

Hey, you've only read a few pages, and already you can turn your iMac on and off! See? This thing's no harder than a toaster.

If your thirst for knowledge is unquenched and you want to slog ahead with this lesson, read on.

Moving things around on the desktop

Take a look around the screen. You've already encountered *menus* (those words *File, Edit, View,* and so on at the top of the screen). Near the upper-right corner of the screen, you see an *icon.* (Remember? — a small symbolic picture.) Unless you've changed it, that icon is called *Macintosh HD*.

Icons represent everything in the Mac world. They all look different: One represents a letter you wrote, another represents the Trash can, another represents a CD you've inserted. Here are some examples of icons you'll probably be seeing before long:

You can move an icon by dragging it. Try this:

1. **Point to the Trash icon.**

2. **Press and then hold down the mouse button continuously — and, while it's down, move the mouse to a new position.**

   This sophisticated technique is called, by the way, *dragging*. You're dragging the Trash icon now.

3. **Let go of the mouse button.**

Hey, this thing isn't so technical after all, right?

Other than the fact that there's a Trash can, nobody's really sure why they call this "home-base" screen the *desktop*. It has another name, too: the *Finder*. It's where you file all your work into little electronic on-screen file folders so that you can *find* them again later. If you have a recent version of the iMac's built-in software, in fact, the word *Finder* even appears at the top of the screen, as shown in the next illustration.

Used in a sentence, you might hear it like this: "Well, no wonder you don't see the Trash can. You're not in the Finder!"

Icons, windows, and Macintosh syntax

Point to the hard-disk icon (a rectangular box, probably called *Macintosh HD* — for *Hard Disk*) in the upper-right corner of the screen.

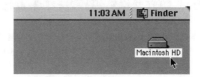

This particular icon represents the giant disk inside your iMac, known as the *hard drive* or *hard disk,* that serves as your filing cabinet. It's where the computer stores all your work, all your files, and all your software.

So how do you see what's in your hard drive? Where do you get to see its table of contents?

It turns out that you can *open* any icon into a window, where you'll see every item inside listed individually. The window has the same name as the icon you opened.

Before we proceed, though, it's time for a lesson in Macintosh syntax. Fear not; it's nothing like English syntax. In fact, everything that you do on the Macintosh has this format: *noun-verb.* Shakespeare it ain't, but it's sure easy to remember.

Let's try a noun-verb command, shall we?

1. Click the hard-disk icon in the upper-right corner of the screen.

The icon turns black, indicating that it's *selected.* Good job — you've just identified the *noun.*

2. Move to the File menu and choose Open.

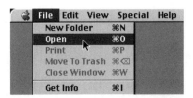

You guessed it — Open is the *verb.* And, sure enough, your hard disk opens into a window, where you can see its contents.

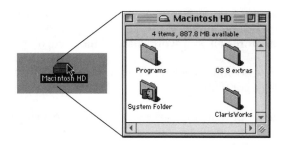

Did any of that make sense? In the world of Macintosh, you always specify *what* you want to change (using the mouse) and then you use a menu command to specify *how* you want it changed. You'll see this pattern over and over again: *Select* something on the screen and then *apply* a menu command to it.

The complete list of window doodads

Look over the contents of your hard-drive window, as shown in the following figure. (Everybody's got different stuff, so what you see on your screen won't exactly match the illustration.)

CLOSE BOX — Click here to close the window, just as though you had chosen Close from the File menu.

TITLE BAR — Drag anywhere in this striped area to move the entire window.

TITLE BAR ICON — Drag this little icon to move the entire window to the Trash, to another disk, or to another window. (In Mac OS 8.5.)

ZOOM BOX — Click here to make the window large enough to show all its contents.

COLLAPSE BOX — Click here to roll the window up like a windowshade so that only the title bar is showing. Click here again to re-expand the window. (In Mac OS 8.5 and later.)

VERTICAL SCROLL BAR — It's white, indicating that you're seeing everything in the window (top to bottom).

SIZE BOX — Drag in any direction to make the window bigger or smaller.

WINDOW EDGES — You can move the entire window by dragging this narrow, puffy strip that runs all the way around.

HORIZONTAL SCROLL BAR — It's gray, indicating that you're not seeing everything in the window (there's something off to the side). You can drag the little square from side to side to adjust your view of the window.

Better yet, look over the various controls and gadgets around the *edges* of this window. Using these controls and buttons, you can do all kinds of neat things to a window: stretch it, move it, or make it go away. (You'll find much more patient descriptions of these controls in Chapter 13.) These various gadgets are worth learning about — you're going to run into windows *everywhere* after you start working.

Go ahead and try out some of the little boxes and scroll bars. Click them. Tug on them. Open the window and close it again. No matter what you do, *you can never hurt the machine by doing "the wrong thing."* That's the wonderful thing about the iMac: It's the Nerf appliance.

All systems are go

In that little window diagram, you may have noticed something peculiar about the item called the *title bar icon* — as shown in the diagram, that little box is present only if your iMac has *Mac OS 8.5 or later.*

And what, you may understandably be shrieking, is *Mac OS 8.5 or later?*

Long story. Every year, Apple Computer piles neat new features onto the behind-the-scenes software that runs your computer. This backstage software was once called the *operating system.* But because everyone's in such a hurry these days, people now just call it the *OS.* (Say it "O-S," not "oss.")

The original, summer 1998 iMac models came equipped with *Mac OS 8.1* — at the time, the newest, trendiest OS around. By the end of the year, though, iMacs came with something even newer: Mac OS 8.5. These days, iMacs have an even more modern software engine called Mac OS 9. (See the end of Chapter 13 for more on this topic.)

I bring up this point here because certain iMac features behave differently depending on which version you have. For example, the name of the program you're currently using is always identified in the upper-right corner of the screen — but only in Mac OS 8.5 and later:

Mac OS 8.1   Mac OS 8.5 and later

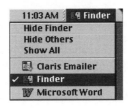

See? The *things* on the screen are pretty much the same; they've just had a makeover on *Oprah*.

In this book, I'll mostly be showing the newer look — don't let it faze you. Even with an older iMac, you'll still find everything where it's supposed to be.

Tell you what: From now on, if something I'm teaching you seems odd, look for an icon like the one beside this paragraph. Then you'll know you're not going crazy.

It would help, I guess, if you knew which OS version *your* iMac uses. Fortunately, finding out is easy.

Get a pencil.

See the logo in the upper-left corner of the screen? It's no ordinary logo. It's actually a menu, just like the ones you've already experienced. Point your arrow cursor tip on the apple, click the button, and watch what happens.

As with any menu, a list drops down. This one, however, includes an extremely useful command. This command is so important that it's separated by a dotted line from the mere mortal list items after it. It's *About This Computer.*

Slide the pointer down until About This Computer turns black and then click the mouse button. A window appears:

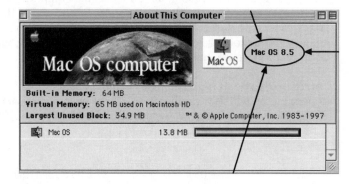

As my subtle drawn-in arrows indicate, this window reveals what version of the System software you have. The version is a number you'll need to know later in this book and later in your life. Therefore, take this opportunity to write it onto your Cheat Sheet (the yellow cardboard page inside the front cover of this book). You'll find a little blank for this information in the upper-left corner of your card, where it says, "Your System version."

When you're finished with this little piece of homework, close the About This Computer window by clicking the little square in the upper-left corner — the Close box — to make the window go away.

Double-clicking in theory and practice

All right, back to the lesson in progress. Make sure your hard-drive window is open.

So far, all of your work in the Finder (the desktop) has involved moving the mouse around. But your keyboard is useful, too. For example, do you see the System Folder? Even if you don't, here's a quick way to find it: Quickly type **SY** on your keyboard.

Presto, the iMac finds the System Folder (which happens to be the first thing that begins with those letters) and highlights it, in effect dropping it in front of you, wagging its tail.

Now try pressing the arrow keys on your keyboard — right, left, up, down. The iMac highlights neighboring icons as you do so.

Suppose you want to see what's in the System Folder. Of course, using your newfound noun-verb method, you could (1) click the System Folder to select it and then (2) choose Open from the File menu.

But that's the sissy way. Try this power shortcut: Point to the System Folder icon so that the tip of the arrow cursor is squarely inside the picture of the folder. Keeping the mouse still, click twice in rapid succession. With stunning originality, the Committee for the Invention of Computer Terminology calls this advanced computing technique *double-clicking*.

If all went well, your double-click opened a new window, showing you the contents of the System Folder. (If it didn't work, you probably need to keep the mouse still or double-click faster.)

Remember this juicy golden rule: *Double-click means "open."*

In your iMac life, you'll be asked (or tempted) to click many an item on-screen: buttons that say "OK;" tools that look like paint brushes; all manner of multiple-choice buttons. In every one of these cases, you're supposed to click *once*.

The only time you ever *double*-click something is when you want to *open* it. Got it?

Multiple windows

Now you should have two windows open on the screen: the hard-disk window and the System Folder window. (The System Folder window may be covering the first one; they're like overlapping pieces of paper on a desk.)

Try this: Click the title bar of the System Folder window (just *one* click). Drag the title bar downward until you can see the hard-drive window behind it, as shown here.

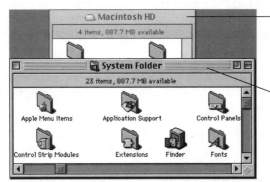

You can tell that this window is in back, because its title bar is solid light gray. Just click anywhere in the window to bring it to the front.

You know that this window is the top window, because its title bar is striped.

Take a stress-free moment to experiment with these two windows: Click the back one to bring it forward; then click the one that was in front to bring it to the front again.

Using a list view

There's one more aspect of windows that will probably make Type A personalities wriggle with delight. Until now, you've been viewing the contents of your disk as a bunch of icons. Nice, but wouldn't it be neat to see things alphabetically?

1. **Make sure the System Folder is the active window (the one in front; "A." in the following figure).**

   We're going to use the System Folder because it's got a lot of stuff in it.

   Next, you're going to use a menu. Remember how to choose a menu command? Click the menu's name and then click the command you want in the drop-down list.

2. **Locate the View menu at the top of the screen; from it, choose "as List" (see "B." in the following picture).**

   Suddenly, the big icons are replaced by a neat alphabetical list of the window's contents (labeled here as "C.").

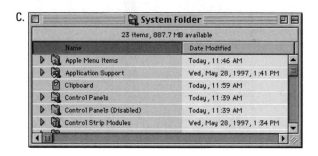

The easiest homework you've ever had

To reinforce your budding mouse skills, here's a pathetically easy assignment: Read the iMac's own version of the lessons in this chapter.

To try out this self-help program, cancel your appointments for the next 20 minutes and turn off your phone's ringer. Now click the Help menu at the top of the screen; from the menu, click Tutorial (older iMacs) or Mac Tutorials (newer ones). You're now treated to an animated, entertaining, Disneyfied version of the lessons in this chapter. The characters in these little movies will never show up in a "Lion King" sequel, but they're a lot better with computers.

Where to get help

Now that you've discovered the Help center, by the way, make a mental note for later. The iMac's Help command stands ready to answer any other questions that may arise. Here's how it works:

When you need answers, click the Help menu at the top of your screen. This time, click the Help *command*. You get a window that looks something like this:

Invasion of the little triangles

When you view a window's contents in a list, each folder *within* the window is marked by a tiny triangle. The triangle points to the right.

You can open one of these folders-within-the-folder in the usual way, if you wish — by double-clicking. But it's much more satisfying for neat freaks to click the *triangle* instead. In the following figure, the before-and-after view of the Control Panels folder (inside the System Folder) shows how much more organized you can be.

When you click the triangle, in other words, your window contents look like an outline. The contents of that subfolder are indented. To "collapse," or close, the folder, click the downward-pointing triangle.

One more trick: See the words *Name*, *Date Modified*, and so on (at the top of the window)? Click any of these words. Instantly the iMac resorts everything in the window, based on the word you clicked. Example: click Size, if it's visible, and you'll see the largest files listed first.

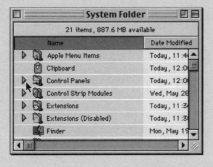

You can use this Help Center in two ways. First, you can type a Help topic into the blank at the top of the window (such as *naming files* or *dialing the Internet*) — and then click the Search button. If you're having a good night, the window will then show you a list of Help pages that might contain the answer you're looking for; click the name of the topic that seems to hold some promise.

Second, you can click your way through this little Help program. In the previous illustration, see all the topics written in blue underlined type?

Of course not. This is a black-and-white book. How silly of me.

But on *your* screen, all those underlined phrases show up in blue lettering. That blueness, and that underlining, means *click me to jump to a different page.* By clicking on successive blue underlined phrases, you can often hone in on the precise Help article you're interested in.

Pit stop

Shut the iMac down now, if you want (flip back a few pages to the section "Shutting down" for complete instructions). Chapter 1½ is something of a chalk-talk to help you understand what's really happening inside the computer's puny brain.

Top Ten Similarities between You and Your iMac

Before you move boldly forward to the next chapter, ponder the following frightening similarities between you and your computer:

1. Both are pulled out of a very special container on Day One.

2. Both have feet on the bottom.

3. Both have slots to provide adequate ventilation.

4. Both react to the movement of a nearby mouse.

5. Both sometimes crash when asked to do too much at once.

6. Both have a button on the front.

7. Both light up when turned on.

8. Both occasionally enjoy a good CD.

9. Both may be connected to a phone line for days at a time.

10. With considerable effort, both may be made to work with Microsoft Windows computers.

iMacs forever

So which iMac did you buy? The Rev B? The DV? The Special Edition?

Unless you're hopelessly overqualified for this book, you probably have no clue what I'm talking about. It turns out that Apple, like a car company, updates the design of its bestseller every year.

August 1998: The first iMacs were teal-colored, ran at 233 miles per hour (or *megahertz,* as the geeks say), had Mac OS 8.1, and cost $1,300. Today, these computers are known as the "Revision A" models.

November 1998: Apple's "Revision B" iMacs looked the same as the originals, but came with Adobe PageMill software (see Chapter 9); for sake of better game-playing, the video-picture circuitry was beefed up (to 6 megs of video memory); and Mac OS 8.5 came installed.

January 1999: The price dropped to $1,200; the hard drive grew from 4 gigs to 6 gigs; the speed was cranked up to 266 miles per hour; Apple introduced a choice of fruit flavors: Grape, Strawberry, Blueberry, Lime, and Tangerine.

Unfortunately, these iMacs, known by the cognoscenti as "Rev. C" or "LifeSavers" iMacs, lost a few goodies, too. Gone were the infrared port and the secret expansion card inside. Well, you know what they say: Apple giveth, and Apple taketh away.

April 1999: The iMac line was quietly zoomed to an even faster speed — 333 mph — without increasing a penny in price. Meanwhile, the mouse gained a subtle groove on the button where your index finger rests. This groove tells you by touch when the perfectly round mouse is correctly aligned with the cord pointing away from you; the previous, un-grooved iMac mouse drove thousands crazy.

October 1999: As an enthusiastic customer somewhere in the world snapped up the 2,000,000th iMac, Apple released its most dramatic improvements yet. This change split the iMac into three lines, all in a slightly smaller, sleeker, and even more transparent plastic case. Each model comes with built-in Harmon Kardon stereo speakers, twice as much memory as before (64 megs), and a CD-ROM drive that doesn't require you to place a CD into a tray. Now you can just slide the disc directly into the front of the machine, like a videocassette into a VCR. (That's why people call this late-1999 series the "CD slot-loading" iMac lineup.)

The least expensive of these iMacs, now available only in Blueberry, dropped in price to $1,000, despite a much faster main chip (350 MHz, almost twice as fast as the original iMac). Pay $200 more, and you get a choice of the five fruit flavors, even more speed (400 MHz), a bigger hard drive (10 gigs), a DVD drive (which lets you watch rented movies that come on discs), and iMovie — the technology that lets you edit your own camcorder movies (see Chapter 10). Yet another $300 gets you the silvery gray Special Edition iMac, with even more memory (128 megs) and hard drive storage (13 gigs). All of these late-1999 models can accommodate an *AirPort card,* an option that lets you connect Macs together, and share an Internet account, without wires. (Chapter 14 has the details.)

But even these iMacs aren't the end of the line. New iMac models are always in the works. Faster ones, models with bigger screens, and lower prices are always on the way. Whatever they do to it, though, it's still an utterly adorable appliance.

Chapter 1½

High-Tech Made Easy

How an iMac Works

I'm a little worried about sticking this chapter so close to the front of the book. Plenty of people firmly believe that the iMac has a personality — that when something goes wrong, the iMac is being cranky; and when a funny message appears on the screen, the iMac is being friendly. Don't let the following discussion of cold, metal, impersonal circuitry ruin that image for you; the iMac *does* have a personality, no matter what the wireheads say.

For the first time, you're going to have to roll up your brain's sleeves and chew on some actual computer jargon. Don't worry — you'll feel coolly in control by the time it's over. Besides, it's a short chapter.

Storing things with disks

Human beings, for the most part, store information in one of two places. Either we retain something in our memory, or we write it down on the back of an envelope.

Computers work pretty much the same way. They can either store what they know in their relatively pea-brained *memory*, which I'll cover in a moment, or they can write it down. A computer writes stuff down on a computer disk.

Conceptualizing the hard disk

Every iMac has a gigantic disk built inside it — a *hard disk.* The concept of a hard disk confuses people because it's hidden inside the iMac's case. Since you can't see it or touch it, it's sort of conceptual — like beta-carotene or God, I guess. But it's there, spinning quietly away, and a hefty chunk of your iMac's purchase price paid for it.

Why all this talk of disks? Because a hard disk is where your life's work is going to live when the computer is shut off. You will, like it or not, become intensely interested in the overall health of your computer's hard disk.

The hard disk isn't the only one you'll encounter in your lifetime, by the way. You may one day decide to buy an *external disk drive* that plugs into the side of the iMac; into such a disk drive, you can insert *removable* disks like floppy disks, Zip disks, and so on. (Unlike most computers, the iMac doesn't have a built-in floppy-disk slot.) Copying your important work onto a pocketable disk is a handy way to *back up,* or make a safety copy of, whatever you've been working on. Details on floppy-disk attachments, Zip drives, and other such removable disks in Chapter 18.

Understanding memory

Okay. Now we get to the good stuff: how a computer really works. I know you'd just as soon not know what's going on in there, but this info is mental broccoli: It's good for you, and later in life, you'll be glad you were forced to digest it. If, at this point, your brain is beginning to hemorrhage, skip this section and find serenity in Chapter 2.

There's actually a significant difference between an *iMac's* memory and *your* memory (besides the fact that yours is probably much more interesting). When you shut down the iMac (not just put it to sleep), it forgets *everything.* It becomes a dumb, metal-and-plastic doorstop. That's because a computer's memory, just like yours, is kept alive by electrical impulses. When you turn off an iMac, the electricity stops.

Therefore, each time you turn *on* an iMac, it has to relearn everything it ever knew, including the fact that it's a computer, what kind of computer it is, how to display text, how many days until your warranty expires, and so on. Now we arrive at the purpose of those disks we've been droning on about; that's where the computer's knowledge lives when the juice is off. Without a disk, the iMac is like someone with a completely hollow skull (and we've all met *that* type). If you're ever unlucky enough to experience a broken hard drive, you'll see how exciting an iMac can be without a disk: It shows a completely gray screen with a small blinking question mark in the middle. (I've met a few people like *that,* too.)

When you turn on a completely shut-down iMac, there's whirring and blinking. The hard disk inside begins to spin. When it hits about 4,500 rpm, the iMac starts reading the hard disk — it "plays" the disk like a CD player. It finds out: "Hey, I'm an iMac! And this is how I display text!" and so on. The iMac is reading the disk and copying everything it reads into *memory*. (That's why the computer takes a minute or so to start up.)

Memory is really neat. After something's in memory, it's instantaneously available to the computer. The iMac no longer has to read the disk to learn something. Memory is also expensive (at least compared to disks); memory is a bunch of complicated circuits etched onto a piece of silicon the size of a piece of Trident by people in white lab coats.

Because it's more expensive, computers have far less memory than disk space. For example, even if your hard disk holds every issue of *National Geographic* ever published, you're probably only going to *read* one article at a time. So the iMac reads "The Nocturnal Nubian Gnat: Nature's Tiniest Vampire" from your hard disk, loads it into memory, and displays it on the screen. So it doesn't matter that your iMac's memory doesn't hold as much as your entire hard disk; the iMac uses the hard disk for *long-term, permanent* storage of *lots* of things, and it uses memory for *temporary* storage while you work on *one thing at a time*.

Who's Meg?

You often hear computer jocks talk about *megs*. Only rarely are they referring to Meg Ryan and Meg Tilly. Meg is short for *megabyte*. So is the abbreviation *MB*. (*Mega* = 1,000,000, and *byte* = an iota of information so small it can only specify a single letter of the alphabet.)

What's highly confusing to most beginners is that you measure memory (fast, expensive, temporary) and hard-disk space (permanent, slower) in the *same units*: megabytes. A typical iMac might have 32 or 64 megs of memory (silicon chips) but 6,000 or 13,000 megs of hard-disk space (spinning platters).

(*Free bonus fact:* If a hard drive's size reaches 1,000 megs, it gets a new measurement name — its size is said to be one *gigabyte*. The abbreviation for one gigabyte is 1GB. Your iMac's hard drive may hold, for example, 6 GB. Computer nerds sometimes use shorthand for this measurement — "My iMac's hard drive has three gigs" — which absolutely bewilders jazz-club musicians.)

With these vital facts in mind, see if you can answer the following paradoxical dinner party question:

"How many megs does your iMac have?"

The novice's answer: "Um . . . say, have you tried those little cocktail weenies?"

Why they call it RAM

You know what an *acronym* is, right? It's a bunch of initials that, together, spell out an actual word, such as M.A.D.D. or SALT Treaty . . . or RAM.

When the Committee for Arbitrary Acronyms (the CAA) ratified the abbreviation RAM, it

probably stood for *R*andom *A*bbreviation for *M*emory. Today, it supposedly stands for *R*andom *A*ccess *M*emory.

Whatever *that* means.

The partly initiated's reply: "I . . . I think 64?"

The truly enlightened response: "What do you mean, how many megs? Are you referring to *memory* or to *hard-disk storage space?* Here, have a cocktail weenie."

Understanding RAM

Let's add another term to your quickly growing nerd vocabulary list. It pains me to teach you this word, because it's one of those really meaningless terms that was invented purely to intimidate people. Trouble is, you're going to hear it a lot. You may as well be prepared.

It's *RAM.* You pronounce it like the sheep. RAM is memory. A typical iMac has 32 or 64 megs of RAM (in other words, of memory).

Incidentally, this might be a good time to find out how much RAM *you* have. Here's how to find out.

Wake up, or turn on, your iMac.

See the logo in the upper-left corner of the screen? It's no ordinary logo. It's actually a menu, just like the ones you've already experienced. Point your arrow cursor tip on the apple, click the mouse button, and watch what happens.

As with any menu, a list drops down. This one, however, includes an extremely useful command. This command is so important that it's separated by a dotted line from the mere mortal list items after it. It's *About This Computer.*

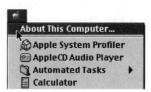

Slide the pointer down until About This Computer turns black, and then click the mouse button. A window appears:

The number labeled Built-in Memory (which I've circled in the picture) is how much actual RAM your iMac has. It's some multiple of eight. (The total amount of usable memory, as listed on the second line, may be higher, thanks to tricks such as RAM Doubler and virtual memory. Chapter 16 explains those memory stunts in painstaking detail.)

In any case, your iMac's RAM endowment is a statistic you'll enjoy reviewing again and again. Therefore, take this opportunity to write this number onto your yellow cardboard Cheat Sheet at the front of the book. There's a little blank for this information.

When you're finished with this little piece of homework, close the About This Computer window by clicking the little square in the upper-left corner — the Close box — to make the window go away.

Putting it all together

Now that you know where a computer's information lives, let me take you on a tour of the computer's guts. Let's get into our little imaginary Disney World tram. Keep hands and feet inside the car at all times.

When you turn on the iMac, as I noted earlier, the hard disk spins, and the iMac copies certain critical information into its memory. So far, the iMac knows only that it's a computer. It doesn't know anything else that's stored on your hard disk. It doesn't yet know about Nocturnal Nubian Gnats, your new screenplay, or how much you owe on your credit card.

To get any practical work done, you now have to transfer the article (or screenplay or spreadsheet) into memory; in Macintosh terminology, you have to *open a file*. In Chapter 2, you'll find out how easy and idiot-proof this process is. Anyway, after you open a file, it appears on-screen. (It's *in memory* now.)

While your document is on the screen, you can make changes to it. This, of course, is why you bought a computer in the first place. You can delete a sentence from your novel or move a steamy scene to a different chapter. (The term for this process is *word processing*.) If you're working on your finances, you can add a couple zeros to your checking-account balance. (The term for this process is *wishful thinking*.) All without any eraser crumbs or whiteout.

Perceptive readers who haven't already gotten bored and gone off to watch TV will recognize that you're making all these changes to what's in *memory*. The more you change the screenplay that's up on the screen, the more it's different from that *permanent* copy that's still on your disk, safe and sound.

 At this point, you're actually in a pretty precarious position. Remember that memory is sustained by electricity. In other words, if your four-year-old mistakes the iMac's power cord for a handy suckable plaything and jerks it out of the wall, then the electricity stops. The screen goes blank, and all the changes you've made disappear forever. You're left with the original copy on the disk, of course, but any work you've done on it vanishes, along with anything else in the iMac's memory.

However, every software program has a simple command, called Save, that saves your work back onto the hard disk. That is, the computer *updates* the original copy that's still on the hard disk, and you're safe. Even if a sun storm wipes out all power plants in the Northern Hemisphere and your iMac goes dark, your novel or letter or spreadsheet is safe on the disk. Most people use the Save command every five or ten minutes so that their work is always up to date and preserved on the disk. (You'll learn how to use the Save command in Chapter 4.)

"I lost all my work!"

So that you'll quit worrying about it, the precariousness of memory accounts for the horror stories you sometimes hear from people who claim that they lost their work to a computer. "I was on volume Y of the encyclopedia I've been writing," they'll say, "and I lost all of it because of a computer glitch!"

Now you can cry crocodile tears and then skip back to your office with a smirk. *You* know what happened. They probably worked for hours with some document on the screen but forgot to use the Save command. Then the unthinkable happened — someone tripped on the power cord — and, sure enough, all the changes they'd made got wiped out. A simple Save command would have stored everything neatly on the hard disk.

Top Ten Differences between Memory and a Hard Disk

May you never confuse memory with a hard disk again.

1. You usually buy memory 32 or 64 megs at a time. Hard disks come in sizes like 4 gigs, 6 gigs, and on up. (A *gigabyte* is 1,000 *megabytes.*)

2. Memory comes on a little minicircuit board. A hard disk is a plastic- or metal-cased box with cables hanging out of it.

3. You can install memory only inside the computer (something Chapter 16 shows you how to do). A hard disk may be either inside the iMac (an *internal* drive) or in a separate box you plug into the side (an *external* drive).

4. Memory delivers information to the iMac's brain almost instantly. The hard disk sometimes seems to take forever.

5. Some disks are removable. When one fills up, you can insert a different one. (Some examples: floppy disks, Zip disks, and SuperDisk disks.) Removing RAM is a more serious proposition, generally involving a knowledgeable geek's assistance.

6. Not every computer on earth has a hard disk. (The earliest Macs used nothing but floppy disks, and pocket organizers such as the PalmPilot have no disks at all.) But every computer ever made has memory.

7. If you listen carefully, you can hear when the iMac is reading information off a hard disk; it makes tiny frantic scraping noises. You can't tell when the iMac is getting information from RAM.

8. As a very general rule, RAM costs about $3 per meg, and hard drive space averages about 15 cents per meg.

9. Memory's contents disappear when you shut down the computer. A disk's contents stay there until you deliberately throw them away.

10. To find out how much *hard-disk space* you have left, look at the top of a window on your desktop, as shown here:

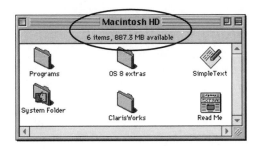

But to see how much *RAM* you have left, you must choose About This Computer from your menu.

The number where it reads Largest Unused Block is roughly how much RAM you're not using at the moment. Details are in Chapter 16.

Chapter 2

Windows, Icons, and Trashes

- -

In This Chapter

▶ All about windows, folders, and icons

▶ Learning keyboard shortcuts

▶ Tips on using windows and disks to raise your social status

- -

Becoming Manipulative

All the clicking and dragging and window-shoving you learned in Chapter 1 is, in fact, leading up to something useful.

Foldermania

I've said that your hard disk is like the world's biggest filing cabinet. It's where you store all your stuff. But a filing cabinet without filing *folders* would be about as convenient to handle as an egg without a shell.

The folders on the iMac screen don't occupy any space on your hard drive. They're electronic fictions whose sole purpose is to help you organize your stuff.

Mr. Folder

The iMac provides an infinite supply of folders. Want a folder? Do this:

From the File menu, choose New Folder.

Ooh, tricky, this machine! A new folder appears. Notice that the iMac gracefully proposes "untitled folder" as its name.

Notice something else, though: The name is *highlighted* (black). Remember our earlier lesson? Highlighted = selected = ready for you to *do* something. When *text* is highlighted, the iMac is ready for you to *replace* it with anything you type. In other words, you don't even have to backspace over the text. Just type away:

1. **Type *USA Folder* and press the Return key.**

   The Return key tells the iMac that your naming spurt is over.

   Now, to see how folders work, create another one.

2. **From the File menu, once again choose New Folder.**

   Another new folder appears, once more waiting for a title.

3. **Type *Ohio* and press Return.**

You're going to create one more empty folder. But by this time, your wrist is probably weary from the forlorn trek back and forth to the File menu. Don't you wish you could make a folder faster?

You can.

Keyboard shortcuts

Open the File menu, but don't select any of the commands in it yet. See those weird notations to the right of some commands?

Get used to 'em. They're *keyboard shortcuts,* and they appear in almost every menu you'll ever see. Keyboard shortcuts let you select certain menu items without using the mouse.

Some people love keyboard shortcuts, claiming that if you're in a hurry, pressing keys is faster than using the mouse. Other people loathe keyboard shortcuts, pointing out that using the mouse doesn't require any memorization. In either case, here's how keyboard shortcuts work.

Unimportant sidebar about other menu symbols

Besides the little keyboard-shortcut symbols at the right side of a menu, you'll occasionally run into a little downward-pointing arrow, like this:

menu that you're not seeing. To get to those additional commands, carefully roll the pointer down the menu all the way to that down-pointing triangle. Don't let the sudden jumping scare you: The menu commands will jump upward, bringing the hidden ones into view.

And then there are the little black triangles pointing to the *right* (left side of the illustration). These triangles indicate that, when selected, the menu command won't do anything except offer you several *other* commands, which pop out to the side (at right in the figure):

That arrow tells you that the menu is so long, it doesn't even fit on the screen. The arrow is implying that still more commands are in the

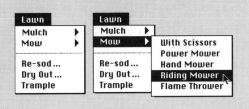

God never closes a window

When you opened the USA Folder, did you notice how its icon changed texture? After you double-clicked it, the icon turned dark and sort of grainy.

It's *supposed* to do that. When you double-click any icon to make its window appear, the icon itself turns into a grainy silhouette. That's your visual clue that it's been opened.

The icon won't collapse back into its normal, more attractive state until you close the corresponding window. (Can't find it? Then double-click the already-opened icon *again*. Its window will pop to the fore.)

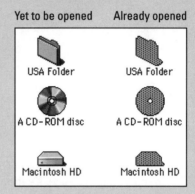

When you type on a typewriter, you press the Shift key to make a capital letter, right? They call the Shift key a *modifier key* because it turns ordinary, well-behaved citizen keys like 3 and 4 into madcap symbols like # and $. Welcome to the world of computers, where everything is four times more complicated. Instead of having only *one* modifier key, the iMac has *four* of them! Look down next to your spacebar. There they are: In addition to the Shift key, one says Option, one says Ctrl, and another has a little ⌘ symbol on it.

It's that little cloverleaf — the *command key* — whose symbol appears in the File menu. Next to the New Folder command, you see ⌘-N. That means:

1. **While pressing the ⌘ key, press the N key and then release everything.**

   Bam! You've got yourself another folder.

2. **Type *Michigan* and press Return.**

   You've just named your third folder. So why have you been wasting a perfectly good afternoon (or whatever it is in your time zone) making empty folders? So you can pretend you're getting organized.

3. **Drag the Ohio folder on top of the USA Folder.**

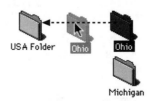

Make sure that the tip of the arrow actually hits the center of the USA Folder so that the folder becomes highlighted. The instant it turns black, let go of the Ohio folder — and watch it disappear into the USA Folder. (If your aim wasn't good, you'll now see the Ohio folder sitting *next* to the USA Folder; try the last step again.)

4. **Put the Michigan folder into the USA Folder in the same way — by dragging it on top of the USA Folder.**

   As far as you know, though, those state folders have *disappeared*. How can you trust me that they're now neatly filed away?

5. **Double-click the USA Folder.**

   Yep. Opens right up into a window, and there are your two darling states, nestled sweetly where they belong.

   If you were to double-click one of the *state* folders, you'd open *another* window. (Having a million windows open at once is nothing to be afraid of. If you're a neatness freak, you might feel threatened, but closing them is easy enough — remember the close box in the upper-left corner of each one?)

   Okay, so how do you get these inner folders *out* again? Do you have to drag them individually? That would certainly be a bummer if you had all 50 folders in the USA Folder.

   Turns out there are several ways to select more than one icon at a time.

6. **Click above and to the left of the Ohio folder (Step 1 in the upcoming picture) and, without releasing the mouse, drag down and to the right so that you enclose both folders with a dotted rectangle (Steps 2 and 3).**

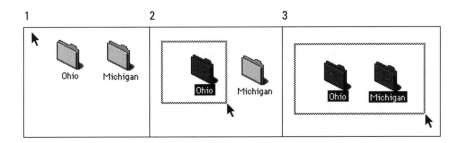

Release the mouse button when you've got both icons enclosed.

Now that you have several folders selected, you can move them en masse to another location.

7. **Drag the Ohio folder outside of the USA Folder window.**

   The Michigan folder goes along for the ride.

Bonus technique for extra credit

The method of selecting several icons by dragging a rectangle around them is fine if all the icons are next to each other. But how would you select only the icons that begin with the letter A in this picture?

The power-user's secret: Click each icon *while pressing the Shift key.* As long as you're pressing Shift, you continually add additional, nonadjacent icons to the selection. (And if you Shift-click one by accident, you can *de*select it by Shift-clicking *again.* Try it!)

You can't very well enclose each A by dragging the mouse — you'd also get all the *other* icons within the same rectangle.

This was a somewhat unproductive exercise, of course, because we were only working with empty folders. It gets much more exciting when you start working with your own documents. All of these techniques work equally well with folders and with documents.

How to trash something

Here's one more icon-manipulation trick you'll probably find valuable:

1. **Close the USA Folder by clicking its close box.**

2. **Drag the folder on top of the Trash can in the lower-right corner of the screen.**

Don't let go until the Trash can actually turns black (when the tip of the arrow cursor is on it). When you do let go, notice how the Trash can bulges or overflows, a subtle reinforcement of how important it thinks your stuff is.

Anyway, that's how you throw things out on the iMac: Just drag them on top of the Trash can. (There's even a keystroke for this: Highlight an icon and then press ⌘-Delete. The chosen icon goes flying into the Trash as though it's just been drop-kicked.)

What's really hilarious is how hard Apple made it for you to get rid of something. Just putting something into the Trash doesn't actually get rid of it; technically, you've really only put it into the Oblivion Waiting Room. It'll sit there forever, in an overflowing trash can. To rescue something, you just double-click the Trash can to open its window; then drag whatever-it-was right back onto the screen.

So if putting something into the Trash doesn't really delete it, how *do* you really delete it? You choose Empty Trash from the Special menu.

But even *then* your stuff isn't really gone; you get a message like this:

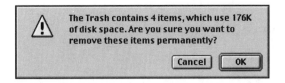

Click OK, and your file is finally gone.

Actually, don't tell anybody, but *even after* you've emptied the Trash, your file *still* isn't really gone forever. Programs like Norton Utilities can unerase a file that's been trashed, as long as you haven't used your iMac much since you threw away the file. That's useful to remember in case (1) you ever trash something by mistake, or (2) you're a spy.

Your basic CD-ROM crash course

You won't get far in life without knowing how to use your iMac's built-in CD-ROM drive. For example, whenever you buy new software to install onto your iMac, you'll get it in the form of a CD-ROM disc.

How you insert a CD depends on what model your iMac is. Examine your computer. Front and center, just below the screen, you have either a six-inch *slot* or a six-inch plastic *panel* with a button in the middle.

Slot models: Insert a CD by slipping it (label side up) directly into the slot, pushing it until the iMac slurps it all the way in. *Be careful* not to insert a CD if there's already one in the machine!

Panel models: To insert a CD, press the colored, capsule-shaped button directly underneath the word "iMac" on the front of the computer. After a moment, the CD tray pops out about an inch.

With your finger, pull it out all the way. Place a CD into it — label side up — and snap the center ring down over the little sprocket in the center of the tray. (Avoid touching the underside of a CD.) Finally, push the tray shut. In a moment, the CD's icon shows up at the right side of your iMac screen.

All models: To get the CD *out* again, don't try pressing that CD-drawer button again — it won't work. Instead, click the CD's icon on the screen. Then, from the Special menu, choose Eject Disk. (Or — shortcut time — drag the CD's icon onto the Trash icon.)

The CD pops out of the slot, or the tray pops open so that you can remove the CD.

Now you can understand why you never hear iMac owners complain of having thrown away some important document by accident — an iMac won't *let* you get rid of anything without fighting your way through four layers of warnings and red tape.

Pretty cool computer, huh?

Top Ten Window, Icon, and Trash Tips

Staggering through the basics of using your iMac unattended is one thing. Shoving around those on-screen windows and icons with grace is quite another. Master the following, and then invite your friends over to watch some evening.

1. To rename an icon, click carefully on its name. Wait for a second or so, until a rectangle appears around the name. That's your cue to type away, giving it a new name. Press Return when you're done.

2. Don't forget that you can look at a window's contents in a neat list (choose "as List" from the View menu). Once in a list view, when a folder is highlighted, you can press ⌘→ to expand it (as though you'd clicked the triangle to view its contents) and ⌘← to collapse it again.

3. Every time you choose Empty Trash from the Special menu, the iMac asks you if you're absolutely sure. If you'd prefer to simply vaporize the Trash contents without being asked for confirmation, select the Trash icon. From the File menu, choose Get Info and then click the "Warn before emptying" check box so that the check mark disappears.

4. If you have a very important document, you can prevent it from getting thrown away by accident. Click its icon. From the File menu, choose Get Info. Turn on the Locked check box. Now, even if you put it in the Trash and try to empty the Trash, the iMac will simply tell you that there's a locked item in the Trash, which it won't get rid of.

5. To make a copy of a file, click the icon and then choose Duplicate from the File menu. Or, while pressing the Option key, drag the icon into a new window or folder.

6. Isn't it frustrating to open a window that's too small to show you all its contents (shown below at left)?

   Of course, you could spend a weekend fussing with the scroll bars, trying to crank the other icons into view. Or, by using trial-and-error, you could drag the lower-right handle (the resize box) to make the window bigger.

   There's a much quicker solution. Click the *zoom box* in the upper-right corner of the window (shown below at right by the cursor). The iMac automatically makes the window *exactly* large enough to show all of the icons.

 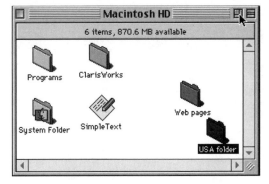

7. You don't have to be content to leave the Trash stranded way down there at the bottom of your screen. You can move it anywhere you want, just by dragging it.

8. Try this sneaky shortcut: While pressing the Control (Ctrl) key, point the cursor tip on an icon, disk, or the inside of a window. Keep the Control key pressed; if you now hold down the mouse button, a pop-up menu appears at your cursor tip, listing commands that pertain only to that icon, disk, or window.

  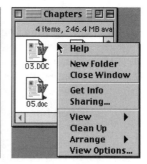

For example, if you Control-click a disk or CD, you'll be offered commands like Eject, Help, and Open. If you Control-click an icon, you get commands like Get Info, Duplicate, and Move To Trash. And if you Control-click anywhere inside a window — but *not* directly on an icon — you're offered New Folder, Help, and Close Window. (The geek term for this phenomenon is *contextual menus* — because the menu is different depending on the context of your click.)

9. When your life overwhelms you with chaos and random events, at least your iMac can give you a sense of control and order.

Want proof? Open a window, such as your Macintosh HD window. From the View menu, choose "as Icons." Note how messy, crude, and slovenly your icons look!

Now, from the View menu, choose View Options. In the window that appears, click Keep Arranged, like this:

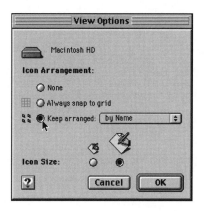

And then click OK. Now, no matter how many icons you add to this window, and no matter what size you make the window, your icons will always remain in neat alignment.

Before   After

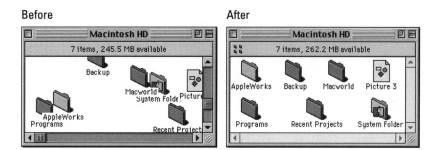

10. You don't have to clean up your windows before you shut down the computer. The windows will be right where you left them the next time you turn on the iMac.

Chapter 3

Actually Accomplishing Something

● ●

In This Chapter

▶ What software is, for those who care

▶ Copying and pasting

▶ Desk accessories and the fruit-shaped menu they're listed in

▶ The pure, unalloyed joy of control panels

● ●

*T*he iMac is like a VCR. The software programs you install on the iMac are like the tapes you slip into your VCR. Without tapes (software), the VCR (iMac) is worthless. But with tapes (software), your VCR (iMac) can take on any personality.

A VCR might let you watch a Western one night, home movies another, and a *60 Minutes* exposé about a corrupt Good Humor man another night. In the same way, your iMac can be a typing instructor, a checkbook balancer, or a movie-editing machine, depending on the software you buy. Each piece of software — usually called a *program,* but sometimes known as an *application* — is like a different GameBoy cartridge: It makes the iMac look, feel, and behave differently. The average iMac user winds up using about six or seven different programs regularly.

Obsolescence Therapy

Your relationship with a software company doesn't end when you buy the program. First, the company provides a technical help staff for you to call when things get rocky. Some firms are great about this relationship — they give you a toll-free number that's answered immediately by a smart, helpful, customer-oriented technician. More often, though, sending out an SOS is a long-distance call . . . and a long-distance five- or ten-minute wait before somebody can help you. How can you find out how good a company's help line is? By asking around and reading the reviews in Mac magazines (such as *Macworld, MacHome Journal,* or *MacAddict*).

Like the computers themselves, software programs are continually being improved and enhanced by their manufacturers. Just as in owning a computer, owning a software program isn't a one-time cash outlay; each time the software company comes out with a new version of the program, you'll be offered the chance to get it for a small "upgrade fee" of $25 or $99, for example.

You'd think people would get fed up with this endless treadmill of expenses and just stick with the version they've got, refusing to upgrade to successive versions. Some manage it. Most people, however, succumb to the fear that somehow they'll be left behind by the march of technology and wind up forking over the upgrade fees once a year or so. Let your budget and sense of independence be your guide.

Credit Card Workout #2: Buying Software

(Credit Card Workout #1, by the way, was buying the computer.)

The iMac comes with a handsome bonus gift of software preinstalled on the hard disk. That's fortunate, because software, for the most part, is expensive.

If you decide to explore the world of Mac software beyond what came with your iMac, for example, you'll discover that the popular word-processing program called Microsoft Word sells for about $300. If you plan to do number crunching, more than 90 percent of Mac users use the Microsoft Excel spreadsheet (another $300). Want a database for handling order forms, tracking phone calls, and creating form letters? Check out the fantastic FileMaker Pro (around $200). (Try, *try* not to focus on the fact that what you *get* for that money is a 50-cent CD and a $3 manual.)

But all that's for later; for now, revel in the fact that you own one of the greats: an *integrated* program called AppleWorks. This single program is actually several programs mashed into one: word processor, database, spreadsheet, drawing program, and so on. (See Chapter 9, "Faking Your Way through the Free Software.")

Your iMac also came with two games, Quicken (for balancing your checkbook), and a Web-page making application. The modern, CD slot-loading iMacs come even more loaded — with an encyclopedia on CD-ROM, a digital movie-making program, a calendar/address book program called Palm

Desktop, and a program that shields young eyes from the Internet's dark side. Chapters 9 and 10 describe all these programs in thrilling detail.

Where to get it

There are two places to buy software: via mail order and at a store. Unfortunately, as you'll quickly discover, today's computer stores generally offer a pathetically small selection of Macintosh software. On the other hand, mail-order companies offer thousands of choices; give much bigger discounts; take returns after you've opened the box; and don't charge sales tax. And, of course, you don't have to fire up the old Volvo. You get your stuff delivered to your door by the next day. (The overnight shipping charge is usually $5 per order.)

The mail-order companies are called things like Outpost.com, Mac Connection, Mac Zone, and Mac Warehouse. They all have toll-free phone numbers and Web pages (see Appendix B, "The Resource Resource," for a listing). Overnight mail-order companies like these are truly one of the bright spots in the computer world. You can call Mac Connection, for example, until *2:45 a.m.* and get your new programs by midmorning (seven hours later). After ordering from these companies, you'll start to wish there were overnight mail-order grocery stores, gas stations, and dentists.

All right, maybe not dentists.

In the next chapter, you're going to do some word processing. As a warm-up, however, let me show you some of the basic principles of using programs on the iMac. To make sure you've got the same thing on your screen that I do, we'll start off by using the built-in programs that came with your iMac.

El cheapo software

Once you've read Chapter 6, and you've decided it might be fun to plug your iMac into the telephone line to dial up faraway computers, you may stumble onto another kind of software: *shareware.* These are programs written by individuals, not software companies, who make their programs freely available on the Internet. You can grab them, via telephone, and bring them to your own iMac. And get this: Only the *honor system,* for heaven's sake, compels you to pay the authors the $15 or $20 they're asking for.

Sure, shareware often has a homemade feel to it. On the other hand, some of it's really terrific. You can search for the kind of shareware program you want (and also for acres of sounds, pictures, clip art, and games) on America Online and on the Internet (such as at *www.macdownload.com* or *www.shareware.com*).

Your very first software

There are several *menus* across the top of the screen (remember these?). As you get to know the iMac, you'll discover that their wording changes from program to program. Right now, they say, for example, File, Edit, View, and Special; in a word processor they might say File, Edit, Font, Size, Format, and so on. The menu names (and the commands listed in those menus) are tailored to the function of the software.

There's one menu that's *always* on your screen, though: our friend the Apple menu (the at the left edge of the menu bar). Among other things, this menu provides immediate access to some useful miniprograms known as *desk accessories.* Desk accessories are surefire, nonthreatening, and fun — perfect for your first baby steps into the world of software.

Desk Accessories

Let's start simple. Move your cursor up to the menu and choose Calculator. The Calculator pops up in a tiny window of its own.

The Calculator

Using the mouse, you can click the little Calculator buttons. The iMac gives you the correct mathematical answer, making you the owner of the world's biggest pocket calculator.

What's neat is that you can also type the number keys on your keyboard. As you press these real keys, you can watch the on-screen keys in the Calculator window get punched accordingly. Try it out!

Take a moment to reinforce your love of windows: By dragging the *title bar* (where it says "Calculator"), move the Calculator window into a new position. If you were tired of looking at it, you could also make the Calculator go away by clicking its close box (in the upper-left corner, like on all windows).

But don't close the Calculator just yet. Leave it open on the screen.

The Note Pad

Now open the menu again. Do you see a command called Note Pad? If so, click its name.

If not, your iMac may have the upgraded operating software called *Mac OS 9* (read all about it at the end of Chapter 13). In that case, skip the menu; your Note Pad has moved to a new address. Double-click your hard drive icon ("Macintosh HD"); then double-click the Apple Extras folder; then double-click the Note Pad icon to open it.

Either way, the world's most frill-free word processor should now be on the screen.

You'll learn more about word processing in the next section. For now, we're just going to do some informative goofing around. With the Note Pad open on your screen, type a math problem, like this:

37+8+19*3-100

(In the computer world, the asterisk [*] means "times," or multiply.) If you make a mistake, press the big Delete key at the upper-right corner of your keyboard. This key means "Backspace."

Now, by dragging the Note Pad's title bar, move it so that you can see the Calculator window, too.

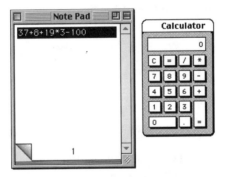

You're going to use two programs at once, making them cooperate with each other — one of the most remarkable features of the iMac.

Selecting text

This is about to get interesting.

Using the mouse, position the pointer at the left side of your equation (below, top). Press the mouse button and drag, perfectly horizontally, to the right (middle). Release the mouse after you've highlighted the entire equation (bottom).

]37+8+19*3-100

37+8+19*3-100

37+8+19*3-100]

You've just *selected* some text. Remember in Chapter 1, when you *selected* an icon — and then used a menu command? Struggling, as always, to come up with a decent analogy, I likened this *select-then-operate* sequence to building a noun-verb sentence.

Well, it works just as well with text as it does with icons. You've now high-lighted, or selected, some text. The iMac now knows what the noun is — what it's supposed to pay attention to. All you have to do is select a verb from one of the menus. And the *verb du jour* is *Copy*.

The cornerstone of human endeavor: Copy and Paste

Choose Copy from the Edit menu.

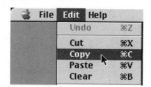

Thunder rolls, lightning flashes, the audience holds its breath . . . and absolutely nothing happens.

Behind the scenes, though, something awesomely useful occurred. The iMac looked at the selected equation and memorized it, socking it away into an invisible storage window called the *Clipboard*. The Clipboard is how you transfer stuff from one window into another and from one program into another. (Some programs even have a Show Clipboard command, in which case I take back the part about the Clipboard being invisible.)

Now then. You can't *see* the Clipboard at this point, but in a powerful act of faith, you put your trust in me and you believe that it contains the high-lighted material (the equation).

The Application menu

See the tiny Note Pad icon at the right end of your menu bar, helpfully identi-fied by the words Note Pad?

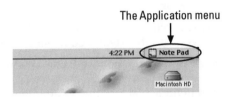

The Application menu

This icon actually represents a menu — the Application menu, of course. It lists all the programs that you have running at once. At this moment, you have *three* programs running at once: the Note Pad, the Calculator, and the famous Finder (or desktop).

You multitasking maniac, you.

Choose Calculator from the Application menu.

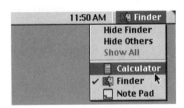

The Calculator window moves to the front, and the icon in the upper-right changes to look like a Calculator.

Those of you still awake will, of course, object to using the Application menu to bring the Calculator forward. You remember all too plainly from Chapter 1 that simply *clicking* in a window brings it to the front, which would have required less muscular effort.

Absolutely right! You may now advance to the semifinals. However, learning to use the Application menu was a good exercise. Many times in your upcom-ing life, the program in front will be covering up the *entire* screen. So *then* how will you bring another program forward, big shot? That's right. You can't *see* any other windows, so you can't click one to make it active. You'll have to use the Application menu.

In any case, the Calculator is now the active application. (*Active* just means it's in front.) Now then: Remember that intricate equation that's still on the iMac Clipboard? Instead of having to type an equation into the Calculator by punching keys, let's just paste it in:

1. **Press the letter C key on your iMac keyboard, or click the C button on the Calculator.**

   You just cleared the display. We wouldn't want your previous diddlings to interfere with this tightly controlled experiment.

2. **From the Edit menu, choose Paste — and watch the Calculator!**

If you looked in time, you saw the number keys flashing like Las Vegas at midnight. And with a triumphant modesty, the iMac displays the answer to your math problem. (It should be 92.)

 Did you get what just happened? You typed out a math problem in a word processor (the Note Pad), copied it to the Clipboard, and pasted it into a number-cruncher (the Calculator). Much of the miracle of the Macintosh stems from its capability to mix and match information among multiple programs in this way.

It's a two-way street, too. You can paste this number back into the word processor:

1. **From the Edit menu, choose Copy.**

   But wait! Something was already on the Clipboard. Where is the iMac supposed to put this *new* copied info?

   On the Clipboard, of course. And whatever was there before (your equation) gets nuked. The Clipboard contains exactly one thing at a time — whatever you copied *most recently.*

2. **From the Application menu, choose Note Pad (or just click the Note Pad window).**

   The Note Pad is now the active application.

3. **Type the following:**

   Dear son: You owe me $

   Stop after the $ sign. Move the mouse up to the Edit menu.

4. **From the Edit menu, choose Paste.**

   Bingo! The iMac pastes in the result from the Calculator (which it had ready on the Clipboard).

   Incidentally, whatever's on the Clipboard stays there until you copy something new or until you turn off the machine. In other words, you can paste it over and over again.

5. **For a second time, choose Paste from the Edit menu.**

   Another 92 pops into the window.

You don't have to use the menu to issue a command like Copy or Paste. If you wish, you can use a keyboard shortcut to do the same thing. You may remember having used the ⌘ key in Chapter 2 to issue commands without using the mouse.

And how are you supposed to remember which letter key corresponds to which command? Well, usually it's mnemonic: ⌘-P means Print, ⌘-O means Open, and so on. But you can cheat; try it right now. Click the Edit menu.

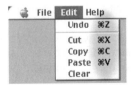

There's your crib sheet, carefully listed down the right side of the menu. Notice that the keyboard shortcuts for all four of these important commands (Undo, Cut, Copy, Paste) are adjacent on the keyboard: Z, X, C, V.

C is Copy. And V, right next to it, is Paste. (I know, I know: Why doesn't *P* stand for Paste? Answer: Because *P* stands for Print! And anyway, V is right next to C-for-Copy on your keyboard, so it *kind of* makes sense.)

Click anywhere else on the screen (to ditch the menu) and let's try it:

Memo to NASA scientists

Don't rely on the little Calculator program for calculating launch times or impact statistics, at least not without understanding how its math differs from yours.

The Calculator processes equations from left to right. It does *not* solve the multiplication and division components before the addition and subtraction, as is standard in math classes worldwide.

For example, consider this equation: 3+2*4=. (The * means "times" in computerland.) The scientific answer is 11, because you multiply before you add when solving such puzzles. But the Mac's answer is 20, because it processes the numbers from left to right.

---

1. **While holding down the ⌘ key, type a V.**

   Bingo! Another copy of the Clipboard stuff (92) appears in your Note Pad. (In the future, I'll just refer to a keyboard shortcut like this as "⌘-V.")

2. **Press ⌘-V again.**

   Yep, that kid's debt is really piling up. He now owes you $92,929,292.

   But after all, he's your son. Why not just let him pay 1 percent down on the amount he owes you? In other words, why not *undo* that last 92 pasting?

3. **From the Edit menu, choose Undo.**

   The most recent thing you did — in this case, pasting the fourth 92 — gets undone.

Rewriting history is addicting, ain't it?

Remember, though, that Undo only reverses your *most recent* action. Suppose you (1) copy something, (2) paste it somewhere else, and then (3) type some more. If you choose Undo, only the typing will be undone (Step 3), *not* the pasting (Step 2).

Control Panels

One item in your menu *isn't* a desk accessory. It says Control Panels, and all it does is open up your Control Panels folder. So what exactly *is* your Control Panels folder? It's a folder that lives inside your System Folder. It contains a bunch of icons, each of which controls some aspect of your iMac. Choose Control Panels from the menu to make the Control Panel window appear.

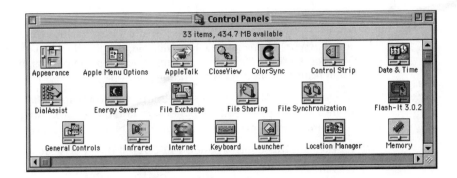

 I'll show you around one control panel; then you can take it from there:

1. **Quickly type *DA* on your keyboard.**

   Remember this handy trick? You can select one icon in a folder just by typing the first couple of letters of its name. In this case, you get the Date & Time icon.

2. **Double-click the Date & Time icon.**

   The Date & Time control-panel window opens. This is where you set the clock — as displayed, for example, at the top right of your screen. To change the time, click a number and then type the correct number in its place.

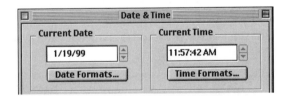

All right — close the Date & Time window by clicking the close box in the upper-left corner.

Top Ten Control Panel Explanations

Dozens of control panels are kicking around in your Control Panels folder. Here are a few national favorites. (Some have different names depending on when you bought your iMac.) For much more detail about all the stuff in your System Folder, see Chapter 12.

1. **Monitors** — Lets you switch your monitor among various color settings (such as *grayscale,* like a black-and-white TV, or various degrees of richness of color). Some games, for example, require that you change your iMac screen to its *256 Colors* setting; when viewing photos, however, you'll want the *Thousands* or *Millions* option.

   (P.S. — If your iMac has a System folder version before Mac OS 9, the Monitors and Sound control panels are combined into a single entity called Monitors & Sound. You'll figure it out.)

2. **Sound** — In this control panel, you can tell the iMac which beep sound you'd like it to use when it wants your attention. You can even record your *own* sounds, as described in Chapter 19.

3. **Mouse** — Controls how sensitive the pointer movement is. Incidentally, the pointer on the screen *always* moves slowly if you move your mouse slowly. This control panel enables you to adjust how quickly the arrow moves if you move your mouse *quickly.*

4. **Appearance** — The various tabs at the top of this massively entertaining control panel let you control the way your iMac's screen looks, feels, and sounds. For a blow-by-blow description of the options here, see "The Control Panels Folder" in Chapter 12. For now, just note that the Appearance control panel is the one that lets you hang a favorite photograph as your on-screen background wallpaper.

5. **Map** — Tells what time it is anywhere in the world. Either click to specify a location or type the name of a major city or country and click the Find button. (If you have Mac OS 9 or later, this control panel *isn't* in your Control Panels folder, although you're free to put it there. It comes instead in the Apple Extras folder in your main hard drive window.)

6. **Speech** — Lets you choose a voice for the iMac to use when *talking to you* (see Chapter 19).

7. **File Exchange** — Lets your iMac use floppy disks from Windows computers (but only if you buy a floppy drive or SuperDisk drive for your iMac).

8. **Energy Saver** — Lets you establish automatic shutoff times (or automatic sleep times) for your iMac, in the name of saving electricity. For example, mine is set to go to sleep if I haven't used the computer in 30 minutes.

9. **General Controls** — Offers a slew of handy customizing features: how fast your cursor blinks when you're word processing, whether or not you want your System Folder protected against marauding children, and so on. Also holds the on/off switches for three of the iMac's most useful features: the Launcher (see Chapter 4), the Documents folder (Chapter 4 again), and self-hiding programs (see Chapter 12, under "General Controls").

10. **Keyboard** — Lets you decide whether holding down a key should type its letter repeatedly — for example, XXXXXXXXXXX — and how fast it repeats.

Chapter 4

Typing, Saving, and Finding Again

. . . .

In This Chapter

▶ Unlearning years of typewriter lessons

▶ Dragging and dropping

▶ How to save your files so they're not lost forever

▶ You — yes, you — the desktop publisher

. . . .

*L*et's not kid ourselves. Yeah, I know, you're gonna use your iMac to do photo retouching, to create 3-D animations, or to compose symphonies. But with the possible exception of e-mail and Web exploits, what you'll probably do the *most* of is good old *word processing*.

But just because everybody does it doesn't mean word processing isn't the single most magical, amazing, time-saving invention since the microwave dinner. Master word processing, and you've essentially mastered your computer.

Your Very First Bestseller

Lucky for you, your iMac comes with a superb word-processing program. It's called AppleWorks, and you can read about it in Chapter 9.

For this quick and dirty typing lesson, though, you may as well use a quick and dirty program: the super-budget word processor known as the Note Pad. Choose its name from the menu to make it appear.

If you don't see it in your menu, then your iMac probably has Mac OS 9, which is described in Chapter 1. You still have the Note Pad, but it's not in the menu. Instead, you'll have to do some double-clicking to find it: Open your hard drive icon. Open the Apple Extras folder. Double-click Note Pad.

All about big fat Launcher buttons

Do you recognize this thing?

If you don't see it, you can make it appear by choosing Launcher from the Control Panels command of your menu.

The Launcher is supposed to make getting into your programs easier. It keeps your favorite programs conveniently collected in a central location. Under the assumption that you generally don't want to waste time launching these programs, Apple designed the Launcher so that *one* click, not the usual two, opens any icon on the Launcher.

The rules for using the Launcher are simple:

1. If there's some program — or document, or folder — whose icon *isn't* on the Launcher window but should be, simply drag its icon into the Launcher window and release. A copy of that icon appears automatically, ready for subsequent one-click launching.

2. If there's some program on the Launcher window that you don't really use, you can get rid of it. While pressing the Option key, drag that sucker right to the trash. (You aren't trashing the *actual* program, wherever it may reside on your computer. You're just getting its *icon* off the Launcher window.)

3. If you'd like to have the Launcher window welcome you every morning, choose Control Panels from the menu. Open the control panel called General Controls. Click the check box called "Show Launcher at system startup" to turn it on.

4. You can make the buttons in the Launcher window bigger or smaller like this: While pressing the ⌘ key, click any white space in the Launcher. A miniature menu pops out, offering you Large, Medium, or Small buttons. Click your choice.

Top three rules of word processing

The first rules of typing on a computer are going to be tough to learn, especially if you've been typing for years. But they're crucial:

> ✔ **Don't press the Return key at the end of each line.** I'm dead serious here. When you type your way to the end of a line, the next word will automatically jump down to the next line. If you press Return in the middle of a sentence, you'll mess everything up.

✔ **Put only one space after a period.** From now on, everything you write will come out looking like it was professionally published instead of being cranked out on some noisy Selectric with a bad ribbon. A quick glance at any published book, magazine, or newspaper will make you realize that the two-spaces-after-a-period thing is strictly for typewriters.

✔ **Don't use the L key to make the number 1.** Your iMac, unlike the typewriter you may have grown up with, actually has a key dedicated to making the number 1. If you use a lowercase L instead, the 1 will look funny, and your spelling checker will think you've gone nuts.

If those statements give you uncontrollable muscular facial spasms, I don't blame you. After all, I'm telling you to do things that you were explicitly taught *not* to do by that high-school typing teacher with the horn-rimmed glasses.

There are a few other rules, too, but breaking them isn't serious enough to get you fired. So let's dig in. Make sure you have a blank piece of electronic typing paper open in front of you — a clean, fresh Note Pad screen.

The excitement begins

You should see a short, blinking, vertical line at the beginning of the typing area. They call this the *insertion point*. It shows you where the letters will appear when you start to type.

Type the upcoming passage. If you make a typo, press Delete, just as you would Backspace on a typewriter. (For a rundown of the iMac's other unusual keys, see Chapter 13.) *Don't* press Return when you get to the edge of the window. Just keep typing, and the iMac will create a second line for you. Believe. *Believe.*

> *The screams of the lions burst Rod's eardrums as the motorboat, out of control, exploded through the froth.*

See how the words automatically wrapped around to the second line? They call this feature, with astonishing originality, *word wrap.*

But suppose, as your novel is going to press, you decide that this sleepy passage really needs some spicing up. You decide to insert the word *speeding* before the word *motorboat.*

Remember the blinking cursor — the insertion point? It's on the screen even now, blinking calmly away at the end of the sentence. If you want to insert text, you have to move the insertion point.

The point of no returns

Why aren't you supposed to hit Return at the end of each line?

First time in print! An actual example of the kind of mess you can get into by pressing Return after each line of text.

At left: the original passage. Suppose you decide to remove Paulson's title, "Chief Executive Officer," since everybody already

knows what kind of guy he is (left). But suppose you'd been foolish enough to press Return after each line of text; if you remove those three highlighted words, the word *Paulson* flops back to the left side of the line, but the rest of the sentence stays where it is, looking dumb (right).

On the other hand, if you *hadn't* put Returns into your text, you'd get the figure below, where everything looks peachy.

You can move the insertion point in two ways. First, try pressing the arrow keys in the lower-right cluster of your keyboard. You can see that the up- and down-arrow keys move the insertion point from line to line, and the right- and left-arrow keys move the insertion point across the line. Practice moving the insertion point by pressing the arrow keys.

If the passage you want to edit is far away, though (on another page, for example), using the arrow keys to move the cursor is inefficient. Your fingers would be bloody stumps by the time you finished. Instead, use this finger-saving technique:

1. **Using the mouse, move the cursor (which, when it's near text, looks like this: I) just before the word *motorboat*, and then click the mouse.**

   The I-beam changes to the insertion point.

   This is as confusing as word processing ever gets — there are *two* little cursors, right? There's the blinking insertion point, and there's this one I, which is called an *I-beam* cursor.

In fact, the two little cursors are quite different. The blinking insertion point is only a *marker,* not a pointer. It always shows you where the next typing will appear. The I-beam, on the other hand, is how you *move* the insertion point; when you click with the I-beam, you set down the insertion point.

In other words, editing stuff you've already typed, on the Macintosh, is a matter of *click and then type*.

2. Type the word *speeding*.

The insertion point does its deed, and the iMac makes room on the line for the new word. A word or two probably got pushed onto the next line. Isn't word wrap wondrous?

Editing for the linguistically blessed

So much for *inserting* text: You click the mouse (to show the iMac *where*) and then type away. But what if you need to delete a bunch of text? What if you decide to *cut out* the first half of our sample text?

Well, unless you typed the challenging excerpt with no errors, you already know one way to erase text — by pressing the Delete key. Delete takes out one letter at a time, just to the left of the insertion point.

Deleting one letter at a time isn't much help in this situation, though. Suppose you decide to take out the *first part* of the sentence. It wouldn't be horribly efficient to backspace over the entire passage just so you could work on the beginning.

No, instead you need a way to edit any part of your work, at any time, without disturbing the stuff you want to leave. Once again, the Macintosh method, noun-then-verb, saves the day. Try this:

1. Using the mouse and its mouse, position the I-beam cursor at the beginning of the sentence.

This takes a steady hand; stay calm.

2. Click *just* to the left of the first word and, keeping the mouse button pressed down, drag the I-beam cursor — *perfectly horizontally,* if possible — to the end of the word *as*.

As you drag, the text gets highlighted, or *selected*. You've done this once before, in your copy-and-paste lesson.

The screams of the lions burst Rod's eardrums as the speeding motorboat, out of control, exploded through the froth.

If you accidentally drag up or down into the next line of text, the highlighting jumps to include a big chunk of that additional line. Don't panic; without releasing the mouse button, simply move the cursor back onto the original line you were selecting. This time, try to drag more horizontally.

If you're especially clever and forward-thinking, you'll also have selected the blank space *after* the word *as*. Take a look at the previous illustration.

All right, in typical Mac syntax, you've just specified *what* you want to edit by selecting it (and making it turn black to show it's selected). Now for the verb:

1. **Press the Delete key.**

    Bam! The selected text is gone. The sentence looks pretty odd, though, since it doesn't begin with a capital letter.

2. **Using the mouse, position the cursor just before (or after) the letter *t* that begins the sentence. Drag the cursor sideways across the letter so that it's highlighted.**

    the speeding motorboat, out of control, exploded
    through the froth.

    Here comes another ground rule of word processing. See how you've just selected, or highlighted, the letter *t?* The idea here is to capitalize it. Of course, using the methods for wiping out (and inserting) text that you learned earlier, you could simply remove the *t* and type a *T*. But since you've selected the *t* by dragging through it, replacing it is much easier.

3. **Type a capital *T*.**

The selected text gets replaced by the new stuff you type. That, in fact, is the fourth ground rule: *Selected text gets replaced by the new stuff you type.* As your iMac life proceeds, keep that handy fact in mind; it can save you a lot of backspacing. In fact, you can select 40 pages of text so that it's all highlighted and then type *one single letter* to replace all of it. Or you could *select* only one letter but replace it with 40 pages of typing.

Take a moment now for some unsupervised free play. Try clicking anywhere in the text (to plant the insertion point). Try dragging through some text: If you drag perfectly horizontally, you select text just on one line (below, left). If you drag diagonally, you get everything between your cursor and the original click (below, right).

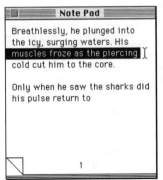 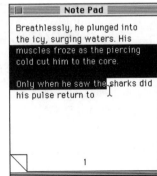

You *deselect* (or, equally poetically, unhighlight) text by clicking the mouse. Anywhere at all (within the typing area).

Here's about the most fabulous word-processing shortcut ever devised: Try pointing to a word and then double-clicking the mouse! You've easily selected *exactly* that word without having to do any dragging.

As you experiment, do anything you want with any combination of drags, clicks, double-clicks, and menu selections. It's nice to know — and you might want to prepare a fine mahogany wall plaque to this effect — that *nothing you do using the mouse or keyboard can physically harm the computer.* Oh, sure, it's possible to erase a disk or wreck one of your documents or something, but none of that requires a visit to a repair shop. You can't *break* the computer by playing around.

Puff, the Magic Drag-N-Drop

You kids today, with your long music and loud hair! You don't know how lucky you are! Why, when I was your age, if I wanted to rearrange a couple of words, I'd have to *copy and paste them!*

But not anymore. Nowadays, you can move text around on the screen just by *pointing* to it! This profoundly handy feature is known as Macintosh *drag-and-drop.*

Unfortunately, drag-and-drop doesn't work in every program, but it works in most of the biggies: the Note Pad; AppleWorks; Microsoft anything; Outlook Express; Palm Desktop; SimpleText; America Online; FileMaker; and so on.

1. **Launch a program that offers drag-and-drop.**

   If you've been following along with the chapter already in progress, just remain in the Note Pad where you've already been. Press the Return key a couple of times to move into an empty part of the page.

A word processing rule-ette

You know, by now, that your mouse pointer looks like this — I — whenever it's near text. And you know, by now, that you use this cursor to *click* wherever you want to type next.

But suppose you want to add some words way down the page, like this:

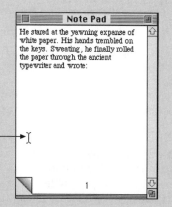

You'll discover pretty quickly that the Macintosh won't let you type there. The rule is: You can click your cursor anywhere on the page *that already has typing on it.* But if you try to click down *below*, in the white space, you're out of luck; the blinking insertion-point cursor simply jumps back up to the end of what you've already typed. In its ornery way, the iMac enforces its own rule of writing: No jumping ahead, bub.

Of course, you *can* skip down the page if you want some words to appear there. But you have to *type your way* down the page first. That's why God invented the Return key. Press it over and over again until your little insertion-point cursor is blinking merrily away at the bottom of the page — or wherever you tell it to go — and *now* start typing.

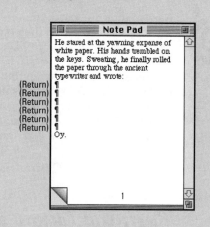

2. **Type up two phrases, as shown here:**

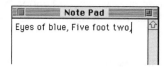

3. **Highlight *Eyes of blue.***

You've done this before: Position the insertion-point cursor just to the left of the word *Eyes* and *carefully* slide directly to the right, highlighting the phrase (below, left).

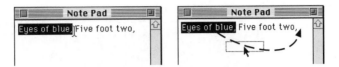

4. **Now position the arrow cursor right smack in the middle of the blackened phrase — hold down the mouse button — and *drag* the arrow to the end of the line (above, right).**

   When your arrow is correctly positioned at the end of the line, you'll see the new insertion point appear there.

5. **Release the mouse!**

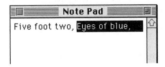

As you can see, you've just *dragged* the first phrase into position after the second phrase! Cole Porter would be very grateful for your correcting his lyrics.

Now how much would you pay? But wait — there's more! Once you've mastered the art of dragging text around your screen, the sky's the limit! To wit:

✔ If you press the *Option* key while you drag some highlighted text, instead of *moving* that phrase, you actually make a *copy* of it, as shown here:

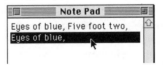

✔ You can actually drag text *clear out of the window* and into another program — for example, from AppleWorks into the waiting Note Pad.

✔ You can also drag text clear out of the window and *onto the desktop*. When you release the mouse button, you'll see that your little drag-and-dropped blurb has turned into a *text clipping*, as shown here:

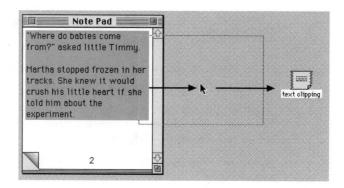

Next time you need that blob of text, you can point to the text clipping and drag it back into your word-processing program, and — presto! — the text appears there, exactly as though you'd typed it again.

Now if they'd only work it out so we could edit our *printouts* using drag-and-drop. . . .

Form and Format

For your next trick, it's time to graduate from the Note Pad to a true word processor. Close the Note Pad window. Open your hard drive; open the Applications folder; open the AppleWorks folder; and double-click the AppleWorks icon.

After a moment, the AppleWorks welcome screen appears, listing six kinds of work you might want to do: Database, Spreadsheet, and so on. (You'll find out what all these things are in Chapter 9.) Double-click the one called Word Processing to open up a new, blank sheet of electronic typing paper. Now you're ready for the lesson.

One of the most important differences between a typewriter and its replacement — the computer — is the sequence of events. When you use a typewriter, you set up all the formatting characteristics *before* you type: the margins, the tab stops, and (for typewriters with interchangeable type heads) the type style.

But the whole point of a word processor is that you can change anything at *any* time. Many people type the text of an entire letter (or proposal, or memo) into the iMac and *then* format it. When you use a typewriter, you might discover, after typing the entire first page, that it's *slightly* too long to fit, and your signature will have to sit awkwardly on a page by itself. With an iMac, you'd see the problem and nudge the text a little bit higher on the page to compensate.

Seeing the unseen

I said that Returns are *usually* invisible. However, every time you press the Return key, the iMac actually does plop down a symbol onto your screen. Same thing with the space bar. Same with the Tab key.

Virtually every word processor lets you see these markings. In AppleWorks or ClarisWorks,

choose Preferences from the Edit or Tools menu to access the Show Invisibles (or View Nonprinting) option. In any case, the result looks something like this:

> ◆   "Alison—my god, not that! Anything but that!"¶
>
> ◆   But it was too late. She had already disappeared.¶

Word processing has other great advantages: no crossouts; easy corrections that involve no whiteout and no retyping; a permanent record of your correspondence that's electronic, not paper, and so it's always easy to find; a selection of striking typefaces — at any size; paste-in graphics; and so on. It's safe to say that once you try processing words, you'll never look back.

The return of Return

With all the subtlety of a Mack truck, I've taught you that you're forbidden to use the Return key *at the end of a line*. Still, that rectangular Return key on your keyboard *is* important. You press Return at the end of a *paragraph,* and only there.

To the computer, the Return key works just like a letter key — it inserts a *Return character* into the text. It's just like rolling the paper in a typewriter forward by one notch. Hit Return twice, and you leave a blank line.

The point of Return, then, is to move text higher or lower on the page. Check out this example, for instance.

¶
¶
¶
¶

Dearest Todd,¶
¶
I have never loved so much as I did last night. Imagine my joy as I watched you plunch your shining scimitar into the greasy flesh of that—that—hideous thing from the deep.¶

Unfortunately, the IRS has determined that you failed to file returns for the years 1982–1986. They have asked that I notify you of ¶

¶
Dearest Todd,¶
¶
I have never loved so much as I did last night. Imagine my joy as I watched you plunch your shining scimitar into the greasy flesh of that—that—hideous thing from the deep.¶

Unfortunately, the IRS has determined that you failed to file returns for the years 1982–1986. They have asked that I notify you of ¶

Return characters move text down on the page. So, if you want to move text up on the page, drag through the blank space so that it's highlighted (above, left); of course, what you've really done is select the usually invisible Return characters. If you delete them, the text slides up the page (right).

Combine this knowledge with your advanced degree in Inserting Text (remember? you *click and then type*), and you can see how you'd make more space between paragraphs or push all the text of a letter down on the page.

Appealing characters

Another big-time difference between word processing and typing is all the great *character formatting* you can do. You can make any piece of text **bold,** *italic,* <u>underlined</u>, all of these, and more. You also get a selection of great-look-ing typefaces — only a few of which look like a typewriter. By combining all these styles and fonts randomly, you can make any document look absolutely hideous.

Here's the scheme for changing some text to one of those character formats: noun-verb. Sound familiar? Go for it:

1. **Select some text by dragging through it.**

   Remember you can select a single word by double-clicking it; to select a bunch of text, drag the cursor through it so that it turns black. You've just identified *what* you want to change.

   Each word processor keeps its Bold, Italic, and Underline commands in its own specially named menu; in AppleWorks, they're in the Style menu. (AppleWorks and Microsoft programs also offer a floating rack of but-tons at the top of the screen, containing B, I, and U buttons. They do the same thing as using the menu commands.)

2. **From the Style menu, choose Bold.**

   You've just specified *how* you want to affect the selected text.

You can apply several of these formats to the same text, too, although you won't win any awards for typographical excellence. Try changing the type-face also; the various fonts are called things like Chicago, Geneva, Times, and so on. Changing fonts works the same way: Select text and then choose the font.

And sizes — same deal: Select some text and then choose a type size from the AppleWorks Size menu. The font sizes are measured in points, of which there are 72 per inch. Works out nicely, too — a typical iMac monitor has 72 *screen* dots per inch, meaning that 12-point type on the screen really *is* 12-point.

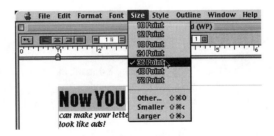

Before you know it, you'll have whipped your document into handsome shape.

Formatting paragraphs

Whereas type styles and sizes can be applied to any amount of text, even a single letter, *paragraph formatting* affects a whole paragraph at once. Usually these styles are easy to apply. To select a paragraph, you don't have to high-light all the text in it. Instead, you can just click *once,* anywhere within a paragraph, to plant the insertion point. Then, as before, choose the menu command that you want to apply to that entire paragraph.

This figure shows some of the different options every word processor pro-vides for paragraph formatting — left-justified, right-justified, fully justified, and centered:

Her heart pounding, she looked toward the door. It swung open with a creak. The stench hit her first—an acrid, rotting swamp smell. She covered her mouth with the blood-soaked handkerchief and stepped backward, her naked back pressed hard against the fourposter.

Left-justified

Her heart pounding, she looked toward the door. It swung open with a creak. The stench hit her first—an acrid, rotting swamp smell. She covered her mouth with the blood-soaked handkerchief and stepped backward, her naked back pressed hard against the fourposter.

Right-justified

Her heart pounding, she looked toward the door. It swung open with a creak. The stench hit her first—an acrid, rotting swamp smell. She covered her mouth with the blood-soaked handkerchief and stepped backward, her naked back pressed hard against the fourposter.

Fully justified

Her heart pounding, she looked toward the door. It swung open with a creak. The stench hit her first—an acrid, rotting swamp smell. She covered her mouth with the blood-soaked handkerchief and stepped backward, her naked back pressed hard against the fourposter.

Centered

(In AppleWorks, you get these effects by clicking a paragraph, and then click-ing one of the four square buttons just above the ruler at the top of the window. You can see these buttons in the previous illustration. If you don't see the ruler, choose Show Rulers from the Window menu.)

The efficiency zealot's guide to power typing

Because you *can* format text after you've typed it doesn't mean you *have* to. Most power-users get used to the keyboard shortcuts for the common style changes, like bold and italic. They're pretty easy to remember: In nearly every word-processing program, you get bold by pressing ⌘-B and italic with ⌘-I.

What's handy is that you can hit this key combo just *before* you type the word. For example, without ever taking your hands off the keyboard, you could type the following:

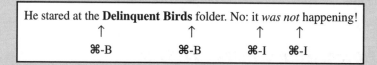

In other words, you hit ⌘-B once to turn bold *on* for the next burst of typing, and ⌘-B again to turn it off — all without ever having to use a menu. (You do the same with ⌘-I.)

You can control paragraphs in other ways, too. Remember in high school when you were supposed to turn in a 20-page paper, and you'd try to pad your much-too-short assignment by making it two-and-a-half spaced? Well, if you'd had an iMac, you could have been much more sneaky about it. You can make your word-processed document single-spaced, double-spaced, quadruple-spaced, or any itty-bitty fraction thereof. You can even control how tightly together the letters are placed, making it easy to stretch or compress your writing into more or fewer pages.

Take this opportunity to toy with your word processor. Go ahead, really muck things up. Make it look like a ransom note with a million different type styles and sizes. Then, when you've got a real masterpiece on the screen, read on.

Working with Documents

It might terrify you — and it should — to find out that you've been working on an imaginary document. Only a thin thread of streaming electrical current preserves it. Your typing doesn't exist yet, to be perfectly accurate, except in your iMac's *memory*.

You may recall from the notes you took on Chapter 1½ that memory is fleeting. (Specifically, I mean *computer* memory, but if you find a more universal truth in my words, interpret away.) In fact, the memory is wiped away when you shut the iMac down — or when a system crash, a rare but inevitable event for any computer, turns it off *for* you. At that moment, anything that exists on the screen is gone forever.

Therefore, almost every program has a Save command. It's always in the File menu, and its keyboard shortcut is always ⌘-S.

When you save your work, the iMac transfers it from transient, fleeting, electronic memory onto the good, solid, permanent disk. There your work will remain, safely saved. It will still be there tomorrow. It will still be there next week. It will still be there ten years from now, when your computer is so obsolete that it's valuable again.

Therefore, let's try an experiment with your ransom note document on the screen. From the File menu, choose Save.

Uh-oh. Something weird just happened: The iMac presented you with a box full of options. It's called a *dialog box,* because the computer needs to have a little chat with you before proceeding.

When you see this box, what the iMac mainly wants to know is: "Under what name would you like me to file this precious document, Massssster?"

And how do you know this? Because in the blank where it says "Save as," a proposed title is highlighted (selected already). And what do you know about highlighted text? *Anything you start typing will instantly replace it.*

The iMac, in its cute, limited way, is trying to tell you that it needs you to type a title. Go ahead, do it: Type *Ransom Note*.

At this point, you could just click the Save button. The iMac would take everything in perilous, fleeting memory and transfer it to the staid, safe hard disk, where it would remain until you're ready to work on it some more.

However, a bunch of other stuff lurks in this dialog box. Especially since this is the Numero Uno source of confusion to beginners, I think a tour of the Save File box is in order.

Navigating the Save File (and Open File) box

You've already learned about the way your computer organizes files: with folders and with folders *in* folders. Remember this little exercise from Chapter 2, where you put state-named folders inside the USA Folder?

Well, all the complicated-looking stuff in the Save File box is a miniature version of that same folder-filing system. Suppose you see this when you're trying to save your file:

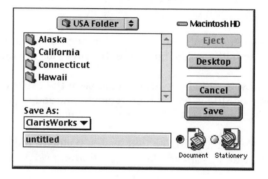

Look at the open-folder "menu" (in a rectangle above the list). It tells you that you're viewing the contents of the USA Folder. In other words, if you click the Save button, you'll file your new Ransom Note document in the USA Folder, mixed in among the state folders.

But suppose that you want to file the Ransom Note document in one of the state folders. You already know how you open a folder — by double-clicking it — so you'd point to Alaska, for example, and double-click.

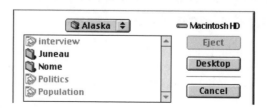

Now the open-folder "menu" above the list says _Alaska,_ and you can see the stuff inside the Alaska folder. Some names are dimmed because they're all _documents;_ the only things whose names are black in this dialog box are folders. (The iMac wants to know where you want to put your new document. Because you can't very well store one document inside _another_ document, the names are grayed out and unavailable, and only the folder names are black and available.)

Okay. So now you're viewing the contents of the Alaska folder. What if you change your mind? What if you decide that the ransom note should really go in the World folder — the one that _contains_ the USA Folder?

You must retrace your steps. That's what the little folder menu is all about (where it now says _Alaska_). They call this doohickey a _pop-up menu:_ It's a menu, but it's not at the top of the screen. The small black triangles beside the name Alaska tell you: "Click me!"

Sure enough, when you click the word Alaska, you see the list of all the nested folders you had to travel through to get here. This is where things get a little weird: The list is _upside-down_ from the path you took!

 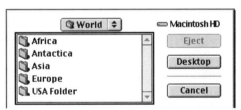

In other words, if you were in the Finder instead of in this Save File dialog box, you'd have started at the desktop level (the colored background). You'd have double-clicked the hard-disk icon (probably called Macintosh HD) to open its window. Then you'd have double-clicked the World folder to open that, and the USA Folder inside of _that,_ and finally the Alaska folder. If you look at the preceding menu picture, you'll see that, sure enough, your entire folder path is listed. You can view the entire hierarchy of folders — as long as you get used to the fact that the list is upside-down, and the outer levels (the hard disk and the desktop) are listed at the bottom.

Therefore, if you wanted to file the ransom note in the World folder (below, right), you'd simply slide down the pop-up menu list and choose World (below, left).

Then, at long last, when you're viewing the contents of the folder you want to save the file in, you can name your file and click the Save button.

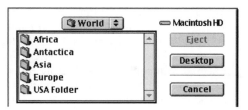

For the purposes of following along with this exercise, double-click a folder — any folder — to store your file in. Type a name for your file, such as *Ransom Note,* in the blank where it probably now says "untitled." And then click Save.

Your file gets snugly tucked away into the folder whose contents you're viewing. Want proof, O Cynic? All you have to do is choose Finder from the Application menu. Remember, the Application menu is the icon at the upper-right side of the screen. It lists all the programs that are running at once.

When you choose Finder, our friends the folders, windows, and Trash can pop up. If you wanted to make sure your file really exists, and it really got put where you wanted it, you could now double-click your hard drive icon (Macintosh HD) and then double-click your way through folders until you found it. In our example, your ransom note would be in the World folder:

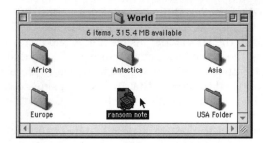

Why are we kicking this absolutely deceased horse? Because the same folder-navigation scheme (where you see an upside-down list of nested folders) is used for *retrieving* files you've already created. You need to know how to climb up and down your folder tree, as you'll see in a moment, if you ever want to see your files again.

Two easy ways to avoid losing stuff

This business about the "Save Where?" dialog box is, as anybody will tell you, the most confusing thing about the Macintosh. After years of experience, a few professional beginners have adopted one of the following cheats — and they never lose another file.

Cheat 1:

Whenever you save a file, and you're faced with the Save dialog box, *click the Desktop button first.* Only then should you click the Save button.

Go ahead, ask it. "What's the point?"

Easy: When you're done working for the day, and you return to the desktop, you won't have to wonder what folder your document's icon fell into. Your new file will be sitting right there, *on the desktop*, in plain sight.

At this point, it's child's play to drag the icon into the folder you *want* it in.

Cheat 2:

So many people complained that they couldn't find their saved documents that Apple invented the Documents folder.

To make yours appear, choose Control Panels from your menu. Double-click General Controls. In the lower-right corner of the resulting

window, select Documents folder (to turn it on) or one of the other choices (to turn it off). Close all the windows you've just opened.

The next time you save a file — or try to open one — the iMac automatically creates this special folder called Documents. It sits in your Macintosh HD window. From now on, *every* time you save a file (or try to open one), you'll always be shown the contents of the Documents folder, like this:

The contents of this special magnet folder will be in your face at all times. You'll never wonder where some file went — it'll always be right in your Documents folder.

Closing a file, with a sigh

You've created a ransom note. It's got all kinds of text and formatting. You've saved it onto the disk so that it'll be there tomorrow. In a moment, you'll get a chance to prove it to yourself.

Switch back into AppleWorks by choosing its name from the upper-right application menu. Click the close box in the upper-left corner of the window. Once.

In the iMac's universal language of love, clicking the small square up there means *close the window*, as you'll recall. If all went well, the window disappears.

Worrywarts' corner

From the way I've described the terrifyingly delicate condition of a document that's on the screen (that you haven't saved to disk yet) — that is, precariously close to oblivion, kept alive only by electric current — you might think that closing a window is a dangerous act. After all, what if you forgot to save some work? Wouldn't closing the window mean losing that critical memo?

Not really — if you try to close a document, the iMac won't *let* you proceed until it asks you whether you're *sure* you want to lose all the work you've done. It will say something like:

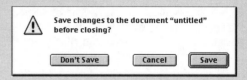

Click Save if you do want to save your work. Click Don't Save if you were only goofing around and don't want to preserve your labors.

Click Cancel if you change your mind completely about closing the document and want to keep working on it.

How to find out what's going on

This gets sort of metaphysical. Hold onto your brain.

Just because you closed your *document* doesn't mean you've left the *program*. In fact, if you pull down the Application menu at the right side of the screen, you'll see that the word-processing program is, in fact, still running. (It's the one with a check mark beside it — such as AppleWorks or Note Pad.)

You could bring the Finder to the front by choosing its name from the Application menu — without exiting the word processor. They both can be running at the same time, but only one can be in front.

In fact, that's the amazing thing about a Macintosh. You can have a bunch of programs all open and running at once. The more memory your iMac has, the more programs you can run simultaneously.

What gets confusing is that one program (say, AppleWorks) may be active, but you'll *think* you're in the Finder. After all, you'll see your familiar icons, Trash, folders, and so on. You need to understand that all this is simply *shining through* the emptiness left by AppleWorks, which has no windows open at the moment. If a window *were* open, it would cover up the desktop behind it.

Right now, for instance, I realize that it's hard for you to believe that you're using a word processor, when there are no words on the screen. But you have several clues as to what program you're using.

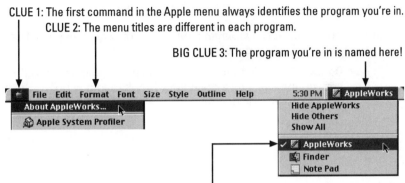

CLUE 1: The first command in the Apple menu always identifies the program you're in.
CLUE 2: The menu titles are different in each program.

BIG CLUE 3: The program you're in is named here!

CLUE 4: The check mark in the Application menu also identifies the program you're in.

For the moment, stay in AppleWorks.

Getting It All Back Again

Okay. You've typed a ransom note. Using the Save command, you turned that typing on your screen into an icon on your hard disk. Now it's time for a concept break.

Crazy relationships: Parents and kids

Two kinds of files are lying on your hard disk right now: *programs* (sometimes called *applications*) and *documents*. A program never changes; it's like a Cuisinart on your kitchen counter, sitting there day after day. Documents are what you *create* with a program — they're the coleslaw, crushed nuts, and guacamole dip that come out of the Cuisinart. You pay money to buy a program. After you own it, you can create as many documents as you want for free.

For example, you could use the Word Proc-S-R program (above, top) to create all the different word-processing documents below it and thousands more like them. If you love analogies as much as I do, you can think of the application as the mommy and the documents as the kiddies.

Here's what their family relationships are like:

- ✔ Double-click the *program* icon when you want to open a brand-new, untitled, clean-slate document.
- ✔ Double-click a document icon to open that document. Unbeknownst to you, double-clicking a document simultaneously opens the program you used to create the document.

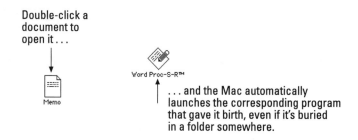

Double-click a
document to
open it . . .

Word Proc-S-R™

Memo

. . . and the Mac automatically
launches the corresponding program
that gave it birth, even if it's buried
in a folder somewhere.

Fetch: How to retrieve a document

Let's pretend it's tomorrow. Yawn, stretch, fluff your hair (if any). You find out that the person you've kidnapped actually comes from a wealthy Rhode Island family, and so you can demand much more ransom money. Fortunately, you created your ransom note on the iMac, so you don't have to retype anything; you can just change the amount you're demanding and print it out again.

But if you've been following the steps in this chapter, then there's *no* document on the screen. You're still *in* your word-processing program, though (or should be; check the name of the program displayed at the upper-right corner of your screen, or look for a checkmark in the Application menu). So how do you get your ransom note file back?

Like this:

1. **From the File menu, choose Open.**

   A dialog box appears. You probably remember dialog boxes — in fact, you probably remember this one. It looks just like the Save dialog box, where you were asked to give your document a title. This one, navigationally speaking, works exactly the same way:

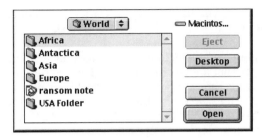

Unfortunately for my efforts to make this as instructional as possible, if you've been following these steps, your ransom note is staring you in the face right now. It's in whichever folder you saved it into. The iMac is nice that way — it remembers the most recent folder you stashed something in and shows you that location the next time you try to save or open something.

If you want to emerge from this experience a better person, pretend that you can't find your ransom note. Pull down the pop-up menu and jump to your hard-disk level (below, left). Now the display changes to show you the contents of your hard disk (below, right).

 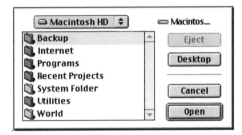

And from here, you know how to get back into the World folder, don't you? Correct — double-click the World folder, and you're right back where you started.

2. **Double-click the ransom note.**

   This is what you've been working up to all this time. The ransom note appears on your screen in its entirety. Now, at last, you can edit it to your heart's content.

Save Me Again!

To continue this experiment, make some changes to your document. Once again, you have to worry about the fact that your precious work only exists in a fragile world of bouncing electrons. Once again, turning the iMac off right now means you'll lose the *new* work you've done. (The original ransom note, without changes, is still safe on your disk.)

Therefore, you have to use that trusty Save command each time you make changes that are worth keeping. (For you desk potatoes out there, remember that ⌘-S is the keyboard shortcut, which saves you an exhausting trip to the menu.) The Save dialog box will *not* appear on the screen each time you use the Save command (as it did the first time). Only the very first time you save a document does the iMac ask for a title (and a folder location).

As mentioned in Chapter 1½, you've probably heard horror stories about people who've lost hours of work when some glitch made their computers crash. Well, usually it's their own darned fault for ignoring the two most important rules of computing:

> **Rule 1. Save your work often.**
>
> **Rule 2. See Rule 1.**

"Often" may mean every five minutes. It may mean after every paragraph. The point is to do it a lot. Get to know that ⌘-S shortcut, and type it reflexively after every tiny burst of inspiration.

Now you know how to start a new document, edit it, save it onto the disk, reopen it later, and save your additional changes. You know how to launch (open or run) a program — by double-clicking its icon. But now you have to learn to get out of a program when you're finished for the day. It's not terribly difficult:

Choose Quit from the File menu.

If AppleWorks was the only program you were running, then you return to the Finder. If you were running some other programs, then you just drop down into the next program. It's as though the programs are stacked on top of each other; take away the top one, and you drop into the next one down.

How to Back Up iMac Files

Duty compels me to keep this chapter going just long enough to preach one other famous word of advice to you: Back up.

To *back up*, or to *make a backup*, means to make a safety copy of your work.

The importance of being backed up

When you're in the Finder, the documents you've worked on appear as icons on the hard disk. Like any of us, these disks occasionally have bad hair days, go through moody spells, or die. On days like those, you'll wish you had made a *copy* of the stuff on the hard disk so your life won't grind to a halt while the hard disk is being repaired.

You know the cruel gods that make it rain when you forget your umbrella? Those same deities have equal powers over your hard disk and an equal taste for irony. That is, if you don't back up, your hard disk will *certainly* croak. On the other hand, if you back up your work at the end of every day or every week, nothing will ever go wrong with your hard disk, and you'll mumble to yourself that you're wasting your time.

Life's just like that.

Where's the floppy drive?

Many computer users back up their work by copying their important icons onto floppy disks. Unless your computer-store salesman was a fast-talking slimeball, however, it should be no surprise to you by now that your iMac *doesn't have* a built-in floppy-disk drive.

There are three reasons the iMac doesn't have a floppy drive. All of them have to do with the changing times (and making the iMac inexpensive):

- ✔ In the olden days, newly purchased software came on floppy disks. Today, all new software comes on a CD instead. And your iMac *does* have a CD player.

- ✔ In the olden days, you needed floppy disks so that you could transfer files to a friend or coworker. These days, you'd probably just send your file by e-mail, over a network cable, or through the air using the iMac's wireless network feature. (See Chapters 8 and 14 for instructions.)

- ✔ In the olden days, you'd use floppy disks to make a safety copy of your work. These days, a floppy's too small to hold much more than a chapter's worth.

Still, you're going to need to make safety copies of your work *somehow*. Some iMac fans use the Internet as a giant backup disk, a trick described in Chapter 6. Others make safety copies of their work by copying them to *another* computer, a scheme described in Chapter 14.

But many break down and *buy* a disk drive for the iMac. You can buy a doodad that accepts floppy disks, Zip disks, SuperDisks, or other kinds of disks. (All these gizmos are described in Chapter 18.)

If you've bought and connected such a disk drive, the next section is for you. If not, skim the following with a look of detached bemusement.

How to insert a disk

Take your first disk (floppy, SuperDisk, Zip, or whatever). You're going to slip it into your extra-purchase disk drive *metal side* first, *label side* up. Put the disk into the disk drive *slot.* Keep pushing the disk in until the disk drive gulps it in with a satisfying *kachunk.*

If it's a brand new floppy disk, or not a Macintosh disk, you'll probably see this message:

Go ahead. Click Initialize. You're then asked to name the disk; type a name, click OK, and then wait about 45 seconds while the iMac prepares the disk for its new life as your data receptacle.

If it's *not* a new disk, its icon shows up on the right side, just beneath your hard-disk icon.

To see what's on the disk, double-click the icon. As you've no doubt tired of hearing repeated, a *double-click* on a disk icon *opens* its contents window.

How to copy stuff onto a disk

Here's how you copy files onto a disk — floppy, Zip, SuperDisk, or whatever. We'll assume that you've already inserted a disk.

1. **Double-click your hard-disk icon to open its window.**

2. **Drag your document icons on top of the icon of the disk you've inserted.**

That's it. On a Macintosh, making a copy of something is as easy as dragging it to the disk you want it copied onto. You can also drag something into the disk's *window* (instead of onto its *icon*).

You can also, incidentally, drag things *from* a floppy (or other kind of disk) *to* your hard drive.

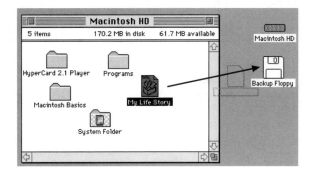

You can make as many copies of a file as you want without ever experiencing a loss of quality. You're digital now, kids.

How to get a disk or CD out again

Okay, so you've made a backup copy of your fourth-quarter report, or you've just copied a new program onto your hard disk. Now what? How do you get the disk out? And if you've inserted a CD-ROM disc into your iMac, how do you get *it* out again?

Just click the disk icon on the screen — and then, from the Special menu, choose Eject Disk. The disk — floppy, Zip, CD-ROM, whatever — pops out of the iMac (or its disk drive) automatically.

When the disk is too shy to come out

Every now and then, you'll be stuck with a disk or CD that won't come out of a CD tray-loading iMac, even if you've tried the usual ways of ejecting it.

In that case, shut down the iMac. While pressing the mouse button continuously, turn the iMac on again. Keep the mouse button pressed until the Trash can appears.

If that trick doesn't pop the disk out, straighten a paper clip. Push it slowly but firmly into the tiny pinhole on the CD-ROM drawer.

If even that radical procedure doesn't force the stuck disk out, here's one last resort. This one applies to stuck CDs only. If a disc is stuck in your iMac, the CD drawer won't open, and even the paper-clip trick fails, you may find that you can pop the drawer open by prying the corner of the drawer *gently* with a butter knife.

If you're weak of stomach, or a lawyer, do not attempt this procedure. Prying too hard will wreck your drive and require a repair.

On the other hand, when the paper-clip trick won't open the CD drawer, your only other alternative to the prying procedure *is* to send the computer in for repair — and you know what the technicians at Apple will do once they get your machine, don't you?

Right: pry open the drawer with a butter knife.

Want a more exciting method? Try this: Drag a disk's icon *to the Trash can!* Yes, yes, I *know* it looks like you're erasing the entire disk. It looks that way to *every* first-time Mac user. But you're not — instead, the disk just pops out of the slot.

When What Was Found Is Now Lost

Okay. You've practiced saving and retrieving files. Yet still it happens: You can't find some file you were working on.

This is nothing to be ashamed of! Thousands of people lose files every day. But through the intervention of caring self-help groups, they often go on to lead productive, "normal" lives.

Here's what to do: Sit up straight, think positive thoughts, and press ⌘-F. Or do it the long way: Choose Sherlock from your menu.

On the screen, you see the Sherlock box: your personal electronic butler who's prepared to spend the next few seconds rummaging through the attics, garages, and basement of your iMac.

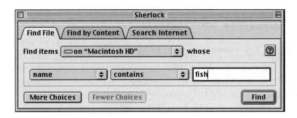

Type a few letters of the missing file's name. (Capitals don't matter, but spaces do!) Then click the Find button (or press Return).

A new window appears, listing everything on your hard drive whose name contains what you looked for. At this point, you can perform any of the following stunts.

Double-click an icon to open it. Or drag it someplace — onto the desktop, maybe, or even directly to the Trash. To open the window a file's in, click the icon and press ⌘-E.

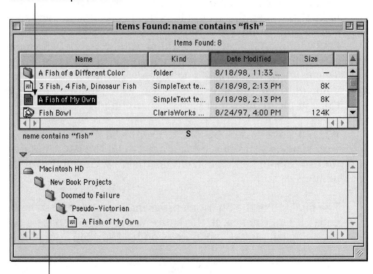

This area shows you where the file is, no matter how many folders deep it's buried. You can double-click a folder, too, to open it.

When you're finished playing with the Sherlock thing, choose Quit from its File menu (or press ⌘-Q).

Seeking wisdom in your own words — and on the Net

In the illustration of the Sherlock window on the previous page, you may notice two other interesting-looking places to click: a tab that says Find by Content and one that says Search Internet.

See, the trouble with the traditional Find command is that it searches only the *names* of your files. If you wrote a 253-page thesis on Wombat Worship Societies, but you accidentally *named* that file "Gift Ideas for Marge," you could search for "Wombat" from now until doomsday without turning up the file.

It would be different, however, if the Sherlock command were smart enough to search for words *inside* your documents. That's exactly what the Find by Content thing does.

But before you can use this feature, the iMac must be allowed to create its own private card-catalog of your hard drive. This process is called *indexing* — spending a couple of hours analyzing every single document you've got. To make this happen, click the "Search by Content" tab of the Find window; click the Index Volumes button, click the name of your hard drive, click Create Index, and then go out to see a nice long movie (such as *Titanic II: The Return*). (If you're *really* into your computer, you could teach yourself to use the Schedule button, which makes your iMac do this kind of thing in the middle of the night, unattended.)

When it's over, you'll be able to use the Find by Content thing to look for words inside your files. (You'll need to let the iMac update that index from time to time to keep it current; fortunately, each index-updating takes only 10 minutes or so.)

The final tab of the Sherlock program, Search Internet, isn't nearly as complicated. It lets you search the entire World Wide Web for a particular plain-English phrase (such as "Wombat Worship Societies"). Details in Chapter 7.

Sherlock goes silver

Got Mac OS 9? (Check Chapter 1 for details.) If so, your Sherlock program looks dramatically different than the preceding illustrations. It's big and silvery, for one thing:

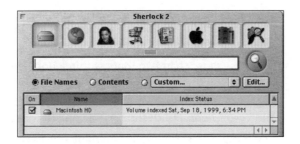

Moreover, the three tabs at the top (Find File, Find by Content, and Search Internet) are missing. You can still perform those three kinds of searches, but the buttons are different: When you want to look for a file by its name, click the File Names button; to look for words inside your files, click Contents; and to search the Internet, click one of the picture buttons at the very top of the window.

I can almost hear you asking: But *which* picture button? And you can almost hear me answering: see in Chapter 7 under the heading "Not just Sherlock — new, improved Sherlock!"

Top Ten Word-Processing Tips

1. Select a word by double-clicking — and then, if you keep the mouse button on the second click and drag sideways, you select additional text in complete one-word increments.

2. Never, never, never line up text using the space bar. It may have worked in the typewriter days, but not any more. For example, you may get things lined up like this on the screen.

   1963   **1992**   **2001**
   Born   Elected President Graduated college

Yet, sure as death or taxes, you'll get this when you print.

   1963 **1992**   **2001**
   Born   Elected President   Graduated college

So instead of using spaces to line up columns, use *tab stops* instead.

3. You can select all the text in your document at once by using the Select All command (to change the font for the whole thing, for example). Its keyboard equivalent is almost always ⌘-A.

4. Don't use more than two fonts within a document. (Bold, italic, and normal versions of a font only count as one.) Talk about ransom notes!

5. Don't use underlining for emphasis. You're a typesetter now, babe. You've got *italics!* Underlining is a cop-out for typewriter people.

6. The box in the scroll bar at the right side of the window tells you, at a glance, where you are in your document.

   By dragging that box, you can jump anywhere in the document.

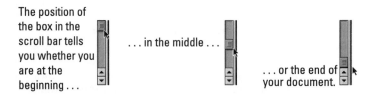

The position of the box in the scroll bar tells you whether you are at the beginning . . .   . . . in the middle . . .   . . . or the end of your document.

You can move around in two other ways, too:

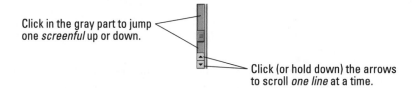

Click in the gray part to jump one *screenful* up or down.

Click (or hold down) the arrows to scroll *one line* at a time.

7. You've already learned how to *copy* some text to the Clipboard, ready to paste into another place. Another useful technique is to *cut* text to the Clipboard. Cut works just like Copy, except it snips the selected text out of the original document. (Cut-and-paste is how you *move* text from one place to another.)

8. It's considered uncouth to use "straight quotes" and 'straight apostrophes.' They hearken back to the days of your typewriter. Instead, use "curly double quotes" and 'curly single quotes' like these.

   You can produce curly double quotes by pressing Option-[(left bracket) and Shift-Option-[for the left and right ones, respectively. The single quotes (or apostrophes) are Option-] (right bracket) and Shift-Option-], for the left and right single quotes, respectively. But who can remember all that? That's why every word processor (AppleWorks, Microsoft Word, and so on) has an *automatic* curly quote feature, which is a much better solution.

(On the other hand, don't type curly quotes into an e-mail message; they come out as bizarre little boxes and random letters at the other end.)

9. If there's an element you want to appear at the top of every page, like the page number, don't try to type it onto each page. The minute you add or delete text from somewhere else, this top-of-the-page information will become *middle*-of-the-page information. Instead, use your word processor's *running header* feature — it's a little window into which you can type whatever you want. The program automatically displays this info at the top of each page, no matter how much text you add or take away. (There's also such a thing as a *running footer,* which appears at the *bottom* of the page.)

10. You know how to select one word (double-click it). You know how to select a line (drag horizontally). You know how to select a block of text (drag diagonally through it). By now, you're probably about to reach Selection-Method Overload.

But none of those techniques will help when you want to select a *lot* of text. What if you want to change the font size for *ten pages'* worth?

Instead, try this two-part tip: First, click at the *beginning* of the stuff you want to highlight so that the insertion point is blinking there.

Now scroll to the *end* of what you want to highlight. Hold down the *Shift key* with one hand and click the mouse button with the other. Magically, every-thing between your original click and your Shift-click gets high-lighted!

Chapter 5

A Quiet Talk about Printers, Printing, and Fonts

In This Chapter

▶ The different kinds of printers and how much they cost

▶ How to hook up and start printing

▶ The truth about fonts

*Y*ou, gentle reader, are fortunate that you waited until now to get into the Mac. You completely missed the era of *dot-matrix* printers, whose printouts were so jagged that they looked like Dante's *Inferno* written in Braille.

The purchase of a printer for your iMac constitutes Credit Card Workout #3, and it probably falls into one of two categories: *laser printers* and *inkjet printers*.

Inkjet Printers

The least expensive kind of printer is called an *inkjet*. Hewlett-Packard (HP) makes a line called DeskJets; Epson makes some terrific color-printing models known as the Stylus Color series. A typical inkjet looks like this:

Inkjet printouts are so good that they almost match a laser printer's. The printers are small, lightweight, and almost silent. You can feed all kinds of nonliving things through them: tagboard, envelopes, sheet metal, whatever. And they cost less than $250, even for ones that can print in color. (If you have a color inkjet, and you want to print out photographs, you can buy fancy shiny paper for this — correction: *expensive* fancy shiny paper — that make the printouts look almost like actual photos.) Some HP and Epson inkjets have USB connectors (see Chapter 14) that plug directly into the iMac; if you have a printer designed for older Mac models, you can plug it into the iMac with an adapter, such as a Farallon iPrint (see Appendix C).

So what's the catch? Well, they're inkjet printers. They work by spraying a mist of ink. Therefore, the printing isn't laser-crisp if your stationery is even slightly absorbent, and you have to replace the ink cartridges fairly often. Note, too, that inkjet-printed pages smear if they ever get the least bit damp, making them poor candidates for use during yacht races.

Still, inkjet printers are so compact, quiet, and inexpensive that they're hard to resist, especially if you want to print in color.

How to hook up a USB inkjet printer

The term *USB* refers to the kind of connector a printer has — and in the iMac world, USB means U Should B thrilled. Anything you plug into your iMac's USB jack works the first time, every time, with no hassle, no figuring out, and no turning the computer on or off. (And if that sounds perfectly normal to you, then you obviously weren't using computers in the 1980's.)

Many Epson and Hewlett-Packard inkjet printers have USB connectors — and that's exactly what you want. In most cases, however, you also need to buy the USB cable (printer-to-iMac), too. Then you're ready to set things up:

1. **Plug the printer into a power outlet. Turn the printer on.**

2. **Connect one end of the USB printer cable to the printer. Connect the other end to the iMac's USB jack.**

   The USB jack is on the left side of the computer, marked by a little three-forked tree icon.

3. **Find the software CD that came with your printer. Place it into the iMac's CD-ROM drive, and run the installation program on the CD.**

   If you have any trouble with this step, call the printer company. When the software-installation process is complete, you'll probably be told to restart the iMac.

Now you're wired, but not yet ready to print. When you first plug a printer into the iMac, it's not smart enough to notice that it's got a new friend; you have to *tell* it.

4. From the ⁪ menu, choose Chooser. It looks something like this:

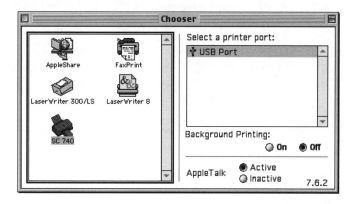

The icons that appear in the left half of the window depend on which *printer drivers* are in your System Folder. A printer driver is a little piece of software that teaches the iMac how to communicate with a specific printer. Its name and its icon match the printer itself, as you can tell, sort of, from the preceding figure. (The highlighted icon corresponds to the popular Epson Stylus 740.)

5. Click the icon that corresponds to your printer.

You've just introduced the iMac to its new printer. All this is a one-time operation, by the way. Close the Chooser window, click OK to dismiss the warning message, and proceed to "After All That: How You Actually Print," later in this chapter.

Unless you have to switch printers or something, you'll never have to touch the Chooser again.

How to hook up an older inkjet printer

In the best of all possible worlds, you bought a USB printer and your iMac at about the same time. A few troublemakers, however, attempt to connect a new iMac with an older printer that doesn't have a USB jack, such as an old Apple StyleWriter.

Tales of dpi

Why have America's scientific geniuses invented all these different kinds of printers?

In a word, they're on a quest for higher *dpi*. That stands for "dots per inch," and it measures the quality of a printout. We're talking about *tiny* dots, mind you — there are about 100 of them clumped together to form the period at the end of this sentence. Clearly, the more of these dots there are per inch, the sharper quality your printouts will have.

Old laser printers manage 300 dpi, and today's generally do 600 dpi. A typical inkjet printer, such as a DeskJet, sprays 720 or even 1,440 dpi onto your paper. Photos printed by a 1,440 dpi printer *look* like photos, let me tell you.

Pretty good, you say? Yeah, well, so's yer ol' man — this book was printed on a *2,400* dpi professional printer!

In such a case, you must buy one more component: an adapter. (The $99 Farallon iPrint SL is a good bet, as described in Appendix C.) It connects to your iMac's Ethernet or USB jack (on the left side of the computer) and provides an old-style round connector, into which you can plug your printer's existing cable.

To use the Farallon iPrint, start by installing the software that came with it (on the included CD disc). When the installation is complete, choose Control Panels from your menu. Open the AppleTalk control panel. From the pop-up menu, chose Ethernet; when you're asked if you want AppleTalk turned on, say yes.

Now return to the Chooser. Click the icon of the kind of printer you want; when your printer shows up on the right side of the window, close the Chooser window, click OK, smile, and jump down to "After All That: How You Actually Print."

Laser Printers

If you can afford to pay something like $600 for a printer, some real magic awaits you: *PostScript laser printers.* Don't worry about the word *PostScript* for now. Just look for the word PostScript in the printer's description, as though it's some kind of seal of approval.

A PostScript printer, like HP's LaserJet series or Apple's discontinued (but ubiquitous) LaserWriters, can print any text, in any style, at any size, and at any angle, and everything looks terrific. The printouts are created much like photocopies: they're crisp and black, heat-fused to white paper. These laser printers can also print phenomenal-looking graphics, like all the diagrams in Macintosh magazines and the weather maps in *USA Today*. They're quick, quiet, and hassle-free; most can print envelopes, mailing labels, and paper up to legal-size (but not tagboard). They're also much bigger and bulkier than inkjets, as you can see by this example.

If you can afford a PostScript printer, get it. If you're a small-time operation — a home business, for example — get the cheapest PostScript laser printer you can find.

Just remember that laser printers, while superior to inkjets for *black-and-white* quality, aren't what to buy if you want color. Sure, you can *buy* a color laser printer — for several thousand dollars — but the printouts aren't even as realistic as color *inkjet* printers' printouts.

How to hook up a modern laser printer

Most modern laser printers include an *Ethernet jack.* That's handy — so does your iMac. Laser printers usually don't come equipped with cables, however. After having collected hundreds of dollars from you, printer companies have charitably recognized that this machine may wind up being *shared* among several different computers. Therefore, laser printers are designed to be *networked,* and therefore printer companies assume your office has a local guru who knows what cables to buy.

If you work in an office, then you probably don't care; ask whatever geek is in charge of your office network to connect your iMac to the existing Ethernet wiring system.

If you *are* the geek in charge of all the equipment, life's a little more complicated. Chapter 14 tells you how to set up an Ethernet wiring network by yourself; all you need to know here is that your laser printer should connect to your Ethernet hub (which you'll read about in Chapter 14) exactly like any other Mac.

1. **Connect your laser printer to the Ethernet hub (see Chapter 14). Connect your iMac to it, too.**

   Again, Ethernet *isn't* for dummies — people get advanced degrees in fig-uring this stuff out — but Chapter 14 should make this step at least as transparent as the iMac's plastic case.

2. **From the menu, choose Control Panels. Open the AppleTalk control panel. From the pop-up menu, choose Ethernet; when you're asked if you want AppleTalk turned on, say yes. Close the control panel window.**

   You've just told your computer which connector it should pay attention to.

3. **From the menu, choose Chooser. If you see a printer driver icon in the Chooser window that matches your printer, you're in luck! Click it.**

   If you don't see your specific model named, try the LaserWriter 8 icon. Either way, if your printer is turned on, you should see its actual name show up in the *right* side of the Chooser window, as shown here; click the printer's name.

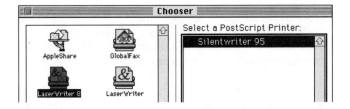

   If the names of *several* printers show up on the right, you're either part of an office network with several printers or you're an unexpectedly wealthy individual. Congratulations. Click the one you want to print on. Close the Chooser window, click OK, and read on.

After All That: How You Actually Print

Suppose that your printer is finally plugged in and, via the Chooser, has been introduced to the iMac. The moment has arrived: You'd actually like to *print* something.

Make sure whatever you want to print (an AppleWorks document, for exam-ple) is on the screen. From the File menu, choose Print. A dialog box appears; it looks different depending on your printer, but this one is typical of what you see if you have an Epson color printer.

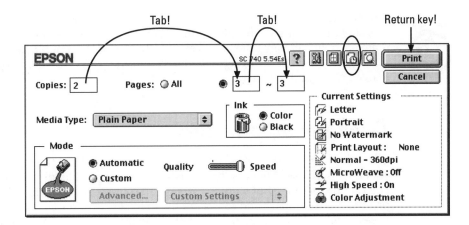

For 95 percent of your life's printouts, you'll completely ignore the choices in this box and simply click the Print button.

For the other 5 percent of the time, the main thing you do in this dialog box is tell the iMac which pages of your document you want it to print. If you just want page 1, type a *1* into *both* the From and To boxes. If you want page 2 to the end, type *2* into the From box and leave the To box empty. (The From: and To: blanks in the Epson dialog box don't have *From:* and *To:* labels, but they're there. They're the two unlabeled boxes, in the preceding illustration, where *3*'s have been typed in.)

Specify how many copies you want by clicking and typing a number in the Copies box.

Using the Tab key in dialog boxes

Now would be a good time, I suppose, to mention what the Tab key does in dialog boxes. Suppose you want to print *two* copies of page 3. Instead of using the mouse to click in each number box on the screen, you can just press Tab to jump from box to box.

Therefore, you'd just type **2** (in the Copies box); press Tab and type **3** (in the From box) and press Tab and type **3** again (in the To box), as shown in the previous illustration. And the mouse just sits there gathering dust.

Anyway, after you're done filling out the options in this box, you can either click the Print button *or* press the Return key. (Pressing Return is always the same as clicking the outlined button.) The iMac should whir for a moment, and pretty soon the printout will come slithering out of your printer.

This handy shortcut — using the Tab key to move around the blanks and pressing the Return key to "click" the OK or Print button — works in *any* dialog box. In fact, any time you ever see a button with a double-thickness outline, as shown in the preceding illustration, you can press the Return key instead of using the mouse.

Background printing

In the Dark Ages of the 1980s, when you printed something, the printer's soul took over your Mac's body. You couldn't type; you couldn't work; you couldn't do anything but stare at the sign on the screen that said, "Now printing." It was a dark and stormy era, a time of wild and rampant coffee breaks. Only when the paper came out of the printer were you allowed to use your computer again.

Since then, some clever engineer at Apple figured out how to allow *background printing*. When you use this handy feature, the iMac sends all the printing information, at a million miles per hour, into a *file* on your hard disk. It then immediately returns its attention to you and your personal needs.

Then, quietly, behind the scenes, the iMac shoots a little bit of that file to your printer at a time. It all happens during the microseconds between your keystrokes and mouse clicks, making it seem as though the iMac is printing in the background. In time, the printer receives all the information it needs to print, the paper comes gliding out, and you've been able to keep working the whole time. This simultaneous-processing bit can slow down your iMac, but it's a great feature to remember when it's 1:55 pm and the meeting starts at 2:00 and you haven't printed your outline yet.

The location of the on/off switch for Background Printing is different on every printer, but I'll do my best. When you choose Print from an iMac program's File menu, you get a dialog box like the one shown in the previous section. If it's an Epson printer, click the tiny second-from-right icon, which I've circled in the previous illustration. If it's some other printer, look for a pop-up menu that contains a Background Printing command.

Either way, you'll wind up with an on/off switch for Background Printing. Click accordingly.

Canceling printing

If you want to interrupt the printing process, ⌘-period does the trick — that is, while pressing the ⌘ key, type a period. Several times, actually. Even then, your printer will take a moment (or page) or two to respond.

A shortcut for multiple-printer owners

As often happens in democracies, the rich sometimes carry special influence. In the case of the Mac, the early 1990s saw the uprising of the powerful People With More Than One Printer lobby (the PWMTOP, as it's known in insider circles). These people — usually people in an office where several different printers are hooked up — resented having to lumber off to the Chooser each time they wanted to redirect their printouts from one printer to another. They asked Apple to come up with some easier method of switching.

Apple complied. When you first turned on your iMac, you may have noticed an icon that matches your printer sitting out *on the desktop,* as shown below. (Such icons generally appear only if you have an Apple brand printer, not Epson, HP, or anything else.)

To create more of these, the PWMTOP members simply select corresponding icons in the Chooser; each time they do so, another printer's icon shows up on the desktop. Thereafter, these lucky folk can direct a printout to a particular printer just by dragging the document's icon onto the appropriate printer icon, like this:

If, on the other hand, you use only *one* printer, this desktop printing thing is a waste of your memory, disk space, and screen space. Here's how you can turn it off:

1. From the menu, choose Control Panels.

2. Double-click the one called Extensions Manager (if you see something called Conflict Catcher, open that instead).

   You should now see a list of a million computer-looking control panels and *extensions,* as they're called. (More about these in Chapter 12.) Click all the ones with the word *Desktop Printing* or *Desktop Printer* in them to turn them off (so that they're no longer highlighted or checked off).

3. Restart your iMac.

Now you can throw away any printer icons that still appear on your desktop (which now probably have a big X through them).

Now *that's* what I call a grass-roots campaign against the rich!

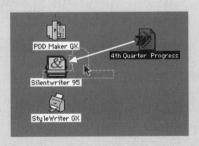

Top Ten Free Fun Font Factoids

The various *fonts* (typefaces) listed in the Font menus of your programs (such as AppleWorks) are amazing. They look terrific on the screen and even better when printed, and they're never jagged-looking like the computer fonts of the early days. You may not realize it, but your fonts are a special kind of idiot-proof, jaggy-free, self-smoothing font that looks great on any printer at any size: *TrueType* fonts.

If you work in the professional printing or graphic design industry, by the way, you may hear about a competing kind of font known as *PostScript* fonts. If you're truly interested in learning about the differences and history of these warring font types, check out a book like *Macworld Mac Secrets*; for now, let's just say that TrueType fonts — the kind that came on your iMac — are easier to manage, handle, and install.

Here are ten examples of the kind of fun you can have with your fonts:

1. Want more fonts? You can, of course, *buy* them. Your friendly neighborhood mail-order joint, like those listed in Appendix B, are only too happy to sell you CD-ROMs crammed with new fonts.

   Those on a budget, however, can still get tons of great fonts. Dial up America Online or the Internet (see Chapter 6), for example, and help yourself to as many fonts as your typographical taste buds can tolerate. (On America Online, use keyword *filesearch;* on the Internet, try *www.shareware.com*; either way, search the resulting page for "fonts.")

2. To install a new font, quit all your programs (if you're running any). Drag the font-file icon (shaped like a suitcase) on top of the System Folder icon. (Do *not* drag it into the open System Folder *window.* Do not drag it to the Trash can. Do not collect $200.)

System Folder   Yer Basic Font Suitcase   Yer Basic Font Suitcase

You'll see a message alerting you that the iMac is going to install the font for you. Just smile, wave, and click OK.

3. Want to see where your fonts live? Open your System Folder and then open the Fonts folder therein. You'll see a list of your fonts in a window. To see what a font looks like, double-click its suitcase icon. You'll get a window showing the individual font sizes, like Times 10 and Times 18; double-click one. A little window opens, displaying a few words to live by (such as: "Cozy lummox gives smart squid who asks for job pen"), displayed in the font you're investigating.

4. To remove a font, quit any programs you're running. Open your Fonts folder (as described in the previous paragraph). Then just drag the offending font — or its entire suitcase — out of the window. Put it onto the desktop. Or put it into some other folder — or right into the Trash can.

5. There are two kinds of people: those who place everything into two categories and those who don't. Among fonts, there are two basic types: *proportional* fonts, where every letter gets exactly as much width as it needs, and *monospaced* fonts, where every letter is exactly the same width, as on a typewriter. What you're reading now is a proportional font; notice that a W is much wider than an I.

   Your iMac comes with two monospaced fonts: Courier and Monaco. All the others are proportional.

   And who the heck cares? You will — the moment somebody sends you, perhaps by e-mail, some text that's supposed to line up, but doesn't. For example, this table that arrived by e-mail:

   ```
   From:      IntenseDude
   To:        pogue@aol.com

   Hello, David! Here are the prices you asked about:

   Item              Features            Price
   ----              --------            -----
   Seinfeld Statuette     Removable hairpiece      $25.00
   Baywatch digital watch     Surfboard sweep-second hand  $34.50
   "60 Minutes" bowtie     Mike Wallace autograph     $65.75
   E.R. BandAid Pak™          100 per box                $ 9.85
   ```

   All you have to do is highlight this text and change it to, say, Courier, and everything looks good again!

   ```
   From:         IntenseDude
   To:           pogue@aol.com

   Hello, David! Here are the prices you asked about:

   Item                  Features                   Price
   ----                  --------                   -----
   Seinfeld Statuette    Removable hairpiece        $25.00
   Baywatch digital watch Surfboard sweep-second hand $34.50
   "60 Minutes" bowtie   Mike Wallace autograph     $65.75
   E.R. BandAid Pak™     100 per box                $ 9.85
   ```

6. For laser-printer users only: From the File menu, choose Page Setup. The Page Setup dialog box offers a handful of useful options — whether you want the paper to print lengthwise or the short way, for example, or how much you want your document enlarged or reduced.

   The Paper pop-up menu near the middle, however, offers one of the most useful controls. If yours says "US Letter Small," your laser printer leaves a half-inch margin all the way around the page, chopping off any part of your printout that extends into it. If that bothers you, choose US Letter from that pop-up menu (and to make your change permanent, hold down Option as you click OK). From now on, your laser can print to within a quarter-inch of the edge of the paper.

7. From your ⌘ menu, choose Control Panels. Double-click the one called Appearance, and click the tab that says Fonts. Turn on the option called "Smooth all fonts on screen."

Now revisit your word processor (or any other program, for that matter). Notice that the edges of your typed letters are drawn with softer and smoother edges, making your entire computer look as though it's an elegantly designed ad.

Before

The Staten Island Fairy

A true story in nine chapters

Once upon a time there was a water sprite named Tia. She lived in New York, near the harbor where

After

The Staten Island Fairy

A true story in nine chapters

Once upon a time there was a water sprite named Tia. She lived in New York, near the harbor where

8. In AppleWorks, Word 98, and some other word processing programs, you can actually see the names of the fonts in your font menu *in* those typefaces, like this:

Font
Arial
Arial MT Condensed Light
Arial Narrow
Arial Rounded MT Bold
Avant Garde
Bauhaw 93
Bodoni MT Ultra Bold
Book Antiqua
Bookman
Bookman Old Style
Bookman Old Style Bold

Problem is, how are you supposed to read the names of *symbol fonts* — fonts where every "letter" is actually a symbol or little picture (such as Zapf Dingbats)? Easy. Hold down the Shift key as you pull down the Font menu. Now every font *doesn't* show up in its own typeface — they're all in the usual menu font now.

9. Want to look good the next time you're hanging out with a bunch of type geeks? Then learn to bandy about the terms *serif* (pronounced SAIR-iff) and *sans serif* (SANNZ sair-iff).

A serif is the little protruding line built onto the edges of the letters in certain typefaces. In the *serif font* pictured in the top example here, I've drawn little circles around some of the serifs.

Terrif serifs
Sans-serif

A *sans serif* font, on the other hand, has no little protuberances, as you can see by their absence in the little square (in the lower example above). Times, Palatino, and the font you're reading are all serif fonts. Helvetica, Geneva, and the headlines in most newspapers are sans serif fonts. And that information, plus 33 cents, will buy you a first-class U.S. postage stamp.

10. This one's techy, but it's good.

When the iMac prints, it matches the placement of each word *exactly* according to its position on the screen. Trouble is, the iMac's screen resolution isn't that good — it's only 72 dots per inch instead of 600 or 1400 dpi (the usual for printers). As a result, you sometimes get weird spacing between words, especially between **boldface** words (see the bottom-left printout on the following page).

The solution: When you print, turn on the Fractional Character Widths feature. This makes words look a little bit cramped on the screen (top right in the figure on the next page) but makes your printouts look *awesomely* professional (bottom right).

	Fractional Widths OFF	Fractional Widths ON
On the screen:	**Bullwinkle's Little Secret**	**Bullwinkle's Little Secret**
In the printout:	**Bullwinkle's Little Secret**	**Bullwinkle's Little Secret**

So how do you find this magical feature? In AppleWorks, Fractional Widths is one of the Preferences (Edit menu). In Word 98, choose Preferences from the Tools menu and click the Print tab. Try keeping it off when you're typing and on when you print.

Part II

The Internet Defanged

INTERNET ACCESS
.50¢ - Min.

In this part . . .

The "i" in *iMac* stands for *Internet*.

I know, I know: If you hear *one more person* start droning on about the Internet, the Web, or the Information Superhighway, you'll tie them to a chair and make them watch 18 hours of the Home Shopping Network.

Actually, though, despite the overwhelming abundance of ridiculous, time-wasting chaff in cyberspace, there's also a lot of useful stuff, plus Dilbert cartoons for free. The next few chapters tell you how to get it.

Chapter 6

Faking Your Way onto America Online and the Internet

- -

In This Chapter

▶ The Internet: What and why it is

▶ America Online, the grocery store; Internet, the farmer's market

▶ How to hang up — and how to get over downloaded-file hang-ups

- -

*I*f you haven't heard of America Online or the Internet by now, you must've spent the last ten years in some Antarctic ice cave. These days, you can't make a move without seeing an e-mail address on someone's business card, a World Wide Web address (like *www.moneygrub.com*) on a magazine ad, or the glazed raccoon look of the all-night Internetter on a friend's face.

Going online gains you endless acres of features: the ability to send e-mail, instantly and for free, to anyone else who's online; incredible savings when you buy stuff (no middleman!); vast amounts of reading and research material (*Time* magazine, *The New York Times*, and so on, *free*); discussion bulletin boards on 29,000 topics (left-handed banjo-playing nuns, unite!); live, typed "chat rooms" that bring you together with similarly bored people from all over the world; and much more.

Before you begin this adventure, though, a grave warning: Going online is every bit as addictive as heroin, crack, or Presidential sex scandals, but even more dangerous. As you explore this endless, yawning new world, filled with surprises at every turn, you're likely to lose track of things — such as time, sleep, and your family. Take it slow, take it in small chunks, and use these services always in moderation.

Above all, remember that the Internet wasn't designed by Apple. It existed long before the Macintosh. It was invented by a bunch of military scientists in the '60s whose idea of a good conversation was debating things like *TCP/IP*, *FTP*, and *ftp.ucs.ubc.ca*. As a result, going online is all quite a bit more complicated and awkward than everyday iMac activities.

In other words, if you can't figure out what's going on, *it's not your fault.*

The birth of the Confusion Superhighway

The Internet began as a gigantic communications network for the U.S. military. The idea was to build a vast web of computer connections all over the country so that, if an enemy bomb destroyed one city, the government's electronic messages could still reach their destinations. (Gee, *that's* reassuring. Yeah, okay, New York is in cinders — but hey!, at least the company picnic memo got delivered.) As a result, you might send an e-mail message to your next-door neighbor — but it might reach him only after traveling from your iMac to Omaha, bouncing down to Orlando, returning to Toronto, and finally reaching the house next door.

There's no central location for the Internet; it's everywhere and nowhere. Nobody can control it; nobody even knows how many computers are connected to it. It's impossible to measure and impossible to control — which is why American teenagers love it, and governments try to ban it.

Anyway, when the U.S. government threw open the Internet to the public, it triggered an incredible explosion of interest, commerce, and nauseating buzzwords like *information superhighway.* There's a lot of useful stuff out on the Internet — and, as a pure time-killer, there's nothing like it. But there's also a lot of chaff to wade through. Let this chapter and the next be your guides to finding your way.

First, the Modem

Your iMac contains a built-in *modem,* the little glob of circuitry that connects your computer to the phone jack on the wall. Fortunately, it's the fastest one money can buy — a so-called *56K* modem, which you can think of as "56 miles per hour."

Now then: When the iMac makes a call, it dials the phone many times faster than, say, a teenager, but ties up the phone line just as effectively. When your iMac is using the modem, nobody else can use the phone. Therefore, you need to figure out how you're going to plug in your modem:

- **Share a single line with the modem.** You can visit your local Radio Shack to buy a *splitter,* a Y-jack, a little plastic thing that makes your wall phone jack split into two identical phone jacks — one for your phone and the other for your iMac. This arrangement lets you talk on the telephone whenever you aren't using the modem and vice versa.

- **Install a second phone line.** This is clearly the power user's method: Give the modem a phone line unto itself.

  Pros: (1) Your main family phone number is no longer tied up every time your modem dials up the latest sports scores. (2) You can talk to a human on one line while you're modeming on the other. (3) If you're in an office with one of those PBX or Merlin-type multiline telephone systems, you have to install a new, separate jack for the modem *anyway.*

Cons: (1) This option is expensive. (2) It involves calling up the phone company, which is about as much fun as eating sand. (3) You run a greater risk of becoming a serious modem nerd.

✔ **Don't use a phone line at all.** If you live in one of a few very lucky cities, your local cable TV or phone company may offer a special way to connect to the Internet, known as *cable modems* or *DSLs* (digital subscriber lines). These services cost around $35 or $45 per month, and require a visit (and a bill) from a service technician to install. But the results are worth slobbering over: Your iMac is online *constantly,* without even using its built-in modem, and without tying up your phone line. Your iMac gets its own direct umbilical to the Net, at speeds several times faster than even the fastest standard phone-line modem.

I'll let you and your checkbook mull that one over. For now, it's worth noting that cable modems, DSL, and similar high-speed connections are the wave of the future.

For the rest of this chapter, I'll assume that you plan to go online the way most of the world does it: by connecting to a telephone line. Plug the included telephone wire into the iMac's modem jack. (The modem jack is on the right side of the computer, marked by a little telephone icon.) Plug the other end into a telephone wall jack. (If you've equipped your iMac with an AirPort Card, the setup is slightly different; see Chapter 14.)

America Online or Direct to the Internet?

When it comes to visiting the vast, seething world of cyberspace, you have two on-ramps. You can become an America Online member, or you can sign up for a direct Internet account with a company like EarthLink. The geeks call Internet-access companies (like EarthLink) *ISPs,* short for *Internet Service Providers.*

I find the term Internet Service Provider — let alone *ISP* — overly nerdy, like calling a writer a "Literature Service Provider." Unfortunately, you can't crack open a magazine or visit a computer club without hearing people talk about ISPs. ("My ISP only charges $15 a month!" "Really? Maybe I'll change ISPs then.") So, with your permission, I'll refer to the companies who rent you time on the Internet as *ISPs,* just like everyone else does.

In this chapter, I'll show you both methods of getting online. Each route has significant pros and cons, however, which you'll find in the following table. Photocopy, distribute to your family members, and discuss over dinner.

America Online	Internet Service Provider (ISP)
$22 per month, unlimited access.	$20 per month, unlimited access.
Frequent busy signals between 6 p.m. and midnight.	Busy signals are rare.
Hangs up on you after several minutes of your not doing anything.	Doesn't hang up on you.
Long hold times for help, but fairly Macintosh-savvy agents are available.	Help agents are sometimes clueless about the iMac.
The one program on your hard drive — the America Online program — does everything: e-mail, World Wide Web surfing, chat rooms, and so on.	You need a separate program for each Internet feature: e-mail, Web surfing, and so on.
Generally safe for kids; no pornography on America Online itself.	Adult supervision required.
Very simple, sometimes frustrating; the geeks look down on people with AOL accounts.	More complex, less limiting; nerds admire you for having a "real" Internet account.

America Online (often called AOL) is an *online service*. That is, its offerings are hand-selected by the company's steering committee and sanitized for your protection. Contrast that with the Internet itself, where the offerings constantly change, nobody's in charge, and it's every iMac for itself.

Going onto AOL is like going to a grocery store, where every product is neatly organized, packaged, and labeled. Going onto the Internet, by contrast, is like going to a huge farmer's market that fills a football stadium, filled with whichever vendors happened to show up with their pickup trucks. At the farmer's market, wonderful bargains may await — but it's hard to find anything particular, the turnips may be rancid, and there's no clerk to ask for help.

On the other hand, don't forget that America Online *also* gives you the actual Internet, in addition to its own hand-picked goodies. That is, the AOL grocery store has a back door into the farmer's market.

America Online (AOL), the Cyber-Grocery

Your iMac came with the America Online (AOL) folder already on the hard disk (inside the Internet folder). Inside this folder is the America Online *program* whose icon you double-click to get started.

The first time you double-click this icon, you'll be guided through a series of setup steps. You'll be asked:

✔ For your name, address, and credit-card number. Remember, though, that you get 100 hours of time online (during the first month) for free. Cancel within the first month, and your card is never charged.

✔ To choose a local *access number* from a list (and a backup number). Fortunately, AOL has worked out a clever scheme that lets you, as one of 90 percent of Americans living near metropolitan centers, make a *local* call to America Online. Somehow, this system carries your call all the way to Virginia for free. (That's where the actual gigantic AOL computers live.)

✔ To make up a "screen name" and a password.

The *screen name* can be ten letters long, but you can't use punctuation. You can use a variation of your name (A Lincoln, MTMoore, Mr Rourke) or some clever CB radio-type handle (FoxyBabe, Ski Jock, NoLifeGuy). Do understand, however, that America Online has over *17 million* members, and *each* of them (including you) can choose up to five different names, one for each family member. In other words, you can pretty much bet that names like Helen, Hotshot, and Mac Guy were claimed some time in the Mesozoic Era.

If you pick a name that someone has already claimed, the program will make you keep trying until you come up with a name that hasn't been used before.

When all this setup information is complete, your modem begins screaming and making a hideous racket, and you see an AOL logo screen that says things like "Checking Password." Finally, if everything goes well, you're brought to this screen.

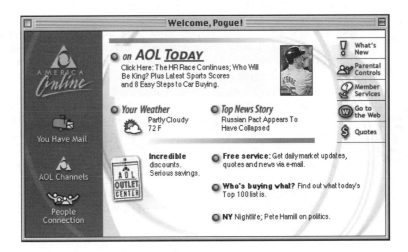

You also get to hear a recording of the famous Mr. Cheerful, the man who says "Welcome!" as though you're *just* the person he's been waiting for all day. If you've got e-mail waiting, he also says "You've got mail!," which he's *really* happy about. (To read the mail, click the "YOU HAVE MAIL" icon.)

Exploring by icon

AOL, you'll quickly discover, is a collection of hundreds of individual screens, each of which represents a different service or company. Each day, several of them (one of which is always News) are advertised on the welcome screen. To jump directly to the advertised feature, click the corresponding icon.

The broader America Online table of contents, however, appears when you click the AOL Channels button on the opening screen. Each of *these* buttons takes you to yet another screen, where you can visit related services — for example:

- ✔ The *Research & Learn* (called *Reference Desk* in some versions) button lets you consult a dictionary, a national phone book, or a choice of encyclopedias.

- ✔ The *Personal Finance* page is stock-market city: You can check quotes, actually buy and sell, get mutual-fund stats, read tax and investing advice, and so on.

- ✔ If you click the *Travel* button, you can actually look up plane fares and even make reservations.

Navigating by keyword

If you poked around enough, clicking icons and opening screen after screen, you'd eventually uncover everything America Online has to offer. In the meantime, however, you'd run up your phone bill, develop mouse elbow, and watch four Presidential administrations pass.

A much faster navigational trick is the *keyword* feature. A keyword is like an elevator button that takes you directly to any of the hundreds of features on AOL, making no stops along the way. Just type the keyword of your choice into the strip at the top of the screen (where it says "Type Keyword/Web address"). When you press Return, you're teleported directly to that service.

Here are a few typical AOL services, along with their keywords. Arm yourself with this list so that you make the most of your free month-long trial.

Keyword	Where It Takes You
Access	A list of local phone numbers for America Online. Use this before a trip to another city.
Banking	Check your accounts, pay bills, and so on (certain banks only).
Beginners	A collection of help topics for Mac newcomers.
Billing	Current billing info, disputes, and so on.
Encyclopedia	Your choice of several different published encyclopedias. You just saved $900!
Help	Assistance about America Online itself.
Homework	A place for students to get live, interactive help with homework and research.
Macgame	Files, messages, and discussions of Mac games.
Star Trek	*Star Trek.*
Stocks	Check the current price of any stock. You can even see your current portfolio value.

And how, you may well ask, do you find out what the keyword *is* for something you're looking for? Easy — just type in keyword: ***keyword!*** You'll get a screen that offers a complete list of keywords.

How to find your way back to the good stuff

With several hundred places worth visiting on AOL — and several *million* places worth visiting on the Internet — it'd be nice if there were a way to mark your place. Suppose you stumble onto this *great* English Cocker Spaniel Owners' area, for example, but you've already forgotten which buttons you clicked to get there.

Simple solution: When you're looking at a screen (or Web page) you might someday like to return to, choose Add to Favorite Places from the Window menu. Thereafter, whenever you want to revisit one of your thus-marked Favorite Places, choose its name from the Favorite Places icon/menu, like this.

To delete something from this list, choose the very first command (Favorite Places) from the Favorites icon/menu. In the resulting window, just click a place's name once and then choose Clear from the Edit menu.

The e-mail connection

One of the best things about AOL is the e-mail — mainly the sheer, ego-boosting joy of *getting* some.

If, in fact, anybody has bothered to write to you (which you'll hear announced by Mr. "You've got mail!"), click the YOU HAVE MAIL button on the welcome screen to see your messages.

After you've read the message, you can (a) reply to it (by clicking the Reply button); (b) send it on to somebody else (by clicking the Forward button); (c) save it on your hard disk (by choosing Save from the File menu); (d) print it (by choosing Print from the File menu); or (e) close its window without saving it. If you do that, the message hangs around in your Old Mail folder for about a week and then disappears forever.

To *send* a message to somebody, click Write on the toolbar. Type your lucky recipient's e-mail address, a subject, and your message in the appropriate blanks. (Don't forget to press the Tab key to move from blank to blank.) When you're done typing, just press Enter (or click the Send Now button).

If you need to look up somebody's screen name, use this keyword: *members*.

The party line

By far the most mind-blowing aspect of AOL is, of course, the *chat rooms*. In a chat room, you'll find up to 23 people chatting away (by typing). The nutty thing is that everybody's talking at once, so the conversation threads overlap, and hilarious results sometimes ensue.

Things to know before entering the Party Zone

If it's your first time in a chat room, you may be nonplused by the gross excesses of punctuation that seem to go on there. Every five minutes, it seems that somebody types {{{{{{{ Jennifer!!!}}}}}}} or ****BabyBones!****

Actually, there's nothing wrong with these people's keyboards. The braces are the cyber-space equivalent of hugging the enclosed person; the asterisks are kisses. That's how you greet friends who enter the room — online, anyway.

Nonetheless, the chat rooms are an unusual social opportunity: For the first time, you can be the total belle of the ball (or stud of the studio) — the wittiest, charmingest, best-liked person — without so much as combing your hair.

To get to the chat rooms, choose Chat Now from the People menu/icon on your toolbar. If you click the button called "Find a Chat," you'll discover that dozens of parties are transpiring simultaneously, each founded on a different topic. Double-click a room's name to go there.

Talking behind their backs

What makes the live chats even more fun is that you can whisper directly into the ear of anybody there — and nobody else can hear you. This kind of behind-the-scenes direct communication is called an Instant Message. To send one, choose Send Instant Message from the Members menu (or press ⌘-I). You get a box like this:

As soon as you type your whispered message and click Send (or press Enter), the window disappears from your screen — and reappears on the recipient's screen! That person can then whisper back to you.

Meanwhile, somebody *else* in the room may have been Instant-Messaging *you*.

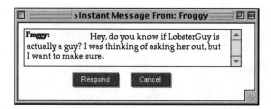

If you try to maintain your presence in the main window *and* keep your end of all these whispered conversations in *their* little windows, the hilarity builds. *Nothing* makes a better typist out of you than the AOL chat rooms.

P.S. You can also carry on Instant-Message chats with people who aren't America Online members — that is, people who have standard Internet (ISP) accounts instead, as described later in this chapter. They, however, must first download and install a free program onto their computers. For details, use keyword: *aim.*

How to find — and get — free software

For many people, the best part of AOL is the free software. Heck, for many people, that's the *only* part of AOL. Just use keyword: *filesearch;* click Shareware; in the Find What? blank, type the name of the file, or kind of file, you're looking for; and click Search.

In a moment, you're shown a complete listing of all files in the AOL data banks that match your search criteria. Keep in mind that roughly 500,000 files hang out on those computers in Virginia, so choose your search words with care.

If you think a file sounds good, double-click its name to read a description. If it *still* sounds good, click Download Now. The iMac asks where you want the downloaded item stashed. If you *click the Desktop button* before clicking Save, you'll avoid the crisis of "Where did my downloaded goodies go?" syndrome suffered by 1 in 6 American adults. When you finish using America Online, you'll see the file you received sitting right on the colored backdrop of your iMac (or, as we say in the biz, *on the Desktop).*

Your modem then begins the task of *downloading* (transferring) the file to your hard drive. (Make sure that you read the section "When You Can't Open Your Downloaded Goodies," later in this chapter, for a follow-up discussion on downloading stuff.)

Signing Up for an Internet Account (ISP)

If you've decided to sign up for a direct Internet connection (instead of going the AOL route), send a thank-you note to Apple; signing up for such an account on an iMac is as easy as signing up for AOL. In fact, if you have a modem, CD slot-loading iMac, you may have set up your Internet account the very first time you turned the machine on, as described in Chapter 1.

If not, open the program called Internet Setup Assistant; it's in the Internet folder on your hard drive. The Internet Setup Assistant asks you if you want to set up your iMac for Internet use; yes, you do. Then it asks if you already have an Internet account; no, you don't.

Now the EarthLink Total Access sign-up program takes over, showing you a series of screens, asking for your name, address, credit-card number, and so on. (Start by clicking the Setup button on this screen.)

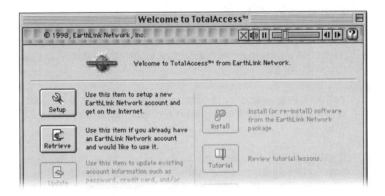

While this goes on, a *voice* starts explaining what's happening. (Scared the bejeezus out of me the first time I heard it.) Your modem dials an 800 number a couple of times. Along the way, you'll be asked to make up a cybername for yourself (such as *SeinfeldNut83*) and a password that protects your account.

When it's all over, you'll be an official, card-carrying member of the Internet. Now you, too, can have an e-mail address with an @ sign on your business card. Now you, too, can banter at cocktail parties about the ghastly new color scheme on the Microsoft Web site. Now you, too, can slowly drift away from family, job, and reality as you recede into cyberhermitdom.

What's on the Internet

In the following pages, you'll read about the various things that you can do on the Internet. The most useful of these features are called *e-mail*, *newsgroups*, and the *World Wide Web*. As you read, keep in mind that all these features are available to you regardless of whether you have an AOL account or a real Internet (ISP) account.

E-mail

If you have America Online, see "The e-mail connection" earlier in this chapter. If you've signed up for an ISP like EarthLink instead, see Chapter 8. Either way, get psyched for a feature that'll change your life; as a technology, e-mail ranks right up there with cable TV, frequent-flyer miles, and microwave popcorn.

Newsgroups

The next important Internet feature is called *newsgroups*. Don't be fooled: They have nothing to do with news, and they're not groups. That's the Internet for ya.

Instead, newsgroups are electronic bulletin boards. I post a message; anyone else on the Internet can read it and post a response for all to see. Then somebody else responds to *that* message, and so on.

By the way: You might notice, in the following illustration, that the writer is somewhat nastier online than he might have been in your living room. That's an interesting Internet lesson — people tend to be ruder than they would in person. There are two reasons: First, you're anonymous — nobody can see you, so it doesn't seem to matter as much if you're a jerk. Second, millions of messages appear here every day; some people think they need to be extra-dramatic just to be noticed.

The little > symbols mean that this portion of the message is being quoted
from a previous message, so everyone will know what this guy is responding to.

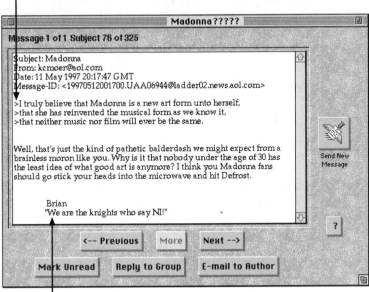

It's typical for Internet weenies to sign their names with some kind of
whimsical quotation. Don't ask me why; personally, it drives me crazy.

There are about 29,000 different newsgroups, ongoing discussions on every
topic — chemists who like bowling, left-handed oboists, Mickey Mouse fans
who live in Bali — anything. Here's how you reach these discussion areas:

- **On America Online:** Use keyword *newsgroups*. If you then click Read
  My Newsgroups, you see a starter list of topics; just keep double-clicking
  topics that interest you until you're reading the actual messages. (To
  add newsgroup topics to your starter list, use the Search All
  Newsgroups button.)

  After you've read a message, you can either respond to it (click the Send
  New Message button) or just keep reading (click the Next>> button).

- **With an ISP:** Use Outlook Express, which came with your iMac. (It's the
  same program you use to read e-mail, as described in Chapter 8.)

  Once you're online and running Outlook Express, click the Microsoft
  News Server icon on the screen. You'll be shown a new window containing dozens of newsgroups that all pertain to Microsoft software.

  Now, I'll be the first to admit that reading about Microsoft products all
  day is not what you'd call, er, realizing the full potential of the Internet.
  Therefore, if you think you're up for the full list of 29,000 discussion
  topics, try this:

From Outlook Express's Edit menu, choose Preferences, click the News icon, click New Server, type *Newsgroup List* (or something similar to that), click OK, tab to the Server Address blank, and type out your ISP's *news server address.* (For EarthLink, it's *news.earthlink.net.* If you have another ISP, call it up and ask what the news-server address is.) Click the Make Default button and then click OK.

From now on, whenever you feel like reading several million bulletin-board notes, launch Outlook Express. You'll see an icon called *Newsgroup List* (or whatever you called it) at the left side of the screen; double-click it. Finally, from the View menu, choose Get Complete Newsgroup List. Wait five minutes for the full list of thousands to arrive on your screen — and then, at last, you can begin reading the messages on the world's largest bulletin board. Just double-click a topic name; choose Refresh Message List from the View menu; and then double-click a message name to read it. (Click the Reply icon at the top of the window if you'd like to respond to something somebody has written. But be nice.)

I realize that this process involves 500 steps, but as I said, nobody ever called the Internet easy.

The World Wide Web

Except for e-mail, by far the most popular and useful Internet feature is the World Wide Web. In fact, it gets a chapter all to itself (the next chapter). For now, all you need to know is this:

- ✔ **On America Online:** A Web browser is built right into your AOL software. In many cases, you wind up on the Web just by innocently clicking some button within AOL — that's how tightly the Web is integrated with America Online these days. (You can tell when you're visiting a Web page, not an AOL page, when the address in the white strip at the top of the window begins with the letters *http.*)

- ✔ **With an ISP account:** You have your choice of two free Web-browsers: Netscape Navigator and Microsoft Internet Explorer, both described in the next chapter.

How to Hang Up

When you're finished with an AOL session, hanging up is no big deal; just choose Quit from the File menu, making your phone line available once again to the other members of your family.

How to use the Internet as a giant backup disk

As described in Chapter 4, *backing up* means making a safety copy of your work. Some iMac fans buy disk drives for this purpose (see Chapter 19). Others send files to themselves as e-mail attachments (see Chapter 8). But one of the cheapest and most convenient ways to back up your iMac is to use an Internet-based service like Freeback.com or MyDocsOnline.com. These special Web pages are easy to use and don't cost a penny.

Here's how these free services work. Using your Web browser (see the next chapter), visit the service's Web page (*http://freeback.com* or *www.mydocsonline.com,* respectively). Click the Register button; you'll be asked to make up a name and password, and to type in your e-mail address. (Freeback asks for a lot of other information, too, and offers you only 10 megabytes of free storage. The easier-to-use MyDocsOnline offers twice as much storage, and requires less personal information.)

Now, when you want to back up some files from your iMac, just click the Upload File button on the same Web page. Click the Browse button to view a list of everything on your hard drive; double-click the file you want backed up. When the screen changes to indicate that the file

transfer was complete, you can repeat the process until all your important files are safely copied onto your own private Internet backup page. A File List screen shows you the list of stuff you've backed up, and special buttons let you retrieve them or delete them.

The 20MB of free storage offered by MyDocsOnline is plenty if you mostly write, crunch numbers, or work in AppleWorks. If you scan huge photos, however, 20MB may not be enough. In that case, you can pay for additional Web storage at a Web site like BackJack.com or iMacBackup.com. These Internet storage services aren't cheap — BackJack.com is $17.50 per month, for example. But they offer two advantages: First, you can set these programs to run *automatically,* backing up specified folders on your hard drive at specified times. And second, there's no limit to the amount of stuff you can back up in this way, although you pay more if you store more.

Whether you use the free Internet backup systems or the pricey ones, you sleep well at night because your backup files are off-site; even if your office is hit by fire, burglar, or plague of locusts, your backup copies are safely somewhere else.

Getting off the Internet if you have a direct Internet account (ISP), however, is trickier. Allow me to propose an analogy: Imagine that you call another branch of your family tree on New Year's Day. You yourself place the call, but then you hand the phone off to various other family members. "And now here's little Timmy! Timmy, talk to Grandma. . . ."

Using the Internet works the same way. Your iMac places the call. But aside from tying up the phone line, your iMac doesn't actually *do* anything until you now launch one of the programs you read about in this chapter: an e-mail program or a Web browser, for example. Each of these Internet programs is like one of your family members, chatting with the Big Internet Grandma for a few minutes apiece.

The point here: When you quit your e-mail or Web program, *the phone line is still tied up,* just as though Timmy, when finished talking to Grandma, put the phone on the couch and wandered out to play. When you're finished Internetting, therefore, end the phone call by doing one of the following:

✔ Choose Remote Access Status from your menu; in the status window, click Disconnect.

✔ Choose Disconnect from the Remote Access tile on your *Control Strip* (see Chapter 12), like this:

✔ Wait. After about 15 minutes of your not doing anything online (or whatever time you've specified in the Remote Access control panel), your iMac hangs up automatically.

When You Can't Open Your Downloaded Goodies

It's easy to download software — either from AOL or the Internet. Maybe you find something on a Web page worth downloading (see the next chapter). Maybe somebody sends you a family picture as a file that's attached to an e-mail. Unfortunately, the first word out of the beginning downloader's mouth, on examining the freshly downloaded loot, is generally this:

"Wha — ?"

First of all, people often can't *find* whatever-it-was that they downloaded. *Hint:* Downloaded stuff usually winds up in a special folder, which you can find like this:

✔ **America Online:** Open the hard drive icon. Open the Internet folder. Open the America Online folder. Open the Online Downloads folder. There's whatever you've downloaded.

✔ **Files attached to Outlook Express e-mails:** Double-click, in sequence: the hard drive icon, the Internet folder, the Internet Applications folder, the Outlook Express folder, and finally the Outlook Express Temp folder. There are your downloaded files. (See Chapter 8 for details on Outlook Express, e-mail, and file attachments.)

Further hint: When downloading stuff from the Web, you can avoid all this folder-burrowing looking if, every time you download something, you click the Desktop button before saving the file onto your hard drive, as mentioned earlier in this chapter. That way, the freshly arrived files will always be waiting for you on your desktop when you get offline.

Second of all, the first thing many people read when they double-click a file they've just downloaded is this: "The application is busy or missing."

And *that's* because of *compression.* As you sit there waiting for your Santa Claus graphic to arrive on your iMac, you're tying up the phone line and drumming your fingers. Therefore, almost everything on America Online and the Internet arrives in a compact, encoded format that takes less time to transfer.

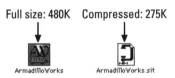

Which is terrific, except for one thing: How are *you* supposed to expand your downloaded file back into usable form?

Any file whose format is indicated by the suffix *.sit* has been "stuffed" using a program called StuffIt. As an added convenience, the America Online software unstuffs these files *automatically* when you log off the service.

But what if (a) you're getting your goodies straight from the Internet, not AOL, or (b) the letters at the end of your precious loot's name *aren't* .sit?

StuffIt Expander: Free and easy

The solution to all of these problems is the set-it-and-forget-it answer to the downloader's prayers: StuffIt Expander. It's free, thank heaven, and already on board your iMac. (Open these icons, in sequence: your hard drive; the Internet folder; the Utilities folder; the Aladdin folder; the StuffIt Expander folder. There it is: the StuffIt Expander program. Want to stash it in a more convenient place? Just drag the StuffIt Expander icon to your desktop, where you'll be able to find it again more easily.)

This little program can gracefully re-expand just about any geeky Internet file, from *.sit* to *.cpt* and *.hqx*, along with such all-time favorites as *.gz*, *.z*, *.ARC*, *.ZIP*, and *.uu* files, too. (This doodad, too, is in the Aladdin folder; it's hidden in the icon called DropStuff with EE Installer.)

After you've got this thing safely installed on your hard drive, here's the handy two-step scheme for expanding something you downloaded from cyberspace.

1. Drag the downloaded mystery item on top of the StuffIt Expander icon.

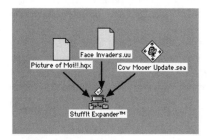

2. Your downloaded mystery item is automatically restored to human form.

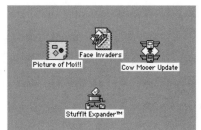

Files you still can't open

Bill Gates, as you may have heard, is the wealthiest human being in the history of everything. He got that way by foisting something called Windows onto all the office computers of the world.

Fortunately, you've got something that works better: an iMac. Unfortunately, sooner or later, you'll encounter files on the Internet intended for Windows people — or files that are meant to be used by *both* Macintosh and Windows. In both cases, you may be befuddled.

The giveaway is the three-letter suffix at the end of a downloaded file's name. As described in the previous section, suffixes like *.sit, .hqx, .zip, .uu,* and others mean that the file is compressed, and can be opened using StuffIt Expander. But sometimes, even *after* being decompressed, a three-letter suffix remains, such as the common ones revealed in this table:

Suffix	How to Open It
.exe	An executable file — in other words, a Windows program. By itself, your iMac can't run Windows programs, just as Windows computers can't run Macintosh programs. All is not lost, however: If you buy and install a program like SoftWindows (*www.insignia.com*) or VirtualPC (*www.connectix.com*), your iMac *can* run Windows programs.
.jpg or *.gif*	You've downloaded yourself a photograph! When you double-click it, you'll probably get a strange list box like this one:

> ⚠ **Could not find the application program that created the document named "6–6.jpg".**
>
> **To open the document, select an alternate program, with or without translation:**
>
> 🏛 **MoviePlayer with QuickTime translation** ▲
> 🎙 **Olympus Utility**
> 📷 **Photoshop**
> 📷 **PictureViewer**
> 🔊 **SimpleSound with QuickTime translation**
> 📝 **SimpleText with QuickTime translation** ▼
>
> ☑ Show only recommended choices
>
> [Cancel] [**Open**]

	To look at the picture, double-click PictureViewer in the list. If you want to make changes to the photo, you need a photo-*editing* program like Photoshop or PhotoDeluxe; if you see such a program in the list, double-click its name.
.pdf	This downloaded item is probably a manual or brochure. It came to you as a *portable document format* file, better known as an Adobe Acrobat file. To open it, you need a free program called Acrobat Reader. The installer for Acrobat Reader is probably on your hard drive already; use the Sherlock command in your 🍎 menu to locate it (search for the word *Acrobat*). If Sherlock comes up empty-handed, visit *www.adobe.com* to download a fresh copy of the free Acrobat Reader Installer. (This computing stuff's a full-time job, isn't it?) When the installation is complete, you'll be able to double-click any .pdf file to open and read it automatically.
.html	A file whose name ends in *.html* or *.htm* is a Web page. In general, Web pages hang out only on the Internet. Every now and then, however, you may find that you've downloaded one to your iMac's hard drive. To view it, launch your favorite Web browser, such as Internet Explorer or Netscape Navigator. From the File menu, choose Open; locate the *.html* file; and double-click it to open.

Top Ten Best/Worst Aspects of the Net

No question: The Internet is changing everything. If you're not on it now, you probably will be within a few years. Here's what to look forward to:

1. Best: Everyone is anonymous, so everyone is equal. It doesn't matter what you look, sound, or smell like — you're judged purely by your words.

2. Worst: Everyone is anonymous, so everyone is equal. You can pretend to be someone you're not — or a *gender* you're not — for the purposes of misleading other Internet surfers.

3. Best: the cost — $20 a month for unlimited access.

4. Worst: the cost — $20 a month is a lot.

5. Best: The Internet connects you to everyone. You're only an e-mail or a Web page away from anyone else on the planet.

6. Worst: The Internet *disconnects* you from everyone. You become a hermit holed up in your room, as family, friends, and relationships pack up and leave.

7. Best: The Internet is drawing people away from TV. Statistics show that as more people discover the Web, they spend less time in front of the boob tube.

8. Worst: The Internet is drawing people away from TV. The TV industry is going crazy wondering what to do.

9. Best: The Internet is complete freedom of speech for everyone. No government agency looks over your shoulder; the Net is completely unsupervised and uncontrolled.

10. Worst: The Internet is complete freedom of speech for everyone. Including pornographers, neo-Nazi groups, and others you may not want your 10-year-old getting chummy with.

Chapter 7

The Weird Wide Web

The most popular part of the Internet is the World Wide Web — you can't help hearing about this thing. Fourth graders run around urging schoolmates to "check out their Web pages." Web "addresses" show up everywhere — on business cards, in newspaper ads, on TV. (Have you noticed *www.sony.com* or *www.spam.com* flashing by at the end of movie ads and car commercials? Those are Web addresses.)

The Web has become incredibly popular for one simple reason: It *isn't* geeky and user-hostile, like the rest of the Internet. It looks friendly and familiar to actual humans. When you connect to the Web, you don't encounter streams of computer codes. Instead, information is displayed attractively, with nice typesetting, color pictures, and interactive buttons.

Internet Made Idiotproof: Link-Clicking

Navigating the Web requires little more than clicking buttons and those underlined blue phrases, which you can sort of see in the following figure.

When you click an underlined phrase, called a *link,* you're automatically transported from one "page" (screen) to another, without having to type in the usual bunch of Internet codes. One page may be a glorified advertisement; another may contain critical information about a bill in Congress; another might have been created by a nine-year-old in Dallas, to document what her dog had for lunch.

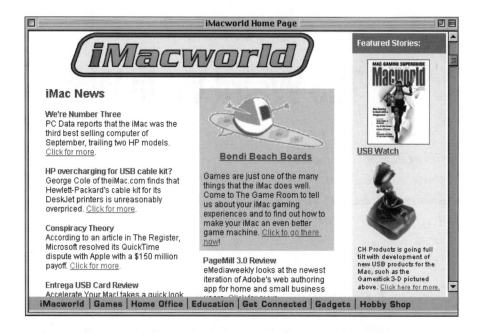

Unfortunately, all of this amazing online multimedia stuff stresses your modem nearly to the breaking point. Even with your iMac's 56 Kbps modem, the fastest standard modem there is, you still wait five or ten seconds for *each* Web page to float onto your screen.

Getting to the Web via America Online

To get to the Web once your online with America Online, choose "Go to the Web" from the Internet icon, as shown here.

If you've been given a particular Web address to visit (such as *www.hamsters.com*), you can also treat it as a keyword. (See Chapter 6 for instructions on using keywords.) That is, type in that Web address into the Keyword box (or the strip at the top of the AOL screen); it'll automatically open up a Web window and take you to the appropriate page.

Getting to the Web via an ISP

If you've signed up for a direct Internet account (such as EarthLink, as described in Chapter 6) instead of America Online, you'll be using a special program for browsing the Web — called, with astounding originality, a *Web browser.*

Most people use either the Netscape Navigator or Microsoft Internet Explorer browser. Both are free; both are on your iMac's hard drive (in the Internet folder).

How do you choose which browser to use? In a nutshell, Navigator is faster, but doesn't have many features. Explorer is slower, but has a lot of nice features (such as the capability to turn off blinking animations on Web pages, which otherwise drive you quietly mad).

To go a-browsing, launch your Web browser. If you have, in fact, signed up for an Internet account (see Chapter 6), the iMac dials the phone automatically, hisses and shrieks, and finally shows you a Web page.

Where to Go, What to Do on the Web

Once you're staring at your first Web page — whether via America Online or an Internet access company — getting around is easy. (The picture below shows Netscape Navigator, but you'll find the same basic elements in Internet Explorer, too.) Just *look* at all the fun things to see and do on the Web!

A. Click the Back button to revisit the page you were just on — or the Forward button to return to the page you were on *before* you clicked the Back button. (Does that make sense?)

B. Type a new Web page address into the thin horizontal strip at the top of the browser window and press Return to go to the site. A Web address, just so you know, is known by the nerds as a *URL* — pronounced "U. R. L."

And where do you find good Web addresses? From friends, from articles, on television, and so on. Look for *http://* or *www* at the beginning of the address — a guaranteed sign that the address points to a Web page.

C. Enjoy the little animated meteor shower in the upper-right-corner logo. It means "Wait a sec, I'm not done painting this Web page picture for you. As long as I'm animating, you'll just have to wait."

D. Clicking a picture or a button often takes you to a new Web page.

E. Clicking blue underlined phrases (called *links*) *always* takes you to a different Web page. (As a handy bonus, these links change to some other color when you see them next. That's to remind you that you've been that way before.)

F. Click in a Search blank and type what you're looking for. (Click the Search button when you're finished typing.) Similar blanks appear when, for example, you're asked to fill out a survey, type in your mailing address, and so on.

G. When you see a picture you'd like to keep, point to it, hold down the mouse button, and watch for a pop-up menu to appear at your cursor tip. From this pop-up menu, choose "Save this Image As" (in Navigator) or "Download Image to Disk" (in Explorer). After you click the Save button, the result is a new icon on your hard drive — a graphics file containing the picture you saved.

H. Use the scroll bar to move up and down the page — or to save mousing, just press the spacebar each time you want to see more. (If that spacebar trick doesn't work, first click any blank area of the Web page.)

Ways to search for a particular topic

Suppose you're looking at the Kickboxing Haiku Web page. But now you want to check the weather in Detroit. Because the World Wide Web is indeed a big interconnected web, you could theoretically work your way from one Web page to another to another, clicking just the proper blue underlined links, until you finally arrived at the Detroit Weather page.

Unfortunately, there are about 200 million Web pages. By the time you actually arrived at the Detroit Weather page, the weather would certainly have changed (not to mention Detroit). Clearly, you need to be able to *look something up* — to jump directly to another Web page whose address you don't currently know.

For this purpose, the denizens of the Web have seen fit to create a few very special Web pages — whose sole function is to search all the *other* Web pages. If you're on the Web, and don't know where to look for, say, information about Venezuelan Beaver Cheese, you can use the Find commands at any of the following sites:

- *www.yahoo.com*
- *www.altavista.com*
- *www.infoseek.com*
- *www.google.com*
- *www.hotbot.com*

All of these search pages work alike. Here, for example, is what it would look like if you used the search page called Yahoo! (the first address listed above) to find information about Venezuelan Beaver Cheese.

After clicking the Search button, you'd be shown a brand-new Web page listing *hits* — that is, Web pages containing the words "Venezuelan," "Beaver," or "Cheese."

See how useful a search page is? This handy Yahoo! thing narrowed down our search to a mere *108,650 Web pages!* You're as good as home!

Not. You can see here, in a nutshell, the problem with the Web: There's so much darned stuff out there, you spend an *awful* lot of your time trying to find exactly what you want. In this case, we probably should have clicked the little Help button on the main Yahoo! screen. It would have told us that to find a page containing the three words "Venezuelan Beaver Cheese" *together,* as a phrase, we should have put quote marks around them. That would have ruled out all the "hits" containing sentences like, "The beaver population has been halved by pollution. In this photo, Venezuelan cleanup engineer José Sanchez says 'Cheese!' for the camera."

Who ever said these things were user-friendly?

Searching from multiple angles

Here's a hair-whitening fact I'll bet the friendly stockholders at Yahoo.com don't want you to know: no single Web search page searches more than about 10 percent of the World Wide Web! Yahoo!, Hotbot, Infoseek, whatever — each knows about only a tiny fraction of the world's Web pages. The task of reading or listing *every* Web page on earth is simply too overwhelming, especially when you consider that hundreds of thousands of Web sites come and go every day.

If you're having no luck finding a certain piece of information online, therefore, try more than one of the search pages listed in this chapter — or just search using a Web site like Mamma.com or MetaCrawler.com, which send your request to ten *other* search pages simultaneously. Or use Sherlock, described in this chapter, which can also search many sites at once.

Searching using Sherlock

When trying to locate a certain piece of information on the World Wide Web, most of the world's citizens use a searching Web page like Yahoo! or InfoSeek. You, as an iMac owner, however, are more fortunate. You can search for stuff on the Web exactly the way you search for files on your own hard drive: by using the machine's built-in Find feature, better known as Sherlock.

It works exactly the way you'd expect: From your menu, choose Sherlock. Click the tab called Search Internet. Type what you're looking for — in plain English — like this:

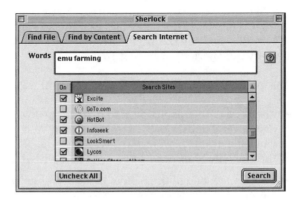

In the lower part of the window, you'll see an assortment of *search engines* (which is geek-speak for "Web pages that search the Internet"). If you were stranded in a desert condominium without Sherlock, you'd have to search each of these Web sites individually. Thanks to Sherlock, however, you can search several search engines simultaneously for a certain morsel of info. (You may find a number of shopping-oriented Web sites listed here, too, such as Amazon.com. No, you won't find much about emu farming or medieval politics at Amazon.com. On the other hand, it may sometimes be handy to search for a certain book or CD from within Sherlock.)

Just turn on the appropriate checkboxes, as shown in the illustration above, and then click Find. Your iMac now connects to the Internet (if it wasn't already), sends your request to the search engines you selected, and displays, in a new window, a list of Web pages that match your search, like this:

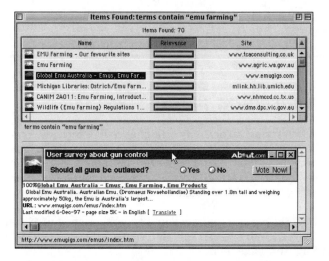

As you'll quickly discover, an advertisement also appears in the results window. On one hand, you may find that the ad slightly dampens the pure giddy joy of searching the Web with such ease. On the other hand, now you know why the Sherlock service is free.

At this point, you can proceed in any of several ways:

- ✔ Click one of the results *once* to read, in the lower pane of the window, the first several lines' worth of text from that Web page (as shown in the previous illustration). Doing so gives you a quick insight into whether or not the Web site Sherlock turned up is actually what you were looking for.

- ✔ *Double-click* one of the results to launch your Web browser program (Internet Explorer or Netscape Navigator), which opens directly to the corresponding Web page.

- ✔ Drag a row of the results directly out of the window and onto your desktop, strange as that gesture may feel.

The iMac automatically creates an icon on your desktop. At any time in the future, you can double-click this icon to open the corresponding Web page. *Handy hint:* Create a folder full of these icons, each representing one of your favorite Web sites. Leave this folder either sitting on your desktop for easy access — or better yet, add it to your menu for quick and easy access at any time. (Instructions for Apple-menu surgery are in Chapter 13.)

Not just Sherlock — new, improved Sherlock!

Every year, Apple makes improvements and additions to the Macintosh *operating system* (the underlying software that lets you turn the thing on, open menus, use windows, and so on). The original iMacs came with the delightful version of this software known as Mac OS 8.1; soon after, however, came Mac OS 8.5, and then even Mac OS 9. No matter what your iMac came with, you can buy and install newer operating-system software at any time. (See Chapter 18 for details on such upgrades.)

If you're used to something earlier, you'll find only two dramatic new features in Mac OS 9. One of them is the ability to share your computer in a family or classroom, such that each person who uses it sees only his or her stuff on the screen. Details on this multiple-user scenario in Chapter 13.

The other major Mac OS 9 feature is *Sherlock 2,* a makeover of the Internet-searching feature described in this chapter. It works exactly as described in the previous section, with two exceptions. First, Sherlock 2 has a handsome new stainless-steel look, guaranteed never to rust, flake, peel, or tarnish:

Second, each icon button at the top of the window searches the Internet for a different *kind* of information. (Apple calls these icon buttons *channels;* I call them *icon buttons.*) When you click the twentysomething brunette's head, for example, you can actually type in a person's name; Sherlock searches the Internet for that person's e-mail address or phone number. (In theory, this icon button gives you a worldwide White Pages right on your screen. In practice, Sherlock often comes up empty-handed. Could be that it's wired only to find twentysomething brunettes.)

Another example: Click the shopping cart button to search shopping Web sites for a particular item. Note, as you click the various icon buttons, that the columns of information in the results window actually change — when Sherlock shows you the results of Web shopping sites, for example, you get a Price column that doesn't normally appear.

Sherlock 2, in fact, is hours of fun for the whole family. Here's what each of the icon buttons does:

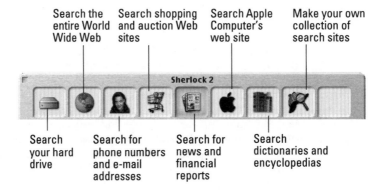

When you click the rightmost icon, you get an empty list of Web search pages. That's because this "channel" is one that you're supposed to build yourself. Click the News icon button, for example; *drag* the CNN item in the checkbox list up and to the right, until your cursor is *on top of* the Sherlock hat. You've just installed that search page onto your very own customizable list.

Nor are you limited to the search pages that show up when you first use Sherlock, by the way. Point your Web browser to *www.apple.com/sherlock/plugins.html*. There you'll find an enormous assortment of additional Web pages that can be searched using Sherlock. You'll find instructions on the Web page for installing your newly downloaded *plug-ins,* as they're called.

Useful Web pages: The tip of the iceberg

But there's more to the Web than getting meaningful work done (as millions of American office workers can attest). Here are some good starting places for your leisure hours. Technically, each of their addresses begins with *http://,* but you and I can both leave that off. Your Web browser will supply those letters automatically when you're finished typing.

(*Disclaimer:* Web pages come and go like New York City restaurants. I guarantee only that these pages existed the day I typed them up.)

- ✔ *mistral.culture.fr/louvre* — The Louvre museum home page, where you can actually view and read about hundreds of paintings hanging there.

- ✔ *amazon.com* — An enormous online bookstore, with three million books available, all at a 20 percent discount (or better). Reviews, sample chapters, the works. Don't freak out about typing in your credit-card number online; you're far more likely to be ripped off by handing your Visa card to the gas-station attendant or restaurant waiter.

- ✔ *www.dilbert.com* — Today's Dilbert cartoon. And a month of past issues.

- ✔ *www.clicktv.com* — Free TV listings for your exact area or cable company. You can customize it to color-code various kinds of shows, to hide the channels you don't want, and so on. Like *TV Guide,* but cheaper.

- ✔ *www.shopper.com* — Here, you can comparison shop among hundreds of computer-stuff mail-order catalogs instantaneously — with the results listed in price order.

- ✔ *pathfinder.com* — The electronic editions of popular magazines like *People, Time, Money, Fortune,* and more. Lots of graphics — nice, if you're willing to wait for the pictures to arrive.

- ✔ *efax.com* — An amazing free service that gives you a private fax number. When anybody sends a fax to your number, it's automatically sent to you by *e-mail.* You read it on your iMac screen with a special free program called EfaxMac, delighted that you've saved the cost of a fax machine, phone line, paper, ink cartridges, and the Brazilian rainforest.

- ✔ *www._____.com* — Fill in the blank with your favorite major company: Honda. Sony. ABC. Apple. CBS. Disney. NY Times. Macworld. McDonald's. Try it — you'll like it.

- ✔ *www.davidpogue.com* — The charming, attractive, and highly entertaining Web page of your eminently modest author.

Navigator vs. Explorer: The Tip-O-Rama

Unless you're an America Online subscriber, you spend much of your Internetting time using the Netscape Navigator or Microsoft Internet Explorer browser.

Their makers, Netscape and Microsoft, are bigger rivals than Rocky Balboa and Apollo Creed (or whatever his opponent's name was). Each company has vowed to keep beating up the other until it crawls out of the ring with puffy black eyes screaming, "ADRIANNN!"

Anyway: Unlike your America Online-subscriber comrades, you, O Internet subscriber, swallowed hard and opted for a hard-core, bona fide *ISP account,* as described in Chapter 6. One of the perks of doing so is a raft of cool features in your Web browser. Here, for example, are some time-savers and little-known features that work in both major browsers.

Choose your weapon

Ever wonder about the icon on your desktop called Browse the Internet? It's been there since the moment you turned on your iMac.

When you double-click that icon, your favorite Web browser launches. Question is, *which is your favorite?* Is it Navigator or Internet Explorer? Here's how you tell the iMac which browser you prefer.

From the menu, choose Control Panels, and then choose Internet. Click the Web tab. See the pop-up menu at the bottom? That's where you choose your browser-of-choice. Close the window, save your changes, and thank me later.

Type almost nothing

As you may have read earlier in this chapter, most Web addresses take the form *http://www.Spam.com,* where *Spam* is the name of the company or place. Thank goodness, you don't have to type all that! Whenever the desired address takes that form, you can type (into that top strip where the address goes) *just the name of the company* — such as Apple, Microsoft, IBM, Snapple, Mentos, Pepsi, McDonalds, Spam, and so on. The browser fills in all the *http:// . . . com* junk for you automatically.

Go get the plug-in

Web browsers can show you text and pictures. But every now and then, you'll stumble onto some page where a *sound* or a *movie* is the main attraction. Unfortunately, Navigator and Explorer don't know how to play these multimedia morsels — but they know somebody who does!

What I'm driving at is *plug-ins* — small add-on programs that, after installed in the Plug-Ins folder on your hard drive, teach Navigator or Explorer how to play those extra goodies like sounds and movies. Plug-ins are free; you just must know where to go to get them on the Web. Lucky you: I'm about to tell you.

Go to the Web address *www.plugins.com* or, if you feel like typing today, *http://home.netscape.com/plugins/index.html*. There you'll find all the little plug-ins looking for a home on your iMac.

I'm not saying you can't live a long, healthy, fulfilling life without any of this stuff. I'm just pointing them out in case you try to visit some Web page and get nothing but an error message saying something like, "Sorry, you can't visit this page until you spend all afternoon downloading and installing Such-N-Such plug-in."

Where's home for you?

Every time you sign onto the Web, your browser starts by showing you the same darned starting page — let me guess: a very complex and daunting-looking Apple page. Wouldn't it be great if you could change the startup page?

You can! From the Edit menu, choose Preferences. Click the icon at the left side of the screen that says Netscape Communicator or Home/Search (in Internet Explorer), as shown here. (If you use Navigator, make this change on the Web tab of your Internet control panel.)

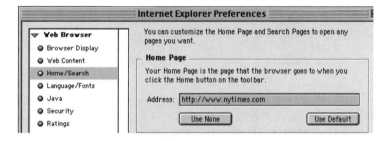

Now just change the Web address in the Home blank to a more desirable starting point. For example, you might prefer *www.dilbert.com,* which is a daily comic strip . . . or *www.macintouch.com,* which is daily news about the Mac . . . or even your own home page, if you've made one.

Faster — please, make it faster!

If the slug-like speed of the Web is making you sob quietly into your late-night coffee, despair no more. You can quadruple the speed of your Web surfing activities — by *turning off the pictures.*

Yes, I realize that graphics are what make the Web look so compelling. But all those pictures are 90 percent of what takes Web pages so darned long to arrive on the screen! You owe it to yourself to try, just for a session or two, turning graphics *off*. You still get fully laid-out Web pages; you still see all the text and headlines. But wherever a picture would normally be — wherever you would have had to wait for eight seconds — you'll see an empty rectangle containing a generic "graphic goes here" logo. Here, for example, is the Macworld magazine page (*www.Macworld.com*, of course) with all its graphics gone.

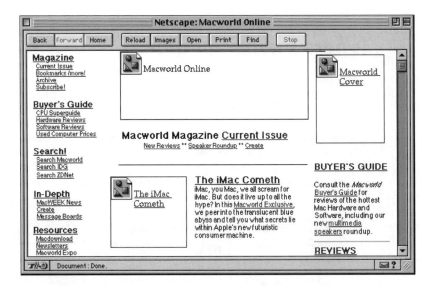

If you like the sound of this arrangement, here's how to make it so:

- ✔ **Netscape Navigator:** From the Edit menu, choose Preferences. Click the Advanced button and then turn off Automatically Load Images.

- ✔ **Internet Explorer:** From the Edit menu, choose Preferences. Click Web Content and then turn off Show Pictures.

The speed you gain is incredible. And if you wind up on a Web page that seems naked and shivering without its pictures, you can choose to summon them all — just on this one page — by choosing Load Images or View Images from the View menu.

Bookmark it

When you find a Web page you might like to visit again, you're not con-demned to writing the address on the edges of your monitor, like some kind of geeky bathroom graffiti. Instead, just choose Add Bookmark from the Bookmarks menu (in Navigator) or Add to Favorites from the Favorites menu (in Internet Explorer).

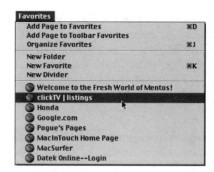

You're rewarded by the plain-English appearance of that page's name in the Bookmarks (or Favorites) menu! Thereafter, the *next* time you want to visit that page, you're spared having to remember *http://www.madmansdream.com* or whatever; you can just choose the page's name from your menu.

To get *rid* of something in your Bookmarks menu, choose Bookmarks from the Window menu (or choose Open Favorites from your Favorites menu). Click the page's name and then press the Delete key. While this bookmark-organization window is open, you can also rearrange (by dragging) or rename (by clicking) your various bookmarks or favorites.

Stop the blinking!

The citizens of the Internet quietly endure the advertising that fills the top inch of almost every Web page. We understand these ads pay for our free TV listings, free *New York Times,* free Internet backup storage, and so on.

But there's a big difference between a calm banner across the top of the screen and a seizure-inducing, blinking, flashing, looping, *animated* advertise-ment that's so distracting, you can't read the actual Web page itself.

If blinking ads make you, too, itch for a sledgehammer, then Internet Explorer should be your browser. From the Edit menu, choose Preferences. Click the Web Content icon; on the right side of the screen, you'll see the options for Animated GIFs. Turn off the Looping option to prevent animated ads from cycling over and over again; turn off Animated GIFs to play *no* animated ads.

Keeping the Net safe for kidlets

If you're worried that the Net's seedy underbelly isn't appropriate for certain people who use your iMac, rest easy. Thanks to Apple's generosity, your iMac came with the EdView Internet Safety Kit — Family Edition, a piece of software that restricts your iMac's surfing to safe, pre-approved Web pages. The Safety Kit also blocks all e-mail and even considers America Online off-limits. (Of course, you, the Person of Maturity, can override these blockades as you see fit.) Step-by-step instructions await in Chapter 9.

(Note: Ironically, some versions of the Internet Safety Kit conflict with Sherlock, the Internet-searching feature described in this chapter. If you discover that your iMac gives you the big bomb-ola whenever you use Sherlock, use the EV menu-bar command to temporarily disable the Safety Kit.)

Chapter 8

E-mail for He-males and Females

In This Chapter

▶ How to get, read, and write e-mail

▶ How to enjoy getting, reading, and writing e-mail

▶ The Anti-Junk-Mail Handbook

*I*f you have any intention of getting the most from your expensive high-tech appliance, you *gotta* get into e-mail. E-mail has all the advantages of the telephone (instantaneous, personal) with none of the disadvantages (interrupts dinner, wakes you up). It also has all the advantages of postal mail (cheap, written, preservable) with none of *its* drawbacks (slow speed, paper cuts).

Chapter 6 covers the glorious world of e-mail on America Online. If you're on the Internet courtesy of an Internet access company (an ISP) like EarthLink, however, read on.

Getting into E-Mail

To read and write electronic mail, you need an e-mail *program.* Microsoft Outlook Express, for example, is sitting right there on your iMac's hard drive (in the Internet folder). There's also a Mail function that's built right into your Web browser (see Chapter 7), but Outlook Express is a much superior e-mail program. It's the one that opens when, for example, you double-click the Mail icon that's sitting out on your desktop when you first turn on the iMac.

The grisliest part of joining the e-mail revolution is setting up your account for the first time. Fortunately, the Internet Setup Assistant (described in Chapter 6) does all of that setup for you. You're all ready to go a-mailing. (If you *didn't* use the Setup Assistant before trying to use Outlook Express, the program asks you to fill in a bunch of evil-looking blanks. Don't say I didn't warn you. Call up your ISP company and ask for help filling them in — or just run the Internet Setup Assistant.)

Sending e-mail

To write an e-mail, choose New Message from the Outlook Express File menu.
An empty e-mail message appears, filled with blanks to fill out. (The To,
Subject, and message areas are the only mandatory ones.) Here's what your
finished message might look like.

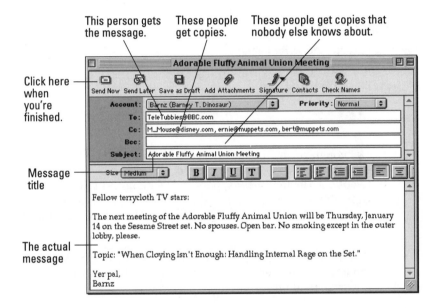

This person gets the message.

These people get copies.

These people get copies that nobody else knows about.

Click here when you're finished.

Message title

The actual message

As you'll quickly discover, e-mail addresses can't include any spaces, always
have an @ symbol in them, and must be typed *exactly* right, even if they look
like *cc293fil@univ_amx.intermp.com*. Capitals don't matter.

When you're finished writing, click one of two buttons at the top of the message window:

- ✔ **Send Now:** Click this button to send the message immediately. If everything's set up right, your modem now dials, connects to the Internet, and
  sends your e-message.

- ✔ **Send Later:** Click this button if you'd rather write several messages that
  you intend to send, later, in a single batch. Each time you click Send
  Later, the program files your newly typed message into its Outbox.

  When you're finally ready to send the pile of Outbox messages, click the
  Send & Receive icon at the top of the Outlook Express window. (If you
  don't *see* the Send & Receive icon, choose Outlook Express from the
  Window menu.)

Three ways not to be loathed online

Like any foreign country, the Net has its own weird culture, including rules of e-mail etiquette that, if broken, will make nasty comments and snideness rain down upon the offender. If you want to be loved online, read up:

✔ Don't type in ALL CAPITALS. They'll *murder* you for that.

✔ Don't ask what LOL means. It stands for "laughing out loud." And while we're at it: IMHO is "in my humble opinion," ROTFL is "rolling on the floor laughing," and RTFM is "read the freakin' manual."

✔ Quote what you're responding to. If someone e-mails you with a question, don't just write back, "No, I don't think so." The question-asker may have long since forgotten his/her own query!

Instead, begin your reply with the question itself. (On the Net, people generally put this quoted portion in <brackets,> like this.) *Then* follow it with your actual answer.

Oh, yeah, one more thing: You'll see these little guys all over the place:

:-)

Turn your head 90 degrees to the left, and you'll see how it makes a little smiley face. That's to indicate, of course, the writer's facial expression (which you can't otherwise see). A thousand variants of that punctuation-face are available — and an equally large number of people who absolutely can't stand those little smileys.

Getting your mail

If the messages you send out to your friends are witty and charming enough, you may actually get a few responses.

To check your e-mail, click the Send & Receive icon on the Outlook Express toolbar. (Can't find it? Then you must have rearranged your windows. From the Window menu, choose Outlook Express to bring the standard toolbar back.) In a spasm of hideous shrieking, your modem then dials cyberspace's home number and fetches any waiting mail. You'll see it in a list, as shown here.

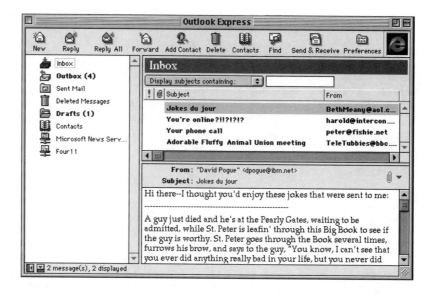

To read one of your messages, just click its name once (to view the incoming memo in the lower pane of the main window, as shown above) or twice (to open it into its own, larger window).

Processing a message you've read

When you're finished reading an e-mail, you have five choices:

> ✔ **Write a reply.** To do so, click the Reply button on the toolbar. Now you're back into I'm-Writing-An-E-mail-Message mode, as described in "Sending e-mail," a couple of pages back. (Your e-mail software thoughtfully pre-types the e-mail address of the person you're answering — along with the date, time, and subject of the message. If I had a machine that did that for my *U.S.* mail, I'd be a much better paper correspondent.)
>
> If you drag your mouse through some pertinent portion of the original message before clicking the Reply button, your e-mail program pre-pastes that passage into the reply window, like this.

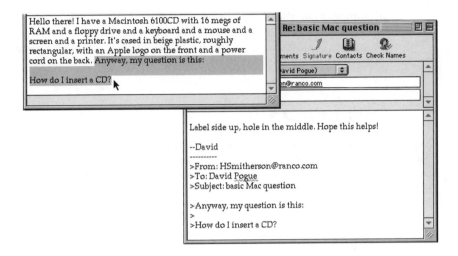

This common Internet technique helps your correspondent grasp what the heck you're talking about, especially since some time may have passed since he or she wrote the original note. As in the illustration, when the original e-mail contains a lot of irrelevant background material, this kind of bracketing helps both of you focus on the actual point (if any).

✔ **Forward it.** If you think somebody else in your cyber-world might be interested in reading the same message, click the Forward button at the top of the window. A new message window opens up, ready for you to address, that contains the forwarded message below a dotted line. If you like, you can type in a short note of your own above the dotted line ("Marge — thought this might annoy you") before clicking the Send Now or Send Later button.

✔ **Trash it.** Click the Delete icon on the toolbar, which sends the message to the great cyber-shredder in the sky.

✔ **Print it.** From the File menu, choose Print.

✔ **Save it for later.** To do so, close the message window. If you want, you can file the message away by dragging its name into one of the folders at the left side of the screen.

By the way: You can, and should, create your own specially named folders. Do that by choosing New Folder from the File menu.

Attaching Files to E-Mail

Fortunately, there's more to e-mail than just sending typed messages back and forth. You can also send files from your hard drive — in the form of *attachments* to your e-mail messages.

Companies use this method to exchange design sketches, movie clips, and spreadsheets. Authors turn in chapters (written in Microsoft Word or AppleWorks) to publishers this way. And families send baby pictures this way, to the eternal boredom of most recipients.

Sending a file

To pull this off, start by writing a normal e-mail message, making sure that you include a phrase like: "By the way, I've attached an AppleWorks file. It's a drawing little Cindy did of a tobacco-company executive in a paroxysm of self-loathing and doubt."

Then locate the icon of the file you want to send. (This may involve opening some folders and rearranging some windows on your screen.) You need to adjust the windows on your screen so that you can see *both* your e-mail message *and* the icon of the file you want to send, like this.

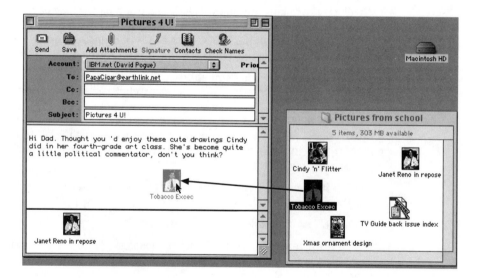

Drag the icons straight into the e-mail window. As in the preceding figure, the icons show up at the bottom of the window to indicate that your dragging was successful.

That's it! When you send the message, the attached iMac files go along for the ride.

Sending files to Windows people

If one aspect of e-mail causes violent gnashing of teeth, it's sending file attachments, as described in this chapter, to Windows computers.

WARNING: As you may have heard, Windows is a more technical computer system than Macintosh. Therefore, the following discussion is by far the most technical one in this book. Fear not, however: This page has been reinforced with invisible microfilaments for added strength.

When you're sending files to Windows PCs, you have to worry about three conditions:

✔ *You must send a file Windows can open.* Just as Betamax VCRs can't play VHS tapes, so Windows programs can't always open files from your iMac. Here are some kinds of files that Windows *can* open: documents created by Microsoft Word, Excel, or PowerPoint; graphics in JPEG or GIF formats; Web pages you've created or downloaded; FileMaker and Photoshop files; and other files where the same application is sold in both Macintosh and Windows formats.

Windows PCs probably *can't* open AppleWorks documents, by the way. If you want to send an AppleWorks document, convert it to Microsoft Word format before sending. To do that, choose Save As from the File menu; from the Save As pop-up menu, choose Microsoft WinWord before clicking the Save button.

If you want to send a picture, such as a scanned photo, to a Windows person, first save it in a format that Windows can understand (JPEG or GIF), using your scanning program's Save As or Export command.

✔ *You must add a three-letter code to the file name.* Every file on every Windows computer has a three-letter computer code that tells the computer what sort of file it is. Without this code, your poor suffering Windows friends won't be able to open what you send them. This table shows a few of the most common codes you might add:

Kind of File	Code	Example
Microsoft Word	.doc	Thesis.doc
Microsoft Excel	.xls	Quarterly results.xls
FileMaker Pro	.fp3	Database.fp3
A JPEG photo	.jpg	Picture of Mom.jpg
A GIF picture	.gif	Banner ad.gif
A Web page	.htm	HomePage.htm

✔ *You must send your file in a format Windows e-mail programs can under-stand.* The Internet, technically speaking, can't transmit files at all — only pure typed text. Behind the scenes, anything else that you transmit, such as photos or AppleWorks documents, must first be converted into a stream of text gibberish that's reconstructed at the other end. Every e-mail program — Mac or Windows — uses a different scheme for con-verting file attachments into codes that can be sent via the Internet. Unfortunately, Macs like the iMac use one format (called *StuffIt* or *BinHex*), and Windows uses another (called *AppleDouble, MIME,* or *Base64*). (I'm perfectly aware that this stuff is technical gobbledygook to you — hey, it's technical gobbledygook to *me* — but it's all for a good cause. Just smile and play along.)

So where do you make such settings? Depends on what e-mail program you're using. Outlook Express, praise be, generally uses the correct format automatically. (To check: From the Edit menu, choose Preferences. Click Message Composition; consult the pop-up menu at the lower-right. If it says AppleDouble, you're all set to send files to *both* Mac and Windows users.)

America Online, unfortunately, *always* compresses files using StuffIt format, which Windows users can't read. Your only option is to send files one at a time, making sure that the "compress Attachments" checkbox *isn't* selected after you click the Attach File icon. (If you try to send more than one file at once, America Online automatically compresses them.)

Getting a file

You may *receive* files as part of an e-mail message, too. The sign that you've received some picture or other file is a paper-clip icon in your In Box list.

If you double-click the name of the message, it opens up into a window of its own. At the bottom, you'll see the attachment file's icon, like this:

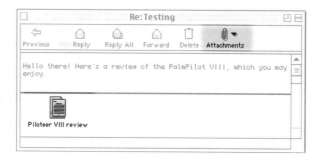

In some cases, you can double-click the file icon to open it. For best results, though, drag it out of the window and onto whatever part of your colored Desktop you can see. Doing so turns the file into an icon on your Desktop; from here, see the section "When You Can't Open Your Downloaded Goodies," in Chapter 7.

The Anti-Spam Handbook

No doubt about it: Unsolicited junk e-mail, better known as *spam*, is the ugly underbelly of e-mail paradise. You'll know it if you've got it — wave after wave of daily messages like "MAKE EZ MONEY AT HOME CARVING TOOTH-PICKS!" and "SEXXXY APPLIANCE REPAIRMEN WAITING FOR YOUR CALL!"

Unfortunately, we can't hunt down the lowlife scum that send out these billions of junk e-mails. Their e-mail doesn't include a phone number or postal address; you're generally expected to visit a Web site or respond by e-mail. Meanwhile, our e-mail boxes fill up with useless crud that makes it harder to find the *real* messages among them.

Whatever you do, *never reply* to a piece of spam e-mail — even if the message says that you can get *off* the e-mail list by doing so! Ironically, your response to the e-mail will simply flag your e-mail address as a live, working account manned by somebody who takes the time to *read* the stuff. Your name will become much more valuable to junk e-mailers, and you'll find yourself on the receiving end of a new wave of spam.

You may have wondered: How did you wind up on these junk lists to begin with? Answer: They get your e-mail address from *you*. Every time you post a message on an online bulletin board, chat in a chat room, or even put your e-mail address up on your Web page, you've just made yourself vulnerable to the spammers' software robots. These little programs scour America Online, newsgroups, and the Web, looking for e-mail addresses to collect.

"But if I can never post messages online," I can hear you protesting, "I'm losing half the advantages of being online!"

Not necessarily. Consider setting up a second mailbox — that is, a second e-mail address for your same America Online or Internet account. (That's easy to do on AOL; go to keyword *names* to set up a new one. If you have an Internet account, call your ISP's help line to arrange an additional mailbox.)

Thereafter, the game is easy to play: Use *one* e-mail address for public postings, chats, and so on. Use your second, private one *for e-mail only*. Spam robots can't read private e-mail, so your secret e-mail address will remain virginal and spam-free.

Part III
Software Competence

The 5th Wave By Rich Tennant

"Great! It comes with Quicken. Now maybe we can figure out where all the money around here is going."

In this part . . .

The next four chapters introduce you to the *software* that came with (or can be added to) your iMac. Including not just AppleWorks, Palm Desktop, games, and that stuff, but also the system software, the heart that beats within your System Folder.

After all, without software, your iMac is little more than an art object — cool-looking and translucent, to be sure, but not much help when it's time to write a letter.

Chapter 9

Faking Your Way Through the Free Software

● ●

In This Chapter

▶ Simulating mastery of AppleWorks, Quicken, and Palm Desktop

▶ Pretending you know how to play Kid Pix, Bugdom, and Nanosaur

▶ Feigning wisdom with the World Book Encyclopedia CD-ROM and Guide to Good Cooking

▶ Appearing to know what you're doing with PageMill and the Internet Family Safety Kit

● ●

Your Personal Software Store

Your iMac came with a gold mine of software programs that, if purchased separately, would have cost you literally *dozens* of dollars. Exactly what you got depends on what model iMac you have.

Software on all iMacs

✓ **AppleWorks** — Swiss Army Knife software. (AppleWorks, by the way, was formerly known as *ClarisWorks* — a useful piece of trivia the next time you hang out with Macintosh old-timers.) Just look at all you get, even if you don't know what they are yet: a word processor, a database, and a spreadsheet. But wait — you also get a graphics program that can even serve as a basic page-layout system. And if you order now, you even get a little telecommunications program — absolutely free!

All these modules are neatly bundled into a single integrated program, which came neatly bundled on your iMac's hard drive at no extra charge. You can write a letter and put a graphic in it, or design a flyer that has a little spreadsheet in it, and so on. Chances are good that you and AppleWorks will get to know each other very, very well in the coming months.

- **Bugdom** — A computer game. You're a noble pillbug-man on a quest to rout the evil Red Ant empire, thus freeing the helpless ladybug hostages. (Politically correct? Forget it.)

- **Nanosaur** — Bugs too small for ya? In this computer game, you're trying to outrun dinosaurs.

- **PageMill** — The Internet is amazing for a hundred reasons, but Reason One is that *anyone* can put up a Web page. Whatever your hobby, interest, passion, or business, you can be represented online. All you need is a program that lets you create Web pages — and Adobe PageMill is it.

Software only on new (CD slot-loading) iMacs

- **EdView Internet Safety Kit, Family Edition** — A piece of software designed to prevent your iMac from connecting to Web sites considered inappropriate for impressionable minds.

- **Palm Desktop** — A calendar and address-book program.

- **World Book Encyclopedia** — The electronic, CD-ROM version of the famous 26-volume book set. Better than the printed version in some ways — weighs a lot less, features occasional movies and sound clips, and is free.

Software only on older (CD tray-loading) iMacs

- **Williams-Sonoma Guide to Good Cooking, Kai's Photo Soap, MDK —** These three programs are a cooking program, a scanned photo touch-up program, and a violent futuristic game, respectively.

As you may have noticed, none of these extra programs come with full printed manuals. Let this chapter, tidily arranged in alphabetical order, be your guide.

AppleWorks

To start up AppleWorks, double-click your hard drive icon to open it. Now open the folder called Applications. Inside is a folder called AppleWorks, and inside *that* folder is the actual AppleWorks icon, which you should now double-click. (From now on, you'll be able to launch AppleWorks much more directly by choosing its name from the Recent Applications item in your menu. Or cheat: attach AppleWorks to one of the F-keys at the top of your keyboard, as described in Chapter 13.)

After the logo disappears, the New Document dialog box, shown below, asks you what you want to accomplish. Because you'll face this decision every time you use this program, a rundown may be in order here. If my Executive Summaries don't quite do the trick, don't sweat it; you'll be introduced to each of these modules in this chapter.

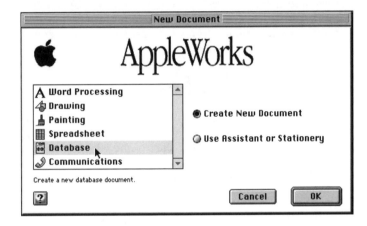

Word Processing: You know what a word-processing document is: something that you type: a memo, a novel, a ransom note.

Drawing: This is a *drawing program*. In this kind of document, you toy around with lines, shapes, and colors to produce such important visuals as logos, maps, and Hangman diagrams.

Painting: This is a painting window. *Painting* is another way of making graphics. But unlike the Drawing mode, where you can create only distinct circles, lines, and squares, the Painting tool lets you create shading, freeform spatters, and much more textured artwork. If you have a scanner or a digital camera, you can use this program to touch up the photos.

Spreadsheet: A computerized ledger sheet designed to help you crunch numbers: You can use it to calculate your car's mileage per gallon, your bank account, how much of the phone bill your teenage daughter owes, that kind of thing.

Database: An electronic index-card file. You type in your lists — household expenditures; record collections; subscriber list to *Regis & Kathie Lee!* magazine — and the program sorts them, prints them, finds certain pieces of info instantly, and so on.

Communications: This rarely used kind of program is useful primarily for dialing up local "electronic bulletin boards" (a rapidly fading memory, thanks to the much zestier Internet) and hacking your grades on the school's computer.

To make AppleWorks strut its stuff, I'll show you how to create a thank-you letter. But not just *any* thank-you letter — this is going to be the world's most beautiful and personalized *form letter*. You're going to merge a list of addresses into a piece of mail, creating what appear to be individually composed letters; thus the technoid term for what you're about to do is *mail merge*.

Even if form letters aren't exactly what you bought a computer to create, follow along. This exercise will take you through most of AppleWorks, and you'll brush up against some features that *will* be useful to you.

Your first database

Suppose that you just got married. You were showered with lovely gifts. And now it's your task to write a charming thank-you note to each of your gift givers. You'll begin by typing a list of the gift givers. The ideal software for organizing this kind of information is a *database*. Therefore, double-click the word Database, as shown in the previous illustration.

Don't be alarmed. The screen that now appears may look complicated, but it's actually not so bad — it simply wants to know what *blanks* you'll be wanting to fill in for each person in your list (name, address, gift type, and so on).

You're about to type names for these blanks (which the program calls *fields*). As always, if you make a typo, just press the Delete key to backspace over it. Here we go:

1. **Type *First Name* and press the Return key.**

   Pressing Return is the same as clicking the Create button.

2. **Type *Last Name* and press Return.**

3. **Type *Address* and press Return.**

   See how you're building a list?

4. **Type *Gift* and press Return.**

5. **Type *Adjective* and press Return.**

   In this blank, you'll eventually type a word that describes the glorious present that this person gave you.

6. **Finally, type *Part of House* (you'll see why in a moment) and press Return.**

   Your masterpiece should look something like this.

Define Database Fields	
Field Name:	**Field Type:**
First Name	Text
Last Name	Text
Address	Text
Gift	Text
Adjective	Text
Part of House	Text

Field Name: `Part of House`   Field Type: `Text ▼`

| Create | Modify | Delete | Options... |

[?] Select a field and click Options to change attributes, or change the name or field type and then click Modify.   **Done**

7. **Click the Done button in the lower-right corner.**

   The dialog box goes away.

When you see what you've created, things should make a little bit more sense. You've just created the blanks (oh, all right, *fields*) to fill in for each person in your list.

First Name	
Last Name	
Address	
Gift	
Adjective	
Part of House	

Accent heaven

Ah, mais oui, mon ami. C'est vrai, c'est la vie, c'est le résumé.

I know what you're thinking: What a smooth, sophisticated guy to be able to speak French like that! Thank you.

But you're also thinking: How did he get those cool accent marks? Very easily — and you, having been smart enough to choose an iMac over all its inferior competitors, can do it, too.

The iMac has a ton of these special characters. Look at your keyboard — I bet you don't see © or ™, or •, or ¢, or any other useful symbols that Mac people use all the time. That's because they're hidden. The secret that unlocks them is . . . the Option key.

It works like the Shift key: While pressing Option, you type a key. Here are some popular ones:

To Get This . . . Press Option and Type This . . .

To Get This	Press Option and Type This
©	g
™	2
ç	c
¢	4
¡	1
£	3
•	8
®	r
†	t

What's nice to know is that you have a complete built-in cheat sheet that shows these symbols' locations on the keyboard. It's the Key Caps desk accessory, which is in your menu.

Open it up and take a look. Now try pressing the Option key.

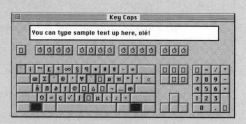

So that's where all those little critters live!

Anyway, there's one more wrinkle to all this. A few symbols, called *diacritical marks* (that's not a computer term; it's a proofreading one, I think) can be placed over any letter. They include the markings over this ü, this é, this è, and so förth. Because the iMac doesn't know ahead of time which vowel you're going to type, creating these marks is a two-step process:

1. While pressing Option, type the key as shown here.

To Get This . . . Press Option and Type This . . .

To Get This	Press Option and Type This
é	e
ü	u
è	`
ñ	n
î	i

When you do this, nothing will happen. In other words, no marking appears on the screen — until you do Step 2.

2. Type the letter you want to appear under the diacritical marking.

Only now does the entire thing — letter and marking — appear on the screen. So if you think about it, typing the six-letter word résumé requires eight keystrokes. *C'est formidable, ça!*

Data entry time

This is important: To fill in the fields of a database (like this one), just type normally. To advance from one field to the next — from First Name to Last Name, for example — *press the Tab key*. Do *not* press the Return key, as every instinct in your body will be screaming to do. You'll discover why in a moment. (You can also move to a new field by clicking in it, but the Tab key is quicker.)

So here goes:

1. **Make sure that you can see a dotted-line rectangle for each field, like the ones in the preceding figure; if not, press the Tab key.**

   The little blinking cursor should be in the First Name blank. (If it's not, click there.)

2. **Type *Josephine* and then press the Tab key to jump to the Last Name field.**

First Name	Josephine
Last Name	
Address	
Gift	

3. **Type *Flombébé* and, again, press Tab.**

   (See the sidebar "Accent heaven" to find out how you make those cool little accents.) Now you're in the Address blank.

4. **Type *200 West 15th Street*.**

   Ready to find out what the Return key does? Go ahead and press Return. Notice that you don't advance to the next blank; instead, the program thoughtfully makes this box bigger so that there's room for another line of address.

First Name	Josephine
Last Name	Flombébé
Address	200 West 15th Street
Gift	New York, NY 10010
Adjective	
Part of	

   If you ever hit Return by *mistake,* intending to jump to the next blank (but just making this blank bigger), press the Delete key.

5. **Go ahead and type *New York, NY 10010* and then press Tab.**

   And don't worry that the second line of the address immediately gets hidden. The information you typed is still there.

6. Type *acrylic sofa cover* (and press Tab); *practical* (and press Tab); and *living room* (and stop).

You've just filled in the information for your first gift sender. So that this won't take all day, let's pretend that it was what they call an *intimate* wedding, and you received gifts from only three people.

But let's see — we need a new set of fields, don't we? Come to think of it, wouldn't life be sweeter if there were a computer *term* for "set of fields"? By gumbo, there is! A set of fields is called a *record*.

I wouldn't bother with that term if it didn't crop up in the next instruction:

1. From the Edit menu, choose New Record.

A new record ("set of fields") appears, and you're ready to type the second person's information.

2. Type anything you want, or copy the example below, but remember to press Tab at the end of each piece of information.

(Oh, and if you want a second line for the address, press Return. Make up a town and state; you're a creative soul.)

First Name	Suzie
Last Name	Khiou
Address	1 Doormouse Ave.
Gift	Harley
Adjective	expensive
Part of	garage

3. Choose New Record from the Edit menu again and type a third set of information, perhaps typing *Ming vase* as the name of the gift.

Fabulous! You're really cooking now.

4. As a final wise step, choose Save from the File menu and type *Gift List* as the name of your database into the Save As text box.

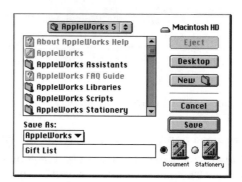

Finding and sorting in AppleWorks databases

After you've got some data typed into an AppleWorks database, you can manipulate it in all kinds of fun and exciting ways. Choose Find from the Layout menu to get what appears to be a blank record. Type what you're looking for into the appropriate blanks. For example, if you're trying to find everybody who lives in zip code 90210, you'd fill out the Find dialog box as shown in the figure below.

Then click the Find button. After about one second, you'll be returned to normal view, where you'll see the results of your search. This is important — AppleWorks is *hiding* the records that *didn't* match your search requirements. You haven't lost them; they're just out of sight until you choose Show All Records from the Organize menu. You can prove this to yourself by consulting the little book at the left side of the screen. It will say "Records: 22 (194)." That means that AppleWorks still knows there are 194 addresses in your mailing list, but only 22 have zip code 90210 (and they're all attractive teenage models on a major TV show).

First Name	
Last Name	
Address	90210
Gift	
Adjective	
Part of House	

Requests: 1

Find from
○ Visible
◉ All

☐ Omit

[Find]

5. **Click the Desktop button, and then the Save button to preserve your database on the hard disk.**

You've just created your first database. Having gone through the tedium of typing in each little scrap of information the way the iMac wants it, you can now perform some stunts with it that'd make your grandparents' jaws drop. You can ask the iMac to show you only the names of your friends whose last names begin with Z. Or only those who live in Texas. Or only those whose gifts you've categorized as *fabulous*. See the sidebar "Finding and sorting in AppleWorks databases" for details.

Forming the form letter

Next, you're going to write the thank-you note. At each place where you want to use somebody's name (or other gift-related information), you'll ask AppleWorks to slap in the appropriate info.

1. **Choose New from the File menu.**

   Again, you're asked to choose the kind of document you want.

2. **Double-click Word Processing.**

   You get a sparkling new sheet of electronic typing paper. You'll start the letter with the address, of course. Yet the address will be different on each letter! This is where mail-merging is handy.

3. **From the File menu, choose Mail Merge.**

   When the little window appears, you'll see your database name, Gift List, prominently displayed.

4. **Double-click Gift List to tell AppleWorks that it's the database you want to work with.**

   Now a strange-looking window appears:

   In the scrolling list you see the *Field Names* from your database. Here's how it works.

5. **Point to First Name and double-click.**

   See what happened? The program popped a placeholder for the First Name right into your letter. When you print, instead of *<<First Name>>*, it will say *Josephine*.

6. **Type a space; in the Mail Merge window, point to *Last Name* and double-click; press Return to begin a new line of the address; then point to the Mail Merge window again and double-click *Address*.**

Before you continue typing, you may want to drag the little Mail Merge window off to the right of your screen as best you can. (To move the window, drag its title bar.) You're going to want to see both it and your typing simultaneously.

7. **Press Return a couple of times and then type** *Dear,* **followed by a space.**

8. **Point to the words** *First Name* **in the Mail Merge window, as you did a moment ago; double-click; then type a comma.**

Your letter should look something like this.

«First Name» «Last Name»
«Address»

Dear «First Name»,

This is where it gets good.

9. **Press Return a couple of times and then type** *I nearly cried when I unwrapped the incredible,* **followed by a space.**

10. **Double-click the word** *Gift* **in the Mail Merge window.**

11. **Continue typing the following:** *you gave me for my wedding. It is far and away the most* **(and now double-click Adjective in the Mail Merge window)** *gift I will ever receive.*

«First Name» «Last Name»
«Address»

Dear «First Name»,

I nearly cried when I unwrapped the incredible «Gift» you gave me for my wedding. It is far and away the most «Adjective» gift I will ever receive.

Are you getting the hang of this? At each place where you want AppleWorks to substitute a piece of information from your Gift List database, you insert a little <<*placeholder*>>.

To see the last field name, Part of House, you may need to use the Mail Merge window's scroll bar. Then finish the letter as follows.

12. **Type** *It will look sensational in the* **(double-click Part of House in the Mail Merge window)** *of our new home.*

13. **Press the Return key twice and finish up like this:** *I had to write this personal note to you and you alone, so you'd know how much I treasure your gift above all the others. Love, Marge*

Specifying your favorite type

Wherever the Intergalactic Committee for Frequently Asked Questions keeps its master list, I'll bet that the first item on the list is this: "I hate having to set up my favorite type style and size every time I open a new AppleWorks word processing document. How do I specify my favorite font once and for all?"

The answer is easy, although you'd never figure it out on your own. From the File menu, choose New; in the New Document dialog box, double-click Word Processing. Now, from the Format menu, choose the font, size, and style you prefer. (If you're into such advanced kinky stuff as double spacing, margin adjustments, a logo in your header, and so on, you can make these changes now, too.)

Finally, from the File menu, choose Save As. Click the Stationery button. Type this name exactly — *AppleWorks WP Options* — and then click Save, and finally click OK.

From now on, every time you indicate that you'd like to begin a new word processing document, your preferred font (and other formatting choices) will be in place before you even type a word.

«First Name» «Last Name»
«Address»

Dear «First Name»,

I nearly cried when I unwrapped the incredible «Gift» you gave me for my wedding. It is far and away the most «Adjective» gift I will ever receive.

It will look sensational in the «Part of House» of our new home.

I had to write this personal note to you and you alone, so you'd know how much I treasure your gift above all the others.

Love, Marge.

Miss Manners would go instantly bald in horror if she thought you were about to send out a letter that says *Dear First Name*. But through the miracle of computers, when these letters are printed, it'll be impossible to tell that each one wasn't typed separately.

Save from the File menu. Type *Thank-You Letter* in the Save As text box and click Save.

The graphics zone: Designing a letterhead

To show you how AppleWorks can tie everything together, let's whip up a quick letterhead in the Drawing module.

Choose New from the File menu. Our friend, the New Document dialog box, appears. This time, double-click the word Drawing.

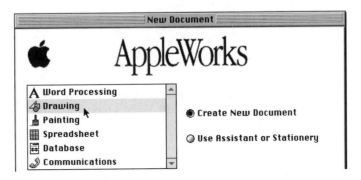

AppleWorks shows you its drawing window. The grid of dotted lines is there to give things a nice architectural look; it won't appear in the finished printout.

1. **Click the Text tool — it looks like a letter A — and release the mouse button; then move your cursor onto the drawing area and drag across the screen, as shown here.**

2. **Use the Font menu and choose Times; use the Size menu and choose 24 Point.**

3. **Type three spaces and then a long dash (to make a long dash, hold down the Shift and Option keys and type a hyphen); type *A Very Personal Note;* type another long dash and then three more spaces.**

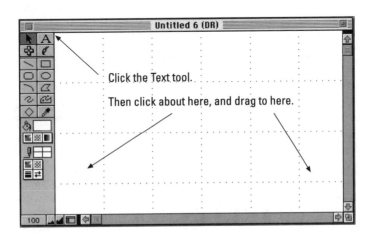

4. **Press the Enter key so that handles appear around your text; using the Alignment submenu of the Format menu, choose Center.**

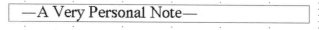

Finally, you'll add that elegant white-lettering-against-black look that shows up on so many corporate annual reports. At the left side of your screen, there's a set of odd-looking icons. Find the one immediately below the tiny pouring paint can icon, as shown by the arrow in this illustration (left).

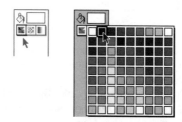

This icon is actually a pop-out palette (right).

5. **Click the paint-can icon but keep the mouse button pressed so that the palette appears (preceding figure, right); drag carefully to the right until the pointer is on the solid black square; release the mouse.**

You've just used the Fill palette to color in the entire text block with black. Which is just great, except that now the text is a solid black rectangle! To fix the problem, you need to make the text *white*.

6. **From the Text Color submenu of the Format menu, choose White.**

Of course, while you're in the Drawing mode, you could actually do some graphics . . . you could use any of the other drawing tools to dress up your logo. You could draw a box around this letterhead. You could rotate the whole thing 90 degrees. You could make all kinds of insane diagonal stripes across it. You could choose, from the File menu, Library — and select any of the "libraries" full of ready-to-use graphics (flags, stars, flowers, and so on) worthy of dragging into your drawing as an aid to the artistically challenged.

For control freaks only: The View buttons

Before you leave the drawing window, cast your eyes upon the lower-left corner of the screen. There you'll find this odd-looking array of controls.

Hide palette

Pop-up menu | Split the screen

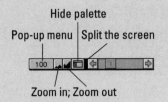

Zoom in; Zoom out

As you can tell, AppleWorks makes blowing up your work extremely easy. (I mean *magnifying* it; *destroying* it is up to you.) A quick click on either of those little mountain buttons makes the artwork smaller or larger. Or jump directly to a more convenient degree of magnification by using the percentage pop-up menu (where it says 100 in the figure to the left). You're not changing the actual printed size — only how it's displayed on the screen.

Keep those creative possibilities in mind when it comes time to design your real letterhead.

The return of Copy and Paste

All that remains is for you to slap this letterhead into your mail-merge letter:

1. **Using the Arrow tool, click your letterhead; from the Edit menu, choose Copy.**

   Now you need to return to your word-processing document. Here's a quick way to pull it to the front.

2. **From the Window menu, choose Thank-You Letter (WP).**

   (*WP* stands for Word Processing document; *DB* stands for Database; *DR* stands for Drawing; *PT* stands for Painting; and *SS* stands for Spreadsheet.)

   Your letter springs to the fore.

3. **From the Format menu, choose Insert Header.**

   (A *header* is an area at the top of every page, above whatever text you've typed. In this case, it looks like an empty text area.)

4. **From the Edit menu, choose Paste.**

   Et voilà . . . your graphic pops neatly into the header.

You've actually done it: combined a database, a word processor, and a drawing program in a single project! For a real kick, click the Print Merge button. It's on the little floating mail merge windowette that should still be on the screen. Watch how the program automatically replaces actual names for the <<*placeholders*>> on the screen.

AppleWorks: The Other Spreadsheet

When most people talk about spreadsheet programs, they usually refer to Microsoft Excel, the $300 program that's universally adored by accountants (especially those who work at Microsoft). Fortunately, AppleWorks comes with a handy spreadsheet program that does most of what Excel can do, requires much less learning, and doesn't add a nickel to the personal fortune of Bill Gates.

A spreadsheet program is for doing math, tracking finances, figuring out which of two mortgage plans is more favorable in the long run, charting the growth of your basement gambling operation, and other number-crunchy stuff.

The not-so-grand total

Suppose, for example, that you're still recovering from the wedding for which you've just sent out handsome thank-you form letters. After enjoying a delightful honeymoon in sunny Tampa, you return home to find a stack of bills reaching to the moon and back six times: from the wedding caterer, from the wedding band, from the wedding photographer, and so on. Before long, the question that has occupied your attention for ten months now — "Is this the person with whom I want to spend eternity?" — has been replaced by a new one: "Is eternity long enough to pay off all these bills?"

As is so often the case in life, software can provide the answer. Start by launching AppleWorks, as you did at the beginning of this chapter. If you see the word AppleWorks in the upper-right corner of your screen, then you're already running AppleWorks; in that case, choose New from the File menu.

Either way, the New Document dialog box now takes center stage on your screen. This time, double-click Spreadsheet.

A blank spreadsheet now appears on your screen. It's a bunch of rows and columns, like a ledger book. The columns are lettered, and the rows are numbered. Each little rectangular cell is called, well, a *cell*. It's referred to by its letter and number: A1, for example, exactly as in a game of Battleship. Here, for example, is how you might calculate your potential for solvency after paying for the wedding:

1. **Click in cell A3. Type** *EXPENSES:* **and then press Return.**

   Notice that as you type, no letters actually appear in the cell. Instead, all the action takes place in the strip above the top row. Only when you press Return or Enter does your typing jump into place in the spreadsheet itself.

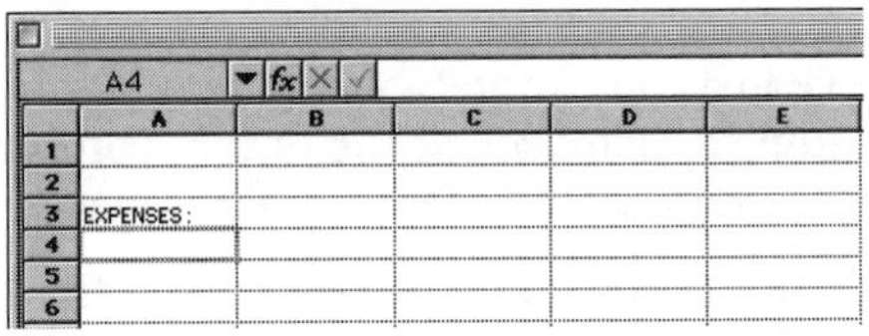

   You should now see that the next cell down, A4, shows a faint colored border, indicating that your next typing will appear there.

2. **Type each of the expenses shown in the illustration below (Caterer, Photographer, and so on); after typing each, press the Return key to jump down into the next cell. In the last cell, type** *TOTAL:* **and then press Return.**

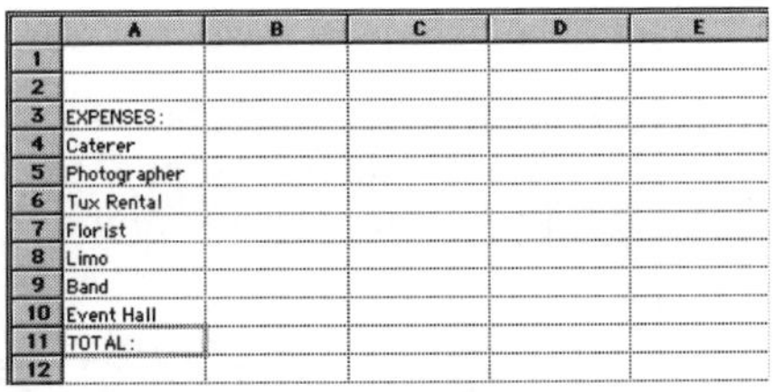

   Having written down everyone to whom you owe money, you should be feeling better already.

3. **Click in cell B4, to the right of the Caterer item. Type dollar amounts for each wedding-money recipient, as shown in the next illustration, again pressing the Return key after each amount.**

   AppleWorks can do far more than just display a bunch of numbers — it can also add them up.

4. Carefully drag your cursor straight down the column of numbers, beginning in cell B4 (where the first number appears) and ending in the empty cell at the bottom of the column (to the right of the word TOTAL:).

	A	B	C	D	E
1					
2					
3	EXPENSES:				
4	Caterer	15232			
5	Photographer	423.22			
6	Tux Rental	150			
7	Florist	235			
8	Limo	75			
9	Band	259			
10	Event Hall	644.23			
11	TOTAL:				
12					
13					

You've just told AppleWorks which numbers you want added up. By including a blank cell at the end of your drag, you also told AppleWorks where you wanted the grand total to appear.

5. Click the Σ button on the toolbar at the top of the screen, as highlighted here:

If you don't see the toolbar, choose Button Bar from the Window menu. If you see a downward pointing black triangle at the left end of the toolbar but you can't find the Σ button, click the black triangle, and then click Default to make the correct toolbar reappear.

When you do finally click the Σ button, an amazing thing happens: AppleWorks adds the correct total of the highlighted numbers in the empty cell at the bottom of the column.

B11	fx X √ =SUM(B4..B10)		
	A	B	C
1			
2			
3	EXPENSES:		
4	Caterer	15232	
5	Photographer	423.22	
6	Tux Rental	150	
7	Florist	235	
8	Limo	75	
9	Band	259	
10	Event Hall	644.23	
11	TOTAL:	17018.45	

Even more amazing, this number is *live* — that is, it checks its own addition thousands of times per second. If you change one of the numbers in the column, the total updates instantaneously. Try it yourself:

The bold accountant

Your spreadsheets aren't limited to the bland and tiny typeface you've been looking at so far. You're welcome to spice up your numbers by formatting them with boldface, italic, different sizes, colors, and so on.

For example, in the wedding-cost example in this chapter, you might decide to show the grand total you owe in boldface red type. To do that, click the cell where the total number appears. Now use the commands in the Format menu, such as Style (to apply boldface) or Text Color (to apply red). You can also make

AppleWorks add the dollar signs and decimal points automatically to highlighted cells, too: From the Format menu, choose Number, and then double-click Currency. (If your toolbar is visible, you can also apply all of these formatting options by clicking toolbar buttons or pop-up menus.)

All the automatic-adding features still work, but now whatever number appears in that total cell will always be red and bold — a cheerful reminder of just how desperate your financial situation is.

6. **Click the cell that shows the Photographer fee. Type a different number, and then press Return.**

   In the blink of an iMac, the Total cell changes to show the new sum.

The good news

So you owe a few thousand dollars. But life doesn't have to end. Surely you have a few assets you could sell to cover the cost of your recent nuptial festivities. Let's see if you could get out of hock by selling, for example, your wedding gifts.

1. **Click in column D3. Type *ASSETS* and then press Return.**

   You're about to begin typing a new column of information.

2. **Type *acrylic sofa cover,* and then press Return; *Harley,* and press Return again; *Ming vase,* and Return. Finally, type *TOTAL:,* and press Return one last time.**

   You might have noticed that "acrylic sofa cover" is too long to fit in the column without spilling over into the next cell. No problem — just make the column wider. Do so by positioning your cursor carefully on the dividing line between the D and E column headings — and dragging to the right.

   Now you need to specify the approximate value of each of your gifts.

3. **Click the cell to the right of *acrylic sofa cover.* Type a dollar amount for each item, remembering to press Return after each one. The result should look like this:**

	A	B	C	D	E	F
1						
2						
3	EXPENSES:			ASSETS		
4	Caterer	15232		acrylic sofa cover	1.79	
5	Photographer	423.22		Harley	5000	
6	Tux Rental	150		Ming vase	12039.44	
7	Florist	235		TOTAL		

4. **Drag through the column of numbers you've just typed, taking care to include one blank cell at the bottom of the column. Click the ∑ button on the toolbar.**

   As you could have predicted, AppleWorks adds up the newly typed numbers, showing your total assets at the moment. Once again, this total is "live" and continually updated. If you change one of the numbers above it, the total changes, too.

The final analysis

The automatic addition you've established is fine when you're stranded on a desert island without a pocket calculator. True spreadsheet nerds, however, don't content themselves with simple totals. In the real world, people use spreadsheets to create totals *of* totals, like this:

1. **In a blank cell beneath all the other numbers — cell C15, for example — type *GRAND TOTAL,* and then press Tab.**

   The Tab key works just like the Return key, except that it jumps to the next cell to the *right,* instead of the next cell *down.*

   The idea here is that you want AppleWorks to combine your two subtotals — to subtract the total amount you owe from the total value of your assets — so that you can see whether or not you'll break even from this wedding deal. To create this elaborate calculation, you'll build a *formula,* which is basically an equation exactly like the ones you used to build in junior high school. Formulas in a spreadsheet always began with an equal sign.

2. **Type an equal sign (=). Click the cell that represents your total assets (cell E7 in the preceding illustration).**

   Up in the formula bar, AppleWorks automatically writes in the name of the cell you clicked.

3. **Type a minus sign or hyphen (-), and then click the total amount you owe (cell B11 in the preceding illustration). Finally, press Return.**

D15	▼	fx	×	√	=E7–B11		
	A	**B**	**C**	**D**	**E**	**F**
1						
2						
3	EXPENSES:			ASSETS		
4	Caterer	15232		acrylic sofa cover	1.79	
5	Photographer	423.22		Harley	5000	
6	Tux Rental	150		Ming vase	12039.44	
7	Florist	235		TOTAL	**17041.23**	
8	Limo	75				
9	Band	259				
10	Event Hall	644.23				
11	TOTAL:	**17018.45**				
12						
13						
14						
15			GRAND TOTAL			
16						

AppleWorks subtracts the second cell from the first, displaying the grand total. This time, you lucked out: selling your gifts will earn you just enough money to cover the costs of the wedding — with enough left over for a bottle of sunscreen.

Amazingly enough, this grand total is also interactively linked to all the other numbers in your spreadsheet. If you change the price of the Ming vase, for example, both your assets total _and_ your grand total cells change automatically.

If you study this example, you'll see that the best way to build formulas in a spreadsheet is say what you're doing out loud. "The number in this cell . . ." (you click the cell where you want the grand total to appear) "equals" (type an = symbol) "this number" (click the assets total) "minus" (type the - sign) "this number" (click the debts total). Muttering softly to yourself as you work may not be the best way to pass yourself off as a financial genius, but you will get your formulas straight.

Other Cool Stuff AppleWorks Does

The little post-wedding mop-up example was only one example of AppleWorks' power. It left plenty of features unexplored, however. For example . . .

A little paint

If you've been following along, you haven't yet tried the Painting window. By this time, I trust that you know how to get there: Choose New from the File menu and then double-click the word Painting.

Suddenly, you're in a pixel-blitzing wonderland, where you can create all kinds of "painted" artwork. This kind of artwork has pros and cons. The pro is that you can change the color of _every single dot_ on the screen (instead of just making circles, lines, rectangles, and text, which is all that you can do in the Drawing window). The con is that you can't move or resize something in a painting after you've laid down the "paint" (which you _can_ do in the Drawing window).

A little slide show

One of the strangest and most delicious things people can do with an iMac is make slide shows. These can be either self-running (a new "slide" every four seconds, say) or controlled by you (a new slide every time you click the mouse button).

All you need to do is choose New from the File menu; select Use Assistant or Stationery; and double-click the Assistant called Presentation. Now AppleWorks asks you a series of questions, such as what kind of message you want to present, what style of slide background you want, and so on. When you're finished answering, you've got a terrific-looking slide show on the screen. Use the scroll bars to move among the slides, changing the (ahem) dummy text on each slide to say what you want it to say.

Mailing labels

AppleWorks is great at mailing labels; the program even walks you through the process. To get started, choose Frequently Asked Questions from the Help menu. Click Continue; double-click the "How do I" item called "make mailing labels?"

Other assistants

While we're on the topic of Assistants, remember that AppleWorks beats the pants off most other programs when it comes to creating certificates, press releases, address books, to-do lists, and so on. The key, after choosing New from the File menu, is to select the Use Assistant or Stationery button, as shown here.

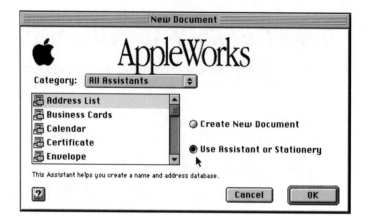

Experiment with the pop-up menu at the top of this screen; some of the most useful ready-made documents (which they call *stationery*) are hiding in here.

Bugdom

You can just hear Bugdom's programmers trying to describe this action game to the committee at Apple Computer: "Well, picture this: it's *A Bug's Life* meets *Rocky III* . . . "

Sure enough, once you launch the game (in your Applications folder), you'll recognize the colorful, 3-D, gigantic backyard setting of 1998's popular animated bug movies. You're a cute, cartoony bug in a world of other cute, cartoony bugs — except that *these* bugs are violent and ruthless. The bug world has been overrun with evil red ants who've locked all the ladybugs in cages, and who now seek to beat you senseless with lethal blades of grass.

Fortunately, having read the Bugdom Instructions file that comes in the Bugdom folder, you know that you're not completely helpless. You move through ten levels of the gamescape, encountering increasingly interesting bug species and situations, kicking red ants and rescuing ladybugs as you go, using these controls:

This control	Does this
Shift key	Makes you move forward.
Mouse	Turns you (drag your finger left or right).
Space bar	Changes you from a standard, walking pillbug into a balled-up pillbug (hence your name, which is Rollie).
Mouse	Makes you kick. (If you're rolled up into a ball, makes you roll into something instead.)
Option	Same thing as with the mouse.
Tab key	Every now and then, you'll discover that some loyal little winged bug is hovering above you wherever you go. It's a Buddy Bug — think of it as an airborne pit bull that you can sic on an enemy bug by pressing the Tab key.

Other than the increasingly oppressed Red Ant minority group, what, exactly, are you supposed to kick or roll into (by clicking the mouse or pressing the Option key)? First, you kick walnuts: When you find one in your path, crack it open. Inside is some kind of clover or other magical amulet that improves your little pillbug's health or weaponry. (After cracking the nut open, move forward to "collect" the treasure inside.) Second, you kick cages: When you spot a ladybug, kick or roll into her cage to shatter it, thus freeing the damsel-bug in distress. The more kicking you do, the more levels you encounter (including a very fishy one).

As rescue plots go, high-tech it ain't. But what do you expect? You're a pillbug.

EdView Internet Safety Kit, Family Edition

In addition to news, sports, jokes, and the Denny's Restaurant Home Page, the Internet also depicts the belly-button lint of the human condition: violence, sex, and other stuff you might not want your eight-year-old reading. The EdView Internet Safety Kit (included with CD slot-loading iMacs) is designed to shield your students, kids, employees, or spouse from such unsavory Internet material. It offers a list of well-organized, certified-safe Web sites — and prevents your iMac from connecting to any Web page not on the list.

Installing the Safety Kit

Insert the iMac Software Install CD-ROM. In the Internet folder is the EdView folder, and inside *that* is an Install EdView Family icon. Double-click it; then, in successive windows, click Continue, Agree, Install, Continue, and finally Restart. Your iMac turns off, and then on again.

During the installation, you'll be asked to make up a password. (I'm assuming that you, dear reader, are the Person In Control. If you, dear reader, are instead the Young Person who Shouldn't Be Exposed to Internet Naughtiness, please take this opportunity to assist your parent or teacher in setting up a password.)

When it comes to, you'll see a tiny red EV icon at the top right of your screen, like this:

We'll get to that icon shortly. In the meantime, there's one more step to sanitizing the Internet for your protection. From the menu, slide down to Control Panels, and then out onto Internet. When the Internet control panel opens, click the Web tab. In the Home Page blank, type *http://home.edview.com,* exactly. Close the window; save changes when you're asked.

Using the Safety Kit

You're ready to roll. Launch your Web browser (Internet Explorer or Netscape Navigator). The first thing you'll notice is that you're taken automatically to EdView's Web page, which is nothing more than a list of approved Web sites, organized by category:

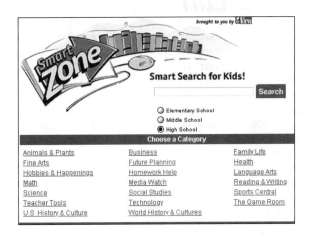

To look up, say, Web sites about basketball, you'd start by indicating (using the three buttons above the list) an age range: Elementary, Middle, or High School. Then, on successive screens, you'd click Sports Central, Basketball, and finally the name of the Web site that interests you. If you try to visit a Web site that's not on EdView's ever-growing list of safe sites, then you get a screen that says:

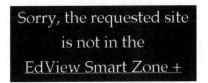

Your only alternative is to mutter, "Drats! Foiled again!" — and click the underlined words "EdView Smart Zone" to return to the list of OK'ed Web pages.

Bypassing the Safety Kit

The Safety Kit is clearly doing its job. But what about you, the Person In Control? What if you want to visit a Web page not on EdView's list — such as CNN or Amazon.com? Even if there's not a breath of smut or ugliness on such pages, they probably aren't on the Master List.

In such cases, you have two alternatives. You can turn off the Web-page blocking for your Internet session — from the EV menu at the top of the screen, choose Disable Channel Lock, confirm your maturity by typing the password, and click OK. Now you can use your browser as usual, without limitation. (Remember to choose Enable Channel Lock from that EV menu when you're finished.)

You can also inform your software that a particular Web page is OK for your kids to visit. Doing so involves a number of geeky steps, but it'll build character. You'll find them in the Manual, which is also in the EdView folder on your iMac Software Install CD.

E-mail, America Online, and other blockades

The Safety Kit not only blocks out unsavory Web sites — it also prevents your iMac from getting any e-mail and doesn't let you get onto America Online!

If you decide to permit access to these Internet features, you'll have to tiptoe through some technical tulips, like this:

1. **From the EV menu, choose Edit Preferences. When asked, type the password and click OK.**

   The Preferences dialog box appears.

2. **Click the Sites tab.**

   You're shown a strange-looking list of *Ports*. Each one represents a particular Internet feature that can be blocked by the Safety Kit.

3. **Turn on the Port options for the Internet features you want.**

   For example, turn on the Port 25 checkbox to permit your iMac to *send* e-mail; turn on Ports 109, 110, 143, and 220 to *receive* e-mail; and turn on Port 5190 to permit access to America Online (and its chat rooms, by the way).

4. **Click OK.**

Your preferences are now in place. The Internet is once again safe for children, students, and small furry animals.

Kid Pix Deluxe

If you know any kids, are one, or act like one, you may find Kid Pix to be the crown jewel of your CD slot-loading iMac's software collection. Start by inserting the Kid Pix CD-ROM; double-click the Kid Pix Studio Deluxe Installer; and keep clicking OK and Install until the job is done. You'll now find a Kid Pix Studio Deluxe folder on your hard drive.

When you launch the actual Kid Pix program, you'll find yourself in a wonderland of painting, sound, and animation tools. The home-base screen offers these activities:

- ✔ **Kid Pix** — The one, the only, the irresistible. Click a tool at the left side of the screen — the paintbrush or rubber stamp, for example — and then start clicking and dragging on your empty white canvas. Use the row of icons across the bottom to change what the paintbrush paints or rubber stamp stamps. The sound effects alone make this program a darling. You can save your work, of course, using the File menu's Save command; but you'll probably find that most people under 20 prefer to clear the screen by *blowing it up*. (Click the Eraser tool — and then the Dynamite icon at the bottom.)

- ✔ **Moopies** — The same as Kid Pix, except that anything you paint wiggles and twitches as though it's alive (or wired).

- ✔ **Stampinator** — This window offers exactly the same kinds of drawing tools as Kid Pix, with one big exception: The rubber-stamp tool creates animations. After clicking one of the animals at the bottom of the screen, drag your mouse across the screen. When you let go, your animal will follow your mouse-dragged path, looping over and over again. You can animate four different characters in this way.

- ✔ **Wacky TV** — Open one of several dozen ten-second movie clips to watch. Not interesting enough? Then click the egg-beater icon below the TV screen to spice things up.

- ✔ **Slide Show** — After you've saved a few animations, pictures, and other creations, you can assemble them into a complete storyboard/movie, using these controls:

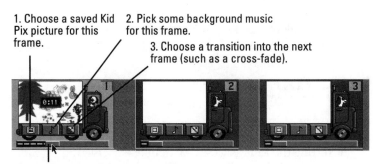

1. Choose a saved Kid Pix picture for this frame.

2. Pick some background music for this frame.

3. Choose a transition into the next frame (such as a cross-fade).

4. Drag this handle to specify how many seconds long this frame should play.

Click each of the frames shown here to select something you've saved. Finally, after having specified how long each "frame" should take to play, click the big triangle at the bottom of the screen to play the entire story-board.

✔ **Digital Puppets** — Pick a character from the Goodies menu. Then whack away at the keys to make your cartoon jerk, twitch, and otherwise respond. Ideal for those under two (or those who've had under two hours of sleep).

Nanosaur

This stunning, 3-D dinosaur shoot-'em up is all about noise, violence, and wiping out endangered species. Kids adore it.

Don't be alarmed when you can't find Nanosaur in the Applications folder with all your other software. Turns out you have to install it yourself. It's on your Software Install CD, in a folder called Applications, in a folder called Nanosaur. Run the Nanosaur installer you'll find within; drag the little Dinosaur head onto your Macintosh HD icon. When the installation is over, you'll find a Nanosaur folder on your hard drive. Double-click the Nanosaur icon inside *that* to play the game, if you're not already worn out for the day.

Just press the arrow keys to move your little dino around, and press the space bar to fire little dino-bullets. Check out the help screen (which appears just after you launch the program) to view the complete keystroke list. You can turn off the sound (or press the + and – keys to adjust the volume) — an excellent idea if you intend to play Nanosaur while in church.

PageMill

Adobe PageMill comes with all iMacs sold after November 1998 (it replaces MDK). It comes on its own CD in your iMac accessory package; insert the CD, run the PageMill Installer, and prepare for creativity.

And what, you may ask, is a page mill? It's a program that lets you make your *own* World Wide Web pages, like those illustrated in Chapter 7. That's the beauty of the Internet: *Anyone* can be represented equally. *Your* personal Web page can be just as prominent on the Web as, say, the Web pages of Sony, General Motors, or the White House — and a lot more entertaining. Maybe you have a small business you'd like to promote; maybe you want far-flung relatives to be able to see your new baby pix; or maybe you just want the world to know what you had for breakfast. With programs like Adobe PageMill, creating a home page of your own requires no knowledge of computer codes; if you've got something to say to the world, you can now stake your claim to a piece of property with frontage on the information superhighway.

The blank canvas

A Web page is made up of several different components: a couple of pictures, say, plus some writing. A solemn word of advice: In your forays into Web-page making, keep all these Web-page files together on your hard drive in a single folder.

You start your Web experiment, then, by creating a new folder on your desktop in which to store all the parts of your magnum opus. Call it "Web Page folder" or something.

Before you begin making your page, figure out what's going to be *on* it. If graphics are involved — and I certainly hope they will be, since the Web is all about pretty pictures — create them in a graphics program like AppleWorks, or grab them from a digital camera or scanner (see Chapter 11). When you save your finished graphics, the iMac usually gives you a choice of *file format* for them. Choose *JPEG* for photos, and *GIF* for non-photos like logos and cartoons.

As you design, remember that *big* graphics and *multiple* graphics make your Web page take forever to appear on your visitors' screens, so design judiciously. Put your finished graphics files into your Web Page folder.

Creating a new, blank page

When you double-click the PageMill icon, you get a shiny, new, blank canvas on which to proclaim yourself to the world. In the blank white strip at the top of the window, type a title for your page (such as *Bullwinkle's Home Page*); once this page is on the Web, this name will appear at the top of your visitors' screens. Now choose Save from the File menu and give a name to your PageMill document — that is, its icon on your hard drive.

PageMill proposes adding *.html* at the end of your document's name. Welcome to the World Wide Web, where, in the spirit of open-hearted fairness, even the users of non-Macintosh computers are allowed online. Because some of those computers are, shall we say, *differently abled,* names of files must meet some very rigid standards. For example:

- **Thou shalt not put spaces in the names of files.** If you feel the absolute need to put a space in the file name of a Web page, use the underline key (shift-hyphen) in place of the spaces, as in "Big_Gray_Poodle.gif" or "Space,_the_final_frontier.html."

- **Every file name shalt end with a suffix.** In other words, a GIF picture should have the letters *.gif* at the end of its name, JPEG should end *.jpg,* and a Web-page document (the kind you're making in PageMill) should end *.html* — for example, *Bullwinkle's_Home_Page.html.*

Meet your toolbar

PageMill's toolbar is crammed with useful gimmicks, most of which are just shortcuts for the menu commands. If you point to some control without clicking, a pop-up yellow label helpfully identifies what you're pointing at. For purposes of this experiment, for example, you'll use these toolbar icons:

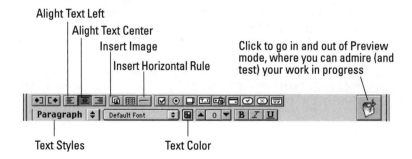

It's all HTML to me

Behind the scenes, Web pages don't look like Web pages. If you open one in a word processor, even a *blank* Web-page document contains enough geeky gobbledygook to curl your toes:

```
<HTML> <HEAD>

<META NAME="GENERATOR" CON-
    TENT="Adobe PageMill 3.0
    Mac">

<TITLE>Untitled
    Document</TITLE> </HEAD>
```

```
<P></P>

</BODY>

</HTML>
```

What you're reading is a computer language called *HTML*, or Hypertext Markup Language. Fortunately, PageMill hides all of this nerdspeak from you. I mention HTML only so that you won't panic if you happen to stumble onto some of it when PageMill isn't looking.

Add the text

At the moment, your blank document is surprisingly drab for the supposedly colorful world of the Internet. Instead of that sickly gray background color, let's choose something that won't look quite so much like a prison cell. See the Inspector panel, the little floating window off to the right of your screen? From the Background pop-up menu, choose the White color. Ahh . . . much better.

Most Web pages start with a headline. Inspect the Text Styles pop-up menu on your toolbar. See the list of Heading types? This pop-up menu offers you a list of various canned text styles. For now, choose Largest Heading. Now click the Center Align Text toolbar icon. Type the headline for your Web page.

The page isn't the only thing that can be colorized, by the way. You can change the color of your text, too. Highlight some of the words in your headline and choose from the Text Color pop-up menu on the toolbar.

Hanging pictures

Adding pictures to your Web page is simple. Just click the Insert Image button on the toolbar. In the Open dialog box, find, and double-click, the graphics file you'd like to slap onto your Web page. (You can also paste in a picture you've copied from another program, such as AppleWorks.) The image appears right there on your Web page, as shown here:

If you click the pic, handles appear, which you can use to change the picture's size. Keep the Shift key pressed as you drag to avoid distorting the image.

A little separation

Back to our Web-page-in-progress: Press Return a couple of times. Click the Align Text Left button on the toolbar. Start typing; now's your chance to spill your guts — as much guts as you'd like to spill in front of a 200-million-person audience, that is.

When you want to introduce a new topic, you might consider drawing a horizontal line between paragraphs. To do so, press Return, and then click the Insert Horizontal Rule button on the toolbar; a 3-D looking line appears on your page, as shown at the bottom of the previous figure.

Linking up

That's certainly enough creativity for one afternoon. From here on in, you can rely on the creativity of others — by creating *links* from your Web page to other peoples' pages. This linking thing, of course, is what the World Wide Web is all about.

Suppose your Web page continues with this common phrase: "If you've enjoyed this Web page, I owe it all to *The iMac For Dummies,* which showed me how to do it. Click here to visit Pogue's Pages."

Highlight the text you want to serve as the link; the idea is for it to turn *blue and underlined,* like the blue, underlined phrases on millions of Web pages all over the universe. Blue underlining tells the visitor: *Click me to move to a different Web page!*

Then, in the "Link To:" strip at the bottom of the window, type the target Web address, like this:

Highlighted text to become the link.

The Web page you're linking to.

After typing the Web address, press Return; you've just created your first Web link. If somebody's looking at your Web page and clicks the "Click here" phrase, their screen will soon fill with *my* Web page.

Getting published

Unfortunately, getting your Web page *on* the Web is almost as much work as *creating* your page. Putting your pages up forces you into encountering such geeky terms as *FTP* and *server.*

If you have an America Online subscription, use keyword: MYPLACE. From here, click the Go To My Place button, click Upload, find your various Web Page Folder files, and transmit them, one at a time, to AOL. (The instructions you'll find at keyword: MYPLACE are much more detailed.) Then start telling your friends your Web page address: It's *http://members.aol.com/skibunny* (substitute your own screen name for *skibunny*).

If you have a direct Internet account instead of AOL — EarthLink, for example — visit its Web page for instructions. (For EarthLink, the instructions await at this Web page: *http://help.earthlink.net/websupport/member/menu.html.* There you'll find out about PageMill's Upload command, which is in the File menu. It's the key to transferring each finished Web page onto the Internet.)

Your Web page address will usually be something like *http://www.earthlink. com/~skibunny,* where *skibunny* is you and *earthlink.com* is the name of your Internet access company.

When it's all over, you, my friend, will be a Web publisher — circulation: 200 million!

Palm Desktop

Don't worry the fact that your friends may say — "Oh my gosh, why are you using that program? That's only for people with PalmPilots!"

Such comments arise because this same software, Palm Desktop, is also included with the *PalmPilot,* a tiny, incredibly popular $200 or $300 handheld computer about the size of an audiocassette. (You can see a photo in Chapter 18.) When you connect a PalmPilot to your iMac, all of your names, addresses, calendar appointments, notes, and to-do lists are automatically sucked into the handheld computer. You can then slip the PalmPilot into your shirt pocket, sock, or undergarment, secure in the knowledge that your electronic little black book is with you at all times.

That convenient arrangement does not, however, mean that you must own a PalmPilot to get mileage out of Palm Desktop. Far from it! Palm Desktop is a perfectly good calendar/phone book program even if you never use a PalmPilot your entire life. It can dial the phone automatically, create reminders that pop up on the iMac screen at specified times, print mailing labels and portable phone books, and save you a lot of time when it comes to typing in your Rolodex.

Installing Palm Desktop

Apple figured that not everybody would want a calendar/phone book program, so Palm Desktop doesn't come pre-installed on your iMac. It's is on your Software Install CD-ROM, tucked away in the Applications folder.

To install it, double-click the icon called Install Palm Desktop. Click every Continue, Install, Agree, or Okie-Dokie button you see. (When you're asked if you want to set up Palm Desktop to sync with a Palm organizer, click Setup Later.) Finally, the iMac restarts, and you're in business.

The Calendar

When you first launch Palm Desktop, you're asked to register the software. If you enjoy getting junk mail, click Next; if not, click Cancel, and then Never Register.

Now you're shown an empty daily calendar. Unless you are the proprietor of a wedding hall, however, you may not necessarily live your life in one-day chunks. Fortunately, the tabs on the right side of the screen (Daily, Weekly, Monthly) let you see one day, one week, or one month at a time, respectively.

Entering appointments in Weekly or Daily view

You jot down events in Weekly or Daily view like this:

1. **Navigate to the day and time of your appointment.**

   To view a different week or day, click the arrow buttons in the upper-right corner of the window. To see the time slots earlier or later in the day, use the scroll bar at the right side.

2. **Using your mouse, drag vertically through the time slot to be consumed by your appointment.**

   For example, to schedule a meeting from 1 p.m. to 3 p.m., click carefully at the 1 p.m. slot — and then, without releasing the mouse, drag down the mouse to the 3 p.m. slot.

   You've just created an empty rectangle.

3. **Type a description for the appointment — for example, "Meet with Janet about impending bankruptcy" — and then press the Return key.**

That's all there is to it: you've just scheduled an appointment. If your schedule later changes — it's been known to happen — you can edit an appointment in any of the following ways:

✔ Delete an appointment by clicking once on its block, and then pressing the Delete key on your keyboard.

✔ Shift an appointment to another time on the same day by dragging the block up or down. In Weekly view, you can also shift the appointment to another day by dragging it sideways.

✔ Adjust an appointment to make it longer or shorter by clicking the block once to make the funny pointy handles appear at the top and bottom. Then drag these funny pointy handles up or down to stretch the appointment block.

✔ Shift the appointment to a completely different time — for example, an entirely different month — by double-clicking its block. A dialog box, cleverly titled the Appointment dialog box, appears:

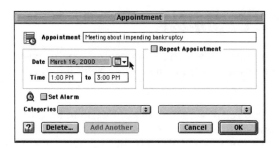

You'll be seeing a lot of this dialog box, so make your peace with it early on. Click the tiny icon to the right of the date (indicated by the cursor in the picture above) to summon a miniature calendar, which you can use to specify the new date for your appointment. (In this box, you can also type in a different time.) Click OK to close this dialog box.

✔ Edit the description for an appointment by clicking once on its block — or by double-clicking the block to open the Appointment dialog box.

✔ Schedule this appointment to repeat (for example, every week or every month) using the Repeat Appointment checkbox. Set up your iMac to remind you about this appointment using the Set Alarm checkbox. Instructions for both of these techniques are in "Fancy appointment tricks," later in this section.

Entering appointments in Monthly View

If you're used to working with paper calendars, you'll probably feel most comfortable in Palm Desktop's Monthly view. (Click the Monthly tab at the right side of the screen to see it.)

![Monthly Calendar - User Data showing March 2000 calendar grid]

March 2000 monthly calendar with appointments including AUSTRALIAN TOUR!, Full Moon, 5 PM Dinner @ Smiths, 11:30 AM Kidlets Play Party, 3 PM Snowboarding rehearsal, Column Due, 11:30 AM Jenkins report, 5 PM Outline development, 12 PM Bus to LGA, 3:30 PM Mom arrives, 6:30 PM Dinner @ Meta, DP's Birthday, 12 PM Lunch 21, 5 PM Dinner/cocktails Hunt club, 1 PM Meeting re: impending bankruptcy, 5 PM Staff Meeting SH, 7 PM Dinner with Geaneys, 1 PM Design mtg, 5:30 PM Staff all call, 10 AM Kelly t-ball tryouts, 2:30 PM Hair Cut with Denise, Times Book Rev Due, 7 PM Ladies night out for Jenn, 4 PM Discuss Taxes, Full Moon.

The squares in the monthly calendar are too small to create new appointments by dragging, as you do in the Monthly or Daily views. Instead, create a new appointment by double-clicking a calendar square. A funny little question box like this appears:

What the iMac is asking is: what kind of thing would you like to add to the calendar square you just double-clicked? You can read about tasks and banners in the next section; to add an Appointment (such as "1:30 p.m.: United Flight #001 to Buffalo"), click the Appointment button.

Now the Appointment dialog box appears, as shown three illustrations ago. Type the name of your appointment, and then press Return (or click the OK button) to close the window. Like magic, your new appointment appears on the appropriate calendar square.

You can change such a Monthly-view appointment in all the usual ways:

- ✔ Delete an appointment by clicking once on its name, and then pressing the Delete key on your keyboard.

- ✔ Shift an appointment to another date by dragging it onto the appropriate calendar square.

- ✔ Change the appointment's time by double-clicking its block. The Appointment dialog box appears; type a different time into the starting or ending time blocks, as you see fit.

  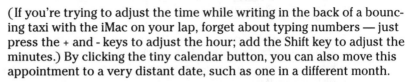

  (If you're trying to adjust the time while writing in the back of a bouncing taxi with the iMac on your lap, forget about typing numbers — just press the + and - keys to adjust the hour; add the Shift key to adjust the minutes.) By clicking the tiny calendar button, you can also move this appointment to a very distant date, such as one in a different month.

- ✔ Edit the description for an appointment by double-clicking the block to open the Appointment dialog box. Change the text in the top box.

Before leaving Monthly view, here's a tip *about* leaving Monthly view. If you double-click the date number in the corner of a calendar square, you open Daily view for that particular day. In other words, you can use Monthly view to get an overview of your schedule, but then jump to a day's Daily view to actually create an appointment (by dragging vertically through a time slot).

Banners

Appointments — in the Palm Desktop sense of the word — are all well and good. But at what time would you schedule, say, *Enid's Birthday* or *Venezuelan Muskrat Festival?* Clearly, you'd feel foolish indicating a starting and ending time for such events. Fortunately, Palm Desktop offers a special kind of notation for these events, one that doesn't require a starting and ending time: a *banner.* A banner appears on a calendar square, or across several calendar squares, as a colored horizontal strip.

In Monthly view, you create a banner by double-clicking a calendar square and then choosing Banner from the "What do you want to create?" dialog box. In Weekly or Daily view, you create a banner by double-clicking the date header (shown here at left).

Before | After

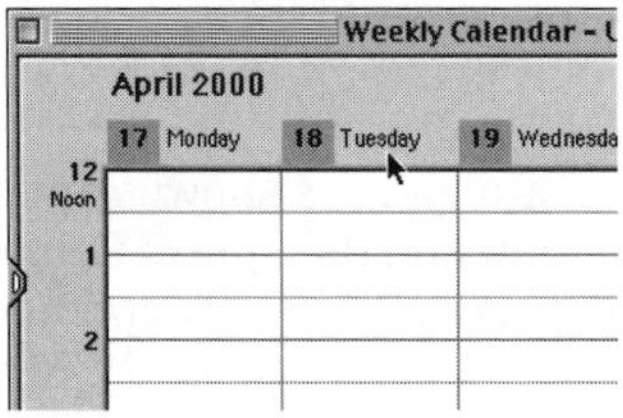

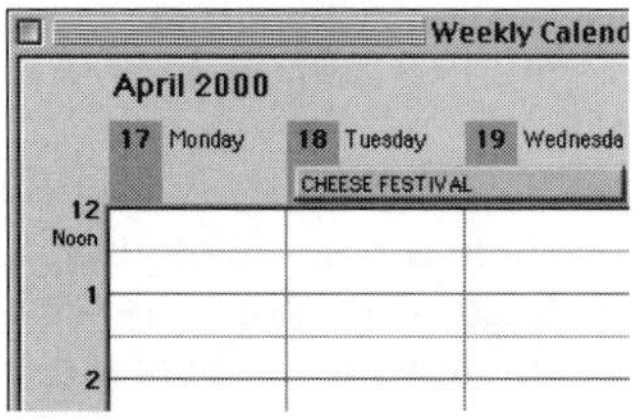

No matter what view you're in, the Banner dialog box now appears, in which you can type a description for this special day. Note, too, the "For __ days" box — by typing a number into this box, you can make your banner stretch across more than one day. People use banners, therefore, to indicate when they're going to be away. For example, you could create a seven-day banner that says "To Cleveland for International Ribs Cook-Off" or "Liposuction recovery in Acapulco."

When you click OK, the banner appears as a strip across the appropriate days (shown above at right).

You manipulate banners exactly the way you manipulate other kind of appointments — you can delete one by clicking it and then pressing the Delete key, reschedule one by dragging it, or change its name or date by double-clicking it.

Fancy appointment tricks

Your deluxe fruit-flavored computer wouldn't be fulfilling its Computercratic Oath if it didn't exploit your electronic calendar by, for example, reminding you when appointments come due. Fortunately, pop-up alarms are only one of the ways Palm Desktop can harness the power of your computerized calendar.

To set up Palm Desktop's three fancy appointment options, double-click an appointment on your calendar. The Appointment dialog box appears, offering these three features:

✔ **Repeat Appointment.** When you turn on this checkbox, a new pop-up menu magically appears, listing commands like Every Day and Every Friday. Using this pop-up menu, you can make this particular appointment write itself into your calendar over and over again according to a regular schedule — the perfect setup for appointments like iMac club once a month, parole-officer visits every week, or trips to the laundry once a year. (Click the tiny calendar next to the "Until" box to specify an ending date for these repeating events.)

✔ **Set Alarm.** When you turn on this checkbox, a new pop-up menu appears. Using the pop-up menu and the blank next to it, you can indicate how much advance notice you want for this appointment — 5 minutes prior (perfect for reminders to watch a certain TV show), 2 hours prior (perfect for driving to the airport for a certain flight), or 3 days prior (perfect for shopping for an anniversary present for a certain someone). When the designated moment arrives, your iMac will beep, and a message will appear on the screen, alerting you of the upcoming appointment. (The message box even contains a Snooze button, for your procrastination pleasure.)

Using this reminder feature, you can set up your iMac as an alarm clock when you're traveling. You wouldn't be the first. (The iMac will beep and show the reminder message even if it's asleep — not if it's shut down, however.)

✔ **Categories.** Using these pop-up menus, you can assign different calendar appointments to certain categories, such as Personal, Business, or None of Your Business. (To add a new category to this list, choose Edit Categories from the Categories pop-up menu.) Later, when you become a big, experienced techno-geek, you can hide certain categories of appointments so that every snooping coworker can't see what you've got planned.

Printing your calendar

The Palm Desktop program is extremely flexible when it comes to printing out your calendar. You can specify how many miniature pages you want printed on each sheet of actual paper; whether you want single-sided or double-sided pages; special formats for Franklin, DayRunner, Day-Timer, and other commercial organizers; whether you want daily, weekly, or monthly calendars; the typeface and size you prefer; and much more.

Fortunately, patient, detailed instructions are built right into Palm Desktop. To see them, from the Help menu, choose Search Index For, and then do a search for Printing. The resulting instructions appear in your screen, complete with illustrations.

The Contact List (Address Book)

As your popularity and circle of friends grow, you'll find it extremely easy to type their names and addresses into Palm Desktop. The program uses several tricks to make such data entry less time-consuming, such as auto-entering your area code and formatting phone numbers automatically. (Visit the Preferences command in the Edit menu, and click the Contacts icon, to see these options.)

And if you already have your phone book in some other computer program, for goodness' sake, don't do *any* re-typing! Palm Desktop can import the entire list in one fell swoop. For instructions, open the Help menu. Choose Search Index For, and search for the topic called Importing.

Typing in names and addresses

To create a new "index card" for your computerized phone book, click the very first icon on the toolbar at the top of the screen. (Alternatively, you can choose New Contact from the View menu.) The Contact dialog box, with which you'll be getting extremely friendly before long, now appears:

You're ready to begin typing in names and addresses. As you go, keep these points in mind:

- ✔ Press the Tab key with your left pinky to jump from blank to blank (from First Name to Last Name, for example). You can jump to a previous blank by pressing *Shift*-Tab. That's much more efficient than using the mouse to click.

- ✔ When you're finished filling in one *block* of information, such as the Phones section, press the Return key twice. Your cursor jumps all the way down to the next block (such as the Primary Address block). So, for example, when you want to record only somebody's name and telephone number — not their title, company, division, and all that jazz — type the first name, and then press Tab; type the last name; and then press the Return key twice. You land in the Work Phone blank, ready to type the phone number.

✔ When you're finished recording somebody's information, click the first
icon on the toolbar again. You're presented with a new, empty phone-
book card, ready to accept the next name. When you're finished typing
names and addresses, click the close box of the Contact window to make
it go away.

Looking up a phone number

Palm Desktop shows your world of names and phone numbers in a tidy list.
To see it, choose Contact List from the View menu — or click the second icon
on the floating toolbar the top of the screen.

You can find somebody in this phone book extremely quickly: just type the
first couple letters of the person's last name. Palm Desktop jumps exactly to
that spot in the list, highlighting the resulting name, like this:

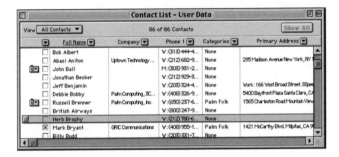

To edit this person's information, double-click his or her row in the list. The
familiar Contact window opens up, ready to accept your changes.

You can do a lot more in the contact list than just looking someone up, however. The built-in Help program (from the Help menu, choose Search Index
For) can tell you how to sort the list by name, city, company, or any other cri-
terion; to rearrange the columns; to adjust the column widths; and so on.

The Task List

Palm Desktop can keep track of your to-do list at no extra charge. To open
your to-do list, click the fourth icon on the toolbar at the top of the screen —
or choose Task List from the View menu. Either way, a list like this appears:

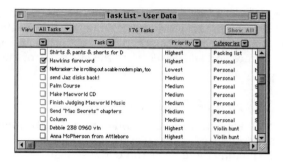

When you finish a task, click the checkbox — or just delete the item entirely by clicking it once and then pressing the Delete key on your keyboard. You can also manipulate the list of to-do items — sort it, change the column arrangement, and so on — exactly as described in "Looking up a phone number" in the previous section.

You can create a new to-do item in several ways:

✔ From the View menu, choose New Task (or click the third icon on the toolbar). This dialog box appears, in which you can type a name, category, reminder, repeat schedule, and other information for your task:

✔ You can also create to-do items when you're looking at your calendar, which is frequently a handy feature. In Monthly view, just double-click the calendar square that represents the deadline for your to-do item; in the "What do you want to create?" dialog box, click Task; and then type the description for your task.

In Weekly or Daily views, double-click in an empty spot at the bottom of the window (where the other to-do items appear) to open the Task dialog box.

The Note List

Thanks to its Notes feature, Palm Desktop can also accommodate driving directions, grocery lists, song lyrics, Shakespearean insults copied from the Web, and other random brainstorms.

You create a new empty note by clicking the seventh icon on the toolbar — or by choosing New Note from the View menu. Give it a title, if you like, and then press the Tab key until you're in the big empty part of the window.

After you've finished pasting or typing your note, click the close box in the upper-left corner of the window. Now you're ready to open the master note: click the sixth icon on the toolbar (or choose Note List from the View menu). As usual with Palm Desktop lists, you can sort this one by clicking its column titles, adjust the column widths, search for a memo by typing a few letters of its name, and so on.

The Magic of Instant Palm Desktop

Instant Palm Desktop is the name of the tiny green icon at the upper-right corner of your screen. Don't be alarmed: I realize that yours isn't there. You have to make it appear.

To do so, launch Palm Desktop. From the Edit menu, choose Preferences. Click the General icon, and then turn on "Show Instant Palm Desktop menu." The next time you restart the iMac, the little green menu appears.

This tiny green thing is a quick-access menu that lets you look up phone numbers and check your schedule without having to launch the Palm Desktop program.

Checking your schedule

After you've spent some time typing in your calendar and to-do list, for example, quit Palm Desktop — and then click the tiny green icon. There, in a convenient list, is your entire schedule for the day, like this:

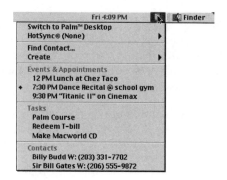

Beneath the dividing line is your to-do list. Delightfully enough, this list is always available, no matter what program you're using, no matter what else you're doing on the iMac.

Finding and dialing a number

After you've put a few phone numbers into Palm Desktop, furthermore, an even more delightful feature is available: the Find Contact command. When you choose this command, type a few letters of somebody's name, and then press the Return key, you're instantly shown a list of names that match what you typed, like this:

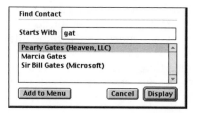

And now, the *pièce de résistance* (French for "piece of resistance"): your iMac can actually *dial the number* you've found. Just double-click the name you want. In the next window, click the tiny telephone icon next to the number. After confirming that you want to dial, Palm Desktop instantly produces the correct touch-tones through your iMac speaker. Just hold up your telephone mouthpiece to the speaker, and presto: you're connected.

Dialing through the modem

Note to the technical: Palm Desktop's automatic dialing feature works even faster and more efficiently if you let the iMac dial through its *modem* rather than its *speaker.* This delightful arrangement requires, however, two preparatory steps.

First, you need to raid your local Radio Shack on a quest for a *line splitter,* a cheap plastic box that lets you keep your iMac and your telephone plugged into the same telephone wall jack simultaneously. Second, launch Palm Desktop. From the Edit menu, choose Preferences, and click the Dialing icon of the left side of the screen. Finally, from the Dial Through pop-up menu, choose Modem Port. Click OK.

Now, when you want to dial a number, just pick up the telephone handset as soon as you hear the iMac finish its dialing. You'll be connected to the number the computer dialed, exactly as though you had dialed the number yourself — except that your index finger, of course, has been free to continue stroking the cat the whole time.

Quicken

Quicken, another free program in your Applications folder, is the ultimate checkbook program. Of course, calling Quicken a checkbook program is slightly understating the case, like calling AT&T a phone company or calling O.J. Simpson a former football player. As you'll discover, Quicken can really be the cornerstone of your entire bank account, credit card, tax, investment, and otherwise financial empire.

The category concept

When you first launch Quicken, it asks you to name the file in which you'll keep all of your financial info. In the same dialog box where you type a name, Quicken makes you choose a set of *categories* before you do anything else — either Home or Business. When it's time to do your taxes; when you want to see where your money's going; when you want to plan ahead for next year; in all of these cases, Quicken can show you a snapshot of your current financial status, organized, as always, by *category.* It's a great system.

 Pick Home, Business, or both to start you off, depending on how you're going to be using Quicken, to get past the opening screen or two. (You can always make up your own categories later.)

When you arrive at this screen, grab your bank account statement.

```
┌─────────────────────────────────────────────────────────┐
│ ▣          Set Up Account                                 │
│  ┌─Account Type───────────────────────────────────────┐  │
│  │  ◉ Bank                    ○ Liability             │  │
│  │    Use for checking, savings, or money  Use for items you owe, such as a loan │
│  │    market accounts.                     or mortgage. │  │
│  │  ○ Cash                    ○ Portfolio             │  │
│  │    Use for cash transactions or petty cash.  Use for brokerage accounts, stocks, │  │
│  │                                         or bonds.   │  │
│  │  ○ Asset                   ○ Mutual Fund           │  │
│  │    Use for valuable assets such as your home.  Use for a single mutual fund. │  │
│  └───────────────────────────────────────────────────┘  │
│                                                           │
│  Account Name:  [                    ]   ☐ Hide in lists  │
│  Description:   [                       ]                 │
│  (optional)                                               │
│                                                           │
│ ┌──────────────────────┐ ┌───────┐ ┌────────┐ ┌────────┐ │
│ │ Enable Online Services│ │ Notes │ │ Cancel │ │ Create │ │
│ └──────────────────────┘ └───────┘ └────────┘ └────────┘ │
└─────────────────────────────────────────────────────────┘
```

Fill in what you want to call this account. *Money-Grubbing Corporate Bank Vermin* is fine, except that it won't fit. *Savings* or *Checking* is a more common title.

The Register

At last you're permitted to see the Face of Quicken: the Register window.

Type in the opening balance — in other words, the ending amount on your last bank statement.

Date	Number	Payee/Category/Memo	Payment	Clr	Deposit	Balance
3/20/99	*Num*	Opening Balance	*Payment*	✓	5,000.00	5,000.00
	▼	[Checking] ▼ *Memo*	Split	Shortcuts ▼		
3/20/99						

Record   Restore   Sort by: Date ▼   Balance Today: $5,000.00
                                            Balance 3/20/99: $5,000.00

Type the date and final amount of your last bank statement, as shown above.

This Register window may look like any normal iMac window, but that's like saying that a jalapeño looks like any normal salad component. There are 1,000 Handi-features to make typing information fast and easy. To wit:

✔ **Change the date by pressing the + and – keys on your keyboard.** Most of The Quicken Experience involves recording money you've spent and money you've made. The first stage of each typing binge is to set the date. Just click there, and then make the date advance or retreat by using + and – ; the longer you hold down the key, the faster the number changes.

Neater yet — after you've clicked the Date blank, you can also type **t** for today's date, **m** or **h** for the beginning or ending date of the **month**, or **y** or **r** for the beginning or ending date of the **year**. Isn't that adorable?

Date	Number	Payee or Description	
		Category	Memo
▶6/7/98		Opening Balance	
	🔲 ▼	[CitiBank Che ▼	

✔ **Press Tab to jump from column to column.** Press *Shift*-Tab to jump *backwards* through the blanks. You can get by for months without ever needing the mouse.

✔ **Don't bother tabbing to the cents place; just hit the decimal.** When you're typing in a dollar amount, leave off the $ sign and just type a decimal point (period) in the usual place. Quicken's smart enough to put the dollars and cents on opposite sides of the dividing line.

✔ **If Quicken recognizes something you're typing, it'll finish the phrase for you.** You do *not* need to type *Metropolitan Light, Power, and Water Authority of Northern California* every time that you cut a check for utilities. By the time you've typed *Metrop,* Quicken will have filled in the rest of the payee for you (assuming that you've typed it before).

If Quicken guesses *wrong,* just keep typing. Quicken will remove its guess.

✔ **After entering a transaction, press Return.** Quicken sets you up with a new blank line, ready to receive the next scrap from your envelope of receipts. Oh, yeah — it also does all the math for you and updates the bottom line at the bottom of the window.

Just another $10,000 day

Now that you've got your register set up, the rest of Quicken is simplicity itself. Suppose that you made a bank deposit today — your weekly paycheck plus the first installment from a lottery you won. (I like to use examples that everyone can relate to.)

Click in the bottom row of the ledger, which is blank. (There's *always* one blank line at the bottom of the register. If you don't see it, maybe you need to scroll down using the scroll bar at the right side.) Use the + and – keys, naturally, to adjust the date (or type **t** for today).

Then type a description of today's event — in this case, *Paycheck and Lottery #1*. Press Tab.

Now type in the *total* amount of your bank deposit — paycheck plus prize money. If this weren't a dual-source deposit, you'd be done — but you're not. Here's where it gets really neat.

See the little *Split* button in the Payment column? Click it. A stack of sub-blanks appears, in which you can break down your total transaction amount:

When you click the Split button, this sub-list appears.

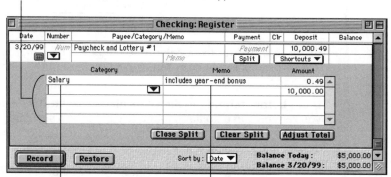

The Category must be on the Category list — generic labels like Tax, Auto, or Insurance.

The Memo can be anything you want.

You've got to choose a category for this part of the split. For the paycheck, no sweat — it would be Salary. If you type the letters *Sa,* Quicken will recognize where you're headed, and it will fill in the rest of the word. (Alternatively, you can press ⌘-L, for *list,* to see Quicken's complete list of categories. You can double-click anything on that list to make it fill in the Category blank here. Or you can choose a category name from the pop-up menu — the tiny black down-pointing triangle at the right edge of the Category blank.)

Press Tab. Then type, for the paycheck, a memo. Anything you want. Or nothing. Press Tab again.

Now enter the amount of the paycheck. In this case, you work as a tollbooth operator for a remote and impoverished township in a debt-ridden South American country, so you make only 49 cents per week. Type *.49.* Press Tab.

Creating a new category

Now you're supposed to enter the category for your lottery money. Yet oddly enough, Quicken doesn't come with a Lottery Winnings category. You're going to need to make it up.

Suppose that you decide to call this category *Prizes*. Type that and then press Tab — and Quicken will tell you that you've colored outside the lines.

Fortunately, Quicken also offers you the easy way out. Click Set Up. Now you can create your new financial category.

When coming up with a name for your new category, think general. Think tax time. Don't create a category called *Beige leatherette camera case, that one with the tassels.* Instead, the IRS would probably be content to see *Equipment* or something.

In the case of the lottery winnings, make sure that you specify the Type — Income — and that, God knows, it's tax-related. In other words, this little baby is definitely going to find a place on your 1040 form. Groceries, on the other hand, will not.

Click Create. You return to your entry, where Prizes is now accepted as a legit category name. Tab over to the Memo blank, type something like **First install-ment,** and you're done. Quicken has already entered $10,000 into the Amount blank to make the split amounts match the grand total.

To close up the Split window, click the Close Split button (or press ⌘-E).

More typical examples

Another great candidate for the Split window: credit-card payments. Suppose that you write a check to pay this month's credit-card bill. (Most people have a separate Checking account, which you can create by choosing New Account from the File menu.)

Choose Write Checks from the Activities menu. You get this representation of America's most recognized piece of paper.

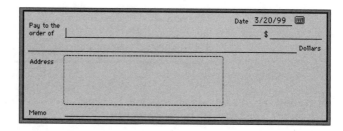

Start typing the payee's name. As you know by now, if Quicken recognizes the name, the program will complete the typing for you. Press Tab and then type in the amount.

This time when you press Tab, you get to see one of the slickest features ever. If you typed *$432.45,* Quicken writes out, in longhand English, *Four hundred thirty-two and 45/100* on the second line.

Tab your way into the Address box and type the mailing address (pressing *Return* after each line, *not* Tab). Then Tab to the Memo blank and type your account number. And *now* (egg roll, please) — choose Memorize from the Edit menu. From now on, when you start to make a check out to *Citib,* Quicken will fill in the payee name *and* the address *and* the account number!

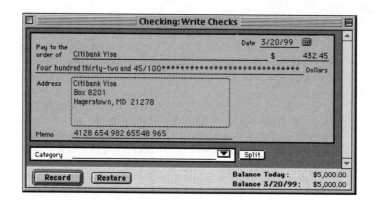

Before you hit Return (or click Record), it's a good idea to note what this credit-card payment *covers*. Just as you did before, click the Split button at the bottom of the check window. Now your expenditures are logged safely in case of disaster (such as fire, flood, or April 15).

The category payoff

The point of all this categorizing, of course, comes at year-end (or any other occasion where a financial snapshot is required). Quicken does some amazing number crunching.

At tax time, for example, choose Reports from the Reports & Graphs command in the Activities menu. Double-click, say, Category Summary. Plug in the year's starting and ending dates; instantly, you've got a detailed breakdown to hand your tax guy (or yourself, as the case may be). The graphs are equally impressive. (Choose Graphs from the Reports & Graphs command.)

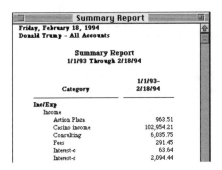

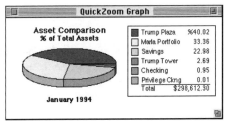

Reconciling for the nonaccountant

Like many of us out in America Land, there was a time when I, too, occasionally failed to compare my checkbook with the bank statement each month. But trusting the bank's computers can be dangerous; they *do* make mistakes. In my six years of using Quicken, I've caught my bank with its computerized hands in my tiller twice — $45 the first time and $200 the second!

Anyway, here's how this feature (called *reconciling*) works. With your bank statement in front of you, choose Reconcile from the Activities menu. Fill in the closing balance from the bank statement; fill in any interest your money earned, too, as well as any finance charges those filthy usurers charged you.

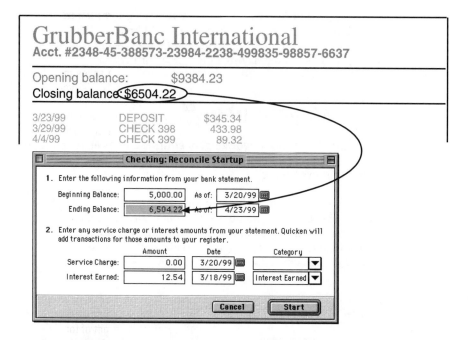

Click OK. Now the fun begins. Read down the transactions listed on your bank statement. Each time that you find one that matches a listing in Quicken's Reconcile window, click it in the Reconcile window so that a check mark appears next to it. Keep going until you've accounted for everything on the statement.

Almost always, Quicken will show transactions that your bank statement doesn't. That's normal. It means that your life didn't stop on the 15th of the month (or whenever the bank's cutoff date for your statement was). The items you're seeing are transactions you've made since the day the statement was printed and mailed.

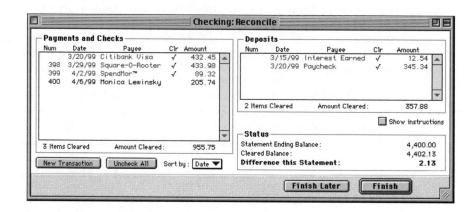

Going electronic

In general, adulthood is a joy. I've got to admit, though, that bill-paying is one of the serious downsides of having to grow up.

As it turns out, though, one of the iMac's most remarkable benefits is *automatic bill paying* — using Quicken in conjunction with your bank. For this service, you usually pay $7 or 10 per month — unless you choose a bank that doesn't charge at all.

In return, you gain a remarkable feature: When you enter a check in your Quicken registry, it becomes a reality! Quicken, at the end of your session, dials a phone number, transmits your check information, and instructs the bank to issue a check to the payee (or, if you're paying a company, to make an electronic transfer), without any further effort on your part.

There are no envelopes, no stamps, and much less record-keeping. The real point here, though,

is that e-banking saves money (and not just in postage). For example, you can input the payment the day your bill arrives, but the check doesn't get *sent* (by your bank) until the date you specify. Suppose that your credit-card, mortgage, utilities, phone bill, cable TV, car payments, and Internet account bills total about $3,500 a month. If that money earns 5 percent interest in the bank, in the three weeks between a bill's arrival and the due date, it could have racked up $10.02 in interest! Yes, $120.24 a year is what you *give away* to those money-grubbing corporations if you pay promptly. Do it electronically, and that's $120 a year in cold, hard cash you save.

Setting up the electronic check-paying thing in Quicken takes a little bit of effort. But electronic banking is like a gift of four hours (and $10) per month with no strings attached.

If the statement has extra items

But what if the bank lists some deposit or payment that Quicken doesn't know about? In most cases — forgive me — this is your mistake; you probably forgot to record something in Quicken. (Or, as they say in the biz, PBKC: *problem between keyboard and chair*.) On the other hand, as I've noted, once in a blue moon, you'll catch a genuine bank mistake.

If you notice discrepancies as you go, use one of these two techniques:

- **Double-click any transaction listed in Quicken's Reconcile window.** You'll be teleported directly to the Register entry for that item so that you can read the description and try to get more information. For example, if you have two different entries for "New co-op in St. Thomas," the odds are pretty good that you entered it twice. Unless you truly did buy two, delete one of them (by using Delete Transaction in the Edit menu).

- **Pull the Register window to the front.** If you discover a transaction on the statement that you forgot to plug into Quicken during the month, click the New Transaction button and type it in. Then return to the Reconcile window and click it off.

What's *supposed* to happen is that the Difference this Statement line (see the previous illustration) winds up at zero. If it does, click OK and bask in the warm sunny feeling of Quicken's little congratulatory message.

If the Difference this Statement doesn't come out to zero, you can either squirm for another 20 minutes trying to find out why your computer doesn't match the bank's, or you can take the fatalistic approach and click the OK button.

In that event, Quicken creates a new entry in your register called, ahem, Balance Adjustment. Try, *try* not to think of it as shouting in huge capital letters, *"This is where you screwed up, you numerically incompetent clod!"* every time that you look at it for the rest of your life.

In my experience, by the way, the temptation to simply accept the discrepancy is much greater when it's in your favor.

World Book Encyclopedia

When I was a kid, my parents forked over big dollars every few years for a bookshelf full of blue, hardbound books: the World Book Encyclopedia. These books were great for homework-writing, debate-settling, and curiosity-slaking. They had only two drawbacks: first, they got out of date quickly; second, we got in trouble when we drew in them.

Today's slot-loading iMacs come with a much, much better version of the World Book — an electronic version that comes on a CD. It's better because it's in color, it's modern, it's got sounds and movies, you can search it electronically, and the articles are beautifully written. And you won't get in trouble for marking it up — in fact, the program includes electronic sticky notes and yellow highlighting pen just for that purpose.

Installing the World Book program

Begin your World Book exploration by inserting the Disc 1 CD into your CD-ROM drive. When the WB Disk 1 window appears on the screen, double-click World Book Installer. On successive screens, click Continue, then Agree. Now type in the serial number from the back of the CD envelope; use all capital letters and no spaces. Click OK. In the next window, click Install; finally, click the Desktop button and then Install.

When it's all over, you'll find a new folder on your desktop called World Book. Inside is the actual World Book program; double-click its icon when you want to look something up.

Note, by the way, that the World Book disc must actually be *in the iMac* if you hope to look up any actual articles.

Looking up a topic

As you'll soon discover, the World Book program lets you look up information in a million different ways. On the main screen, for example, you'll find two columns of buttons: **Browse,** which offers various ways to sample the articles, pictures, sounds, and movies on the CD-ROM, and **Search,** which lets you type in a topic you're looking for.

If you're used to using a traditional encyclopedia, you flip through the alphabetical listings of the CD version like this:

1. **Click the World Book button (in the Browse column).**

   You're shown a little doodad (shown in the upcoming picture).

2. **To jump to a topic, type the first few letters of its name into the white blank.**

   For example, type *ROD* to see if there's an article on Rodents.

3. **To scroll through the list of every topic in the World Book, click the pop-up triangle at the right side of the empty white blank.**

   As shown here, a little popup list appears:

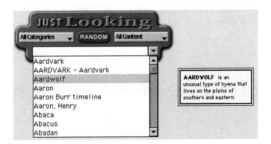

   Scroll through it using the scroll bar, if you like.

4. **When you see an article you'd like to read, click its name once.**

   A little poster version of that article appears, revealing the first part of the entry (such as "Aardwolf," as shown in the preceding picture).

5. **Click the little poster to read the article.**

In some articles, by the way, you'll get lucky: the Article Media icon (to the left of the text) is joined by a down-pointing arrow. That's your cue to click the Article Media icon — a movie, picture, sound, or map lies in store.

Some of them are really neat. Look up Colosseum, for example; when you open the accompanying photograph, you'll find that you can actually *change the camera angle* by dragging your cursor up, down, left, or right inside the photo. You Are There, baby!

Getting more help

You can learn more about the World Book by reading the "World Book-Mac Users Guide" document on the CD, or by choosing Help Topics from your Help menu. In essence, though, you won't find the World Book difficult to figure out. As I always tell my kids: click long enough, and everything good in life will come to you.

Photo Soap, Good Cooking, and MDK

If you have an older (CD tray-loading) iMac, don't be jealous of the CD slot-loading people just because they get Palm Desktop, the encyclopedia, and other stuff that didn't come with your model. You, after all, got stuff that *they* didn't get: the Williams-Sonoma Guide to Good Cooking, Kai's Photo Soap, and MDK, for example.

Here's a crash course. You'll find these programs in the Applications folder on your hard drive. Also note: Except for Nanosaur, the CD containing the program must be *in the iMac* whenever you want to use the program. For example, you can't launch Photo Soap unless the Photo Soap CD is inserted into the iMac.

Williams - Sonoma Guide to Good Cooking

This CD is gorgeous, richly photographed, and saliva-inducing — it's got 1,000 illustrated recipes in a searchable electronic card catalog.

The main WS Guide screen is a photo of several books: Glossary, Recipe Finder, Menu Planner, Recipe Index, and Favorite Recipes. For best results, try the Recipe Finder, which lets you search for specific recipes among the 1,000 available on the CD.

The other highlight of the CD is the Glossary. Not only is it a treat for the eye, but many of the entries also feature actual *movies* that play right on your screen, illustrating how to carve meat, fold calzones, and perform other mission-critical techniques.

MDK

I can't tell you what MDK stands for. I can, however, tell you that it's a dazzling 3-D adventure game that came with only the very first iMac models of 1998.

You control your guy, Kurt, by pressing keys on the keyboard (the arrow keys to move, for example, the Control key to fire your gun, and so on). Press the F1 key on your keyboard to view a full cheat sheet of the keystrokes that make MDK go. If you make it to the very end — via arenas, corridors, freefalls, streams, and just generally blowing up scary-looking customers who wander by — congratulations. If you get stuck, visit *www.playmatestoys.com/pie/mdk/mdkfaq.htm* on the Web for some hints and tips.

Kai's Photo Soap

The purpose of this strange, confusing, wonderful program is to fix photos: remove redeye from snapshots, repair tears or specks from existing photos, fix over- or underexposure, and so on. If you don't have a digital camera or scanner as a source of photos, you can still have fun wreaking havoc on the sample pictures included with the program.

The concept: You're supposed to bring a photo into the program and then repair it in a succession of "rooms" (different screens), each of which handles one kind of fixing. To view the list of different rooms, point to the word Map at the top of the screen, as shown here.

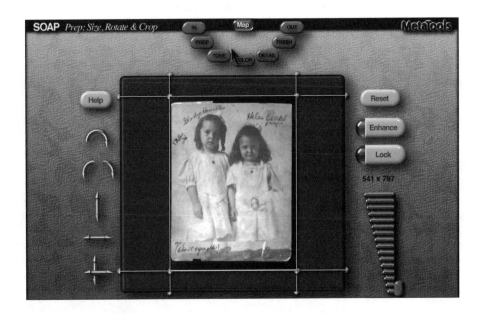

Then click the name of the screen you want to visit next. Here's what they do:

- ✔ **In** — A home-base view where you choose a photo to transmogrify. Click the File button (top left) to view your hard drive's contents; double-click a photo file to work with. If you're feeling particularly organized, you can also drag your photos around into "albums" on this screen.

- ✔ **Prep** — Drag the horizontal and vertical lines, as shown above, to chop off excess edges of a picture. The various buttons on the left side of the photo can flip it mirror-image or upside-down; the Enhance button on the right side fixes over- or underexposure. And the scale slider at the lower-right enables you to make the picture larger or smaller (although you'll see the difference only when you print).

- ✔ **Tone** — On this screen, you can adjust the brightness and contrast levels of the whole photo — or just parts of it. Use the weird-looking, three-slider doodad below the photo to set up the effect you'd like. (They correspond to intensity, brightness, and contrast.) If you'd like to apply these effects to only a *part* of the photo, click the ribbed left side of the photo frame and then click the picture of painting tools. You'll be offered a couple of paintbrush icons that, when clicked and then dragged across your photo, apply your tone changes only to the parts that the brush touches. (The eraser *removes* the tone changes.)

- ✔ **Color** — This screen adjusts the intensity and hue of the colors in your photo. Again, don't miss the ribbed "drawer" of painting tools at the left edge of the photo; these brushes let you apply the color shifts only where you drag.

- ✔ **Detail** — In this room, you can perform astonishing transformations to your photo — or ruin it completely. The Sharpen and Smooth modes bring the picture into, or out of, focus; the Red Eye heals the red-pupil effect in flash photos; Heal fixes tears and blotches; and Clone lets you duplicate an element of the photo, thus turning twins into triplets, for example. (To use this last feature, click once to indicate *what* you want to duplicate; click again to indicate *where* you want the copy placed — and begin painting.)

  After clicking one of these effect buttons, your cursor becomes target-shaped so that you can click *where* on the photo you'd like to operate. (The program automatically enlarges the photo to actual size as you dab away.)

- ✔ **Finish** — In this final room, you can add predrawn, colorful frames or accent graphics to your finished photo. Click the Backgrounds, Edges, or Objects buttons to summon corresponding palettes filled with choices. (Double-click the edge of a palette to make it go away again.) This "room" is also where you'll find Save and Print buttons, thus preserving your edge-cropped, tone-shifted, color-tweaked, rip-fixed, twin-cloned, frame-added photo for future generations.

In most of the rooms, you'll find three important consistent elements. The magnifying glass, when selected, lets you click your photo to enlarge it for detail work (or Option-click to zoom out). The weird-looking remote-control thing (in the lower-right) offers access to many of the program's overall options (such as whether you'd like an extra-large cursor or the normal iMac one). And the Help button summons explanations of the tools.

When on a Help screen, don't miss the ribbed slots at the left side of the screen, as shown in the preceding figure. As you point to these tabs with your mouse, you're offered a selection of Help topics — including the all-important Exit Help button (at the bottom), without which you'd be stuck in Help mode forever.

Speaking of being trapped in a software room for eternity, by the way: In the absence of menus, you may wonder how the heck you're supposed to *leave* this program, neato though it is. *Solution:* Press ⌘-Q, the universal iMac shortcut for the Quit command.

Chapter 10

iSpielberg: Digital Movies with iMovie

*Y*ou lucky, lucky soul. You may have read that in 1986, Apple Computer changed the world by popularizing *desktop publishing,* the simple act of churning out professional-looking publications with a Mac and a laser printer. Now Apple intends to make popular another expensive, rarefied art: video editing. And you, O Fortunate Moviemaker, are alive to see the dawn of this era.

Making digital movies on a computer isn't a new thing. Companies have been selling the $5,000 add-on circuit boards and $800 software programs to do so for several years. But the results weren't anything like what you'd see on TV. The finished movies played on your screen in a window the size of a Triscuit. And they were jerky. If you wanted full-screen, smooth video, you'd have had to assemble $100,000 worth of equipment. Not many people bothered.

Turns out the DV in "iMac DV" means that the $100,000 worth of equipment is *built in.* With an iMac DV, its iMovie software, and a digital camcorder, you can edit your own footage as often as you like. As you transfer it back and forth between the iMac and the camcorder, the film retains 100 percent of its quality, always playing full-screen, smooth, bright, and vibrant.

Got What It Takes?

This chapter is exclusively for people with an iMac DV model — either a fruit-flavored or Special Edition graphite-colored one. This kind of moviemaking doesn't require the mountains of gear it once did, but it does require one additional item: a *digital* camcorder.

Camcorders that accept only VHS, VHS-C, 8 millimeter, or Hi-8 tapes are *not* digital. If you bought your camcorder before 1997, it's not digital, either. True digital camcorders, which start at around $600, are very compact. Sony, Canon, JVC, and Panasonic make them. These cameras accept one-hour tapes called *Mini DV* cassettes, which record CD-quality sound and video of absolutely breathtaking quality. The tapes look like this:

I realize that $600 is a lot to pay for your next iMac accessory. Before you take the plunge, test the waters by (a) reading this chapter and (b) taking the iMovie tutorial. To do that, launch iMovie. From the Help menu, choose Tutorial; you'll be led through the construction of a short Kids Washing the Dog movie using film clips that are already on your hard drive.

If you do decide to buy a camcorder, do your shopping on the Internet. At Web sites like *www.amazon.com* and *www.netmarket.com,* you can survey long lists of digital camcorders and buy one at a discount — with no sales tax.

The last item you need is a FireWire cable. *FireWire* is one of the built-in iMac DV technologies that makes all this possible; it's a high-speed cable that plugs into the FireWire jacks on the right side of your computer. (See Appendix A for a picture.) Your iMac DV may have come with a FireWire cable right in the box. Hook the tiny end up to the corresponding jack on your camcorder (this jack may be concealed by a plastic cover), and the other end to your iMac's FireWire jack, as shown in Appendix A.

Filming Your Life

Not many people actually make *films* with their digital camcorders — writing a script, getting actors together, and all that jazz. Most people wind up just editing their home-movie footage, and that's a very good thing. If you've ever spent time at a friend's house watching six consecutive hours of little Goober spitting up, you know that a *good* home movie is an *edited* home movie.

The first step in making movies on your iMac is capturing life with your camcorder. There's not a lot to it, actually: press the red button to start filming, press it again to stop. Oh, and take off the lens cap.

But the quality of your equipment is so good, and the results are so exciting, that it's worth learning a few tricks to make your stuff look more professional:

- **Go easy on the zooming.** Yes, I know, your camcorder has a zoom in/zoom out button that's really fun to use. It's also really nauseating to watch later. Try to limit yourself to a single zoom — or none — per shot. Use the zoom mostly when it creates a visual punch line: there's little Timmy with a kite string in his hands, but your zoom-out reveals that the other end is, in fact, tied to the collar of a goat that's pulling him down the street on rollerblades.

- **Try a tripod.** For sure, turn on your camcorder's "image stabilization" feature, if it has one. But the biggest difference between home footage and pro TV footage is the tripod. These things are cheap — I found one for $15 at *www.netmarket.com* — and the resulting stability makes an enormous difference to the quality of the finished movie.

- **For dialog, use a clip-on microphone.** The other hallmark of amateur work is the sound. The camcorder's built-in mike not only picks up its own machinery, but sounds lousy if you're more than six feet from the speaker. A tie-clip mike is about $20 at Radio Shack; pick up a couple of extension cords for it, too, plug them into your camcorder's microphone jack, and you won't believe how much better your flicks sound.

- **For iMovie movies, shoot too much.** MiniDV cassettes are expensive — maybe $12 per one-hour tape. If you didn't have an iMac, I'd suggest that you be very selective in what you film. But the beauty of iMovie is that it lets you *edit down* your video, and then *put it back* onto the videotape! You don't lose any quality in the process. For that reason, it's safe and smart to keep the camcorder running more liberally than you would otherwise. Doing so improves the chances that you'll catch really good stuff (especially if you're filming children, animals, or hurricanes). You can always cut the boring stuff and re-use the original tape later.

Step 1: Dump the Footage into iMovie

Once you've filmed got some good scenes, you're ready for the fun to begin. Connect your camcorder to one of the FireWire jacks on the side of your iMac. Put the camcorder into what's usually called VTR mode (also known as VCR or Playback mode). Launch iMovie, which is in your Applications folder. Then click the Camera icon, shown here:

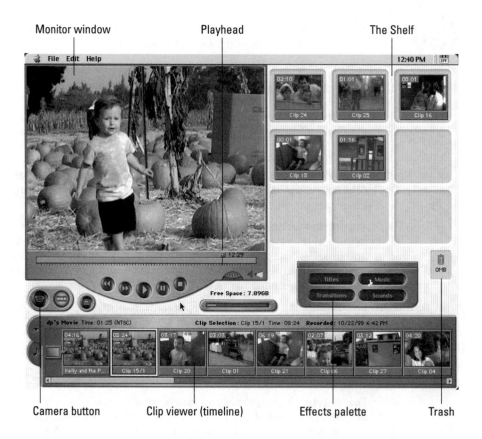

If all is well, you'll see a big blue screen at the upper-left with the words "Camera Connected" prominently displayed. You're ready to begin grabbing choice scenes from the camcorder for storage on the iMac.

Unless you have some weirdo off-brand camcorder, you can actually control the play, stop, rewind, and fast-forward functions of the camcorder using the buttons on the screen of your iMac — an impressive and tingly feature. You do so by clicking the buttons below the big monitor screen, or by pressing the keyboard equivalents, like this:

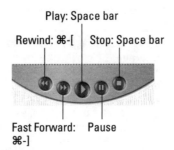

Play: Space bar

Rewind: ⌘-[Stop: Space bar

Fast Forward: Pause
⌘-]

Capturing clips

Here's the deal: As you watch the tape, whenever you see a piece of footage worth including in your movie, capture it! You do that by clicking the Import button once to start, and again to stop, the capturing, while your camcorder plays. Or press the space bar, which is often easier and more accurate: press once to start, once to stop.

Each time you grab a scene from your tape, it appears on the Shelf (see the figure at the beginning of Step 1), where it's represented by what looks like a slide. Congratulations: you've just created a *clip*. The whole business of movie editing, both on your iMac and in Hollywood, boils down to rearranging clips.

You're not limited to nine clips, of course. The Shelf is just a waiting room, a place to store clips temporarily before you start plunking them into the *timeline* at the bottom of the screen. (The timeline can hold as many clips as your hard drive can hold.) Once you've captured enough clips to start assembling your movie, drag them down into the timeline window, thus freeing up space on the Shelf for more clips.

How much footage can your iMac hold?

Considering that this entire book would consume only about 2 megabytes of the 10,000 or 13,000 on your iMac DV hard drive, you may have wondered why these models came with such enormous hard drives. You're about to find out.

Turns out that digital video, once transferred from your camcorder to your iMac, consumes a *huge* amount of hard-drive space. Are you sitting down? You use up 210 megs of your hard drive *per minute* of video! Do the math, and you find out that a Special Edition iMac can hold, therefore, only about 40 minutes of video at a time. The regular, fruit-colored models hold only about 30 minutes.

Speed versus quality

Despite the awe-inspiring power and speed of an iMac DV, it's not quite potent enough to play video, while you're working on it, at full speed *and* with full clarity. When you first start using it, you may encounter annoying skips in video playback in the monitor window where you watch your clips.

Especially when capturing clips from your camcorder, you'll probably have better results if you tell the program not to worry so much about picture quality, but instead to put its emphasis on smoothness. To do so, from the Edit menu, choose Preferences. Click Smoother Motion, and then OK.

Now you'll notice blotchiness in the picture as you build your movie. On the other hand, you won't see any skipping. This arrangement makes it much easier to capture exactly the amount of camcorder footage you want.

Best of all, this tradeoff applies *only* on the iMac screen! Once you send your finished movie back to videotape, or save it as a finished QuickTime movie file, you'll get both stunning picture quality and full smoothness of playback.

This isn't such a big deal, however; the whole object is to edit the stuff on your iMac and then put it *back* onto your videocassettes, where you can play them for friends, family, and backers. Think of your iMac as a temporary operating table, where you work on a little bit of the patient at a time. You can transfer video between your camcorder and your iMac thousands of times; the footage will never, ever deteriorate in quality, as it would with, for example, an audiocassette.

As you work in iMovie, watch the Free Space indicator above the timeline. The graph is blue when you've got plenty of space left, yellow when things are getting tight, and red when your hard drive is nearly full. At that point, it's time to dump your movie back out to a videotape (see the end of this chapter) and then delete the retired clips from your hard drive. (Each file you save from iMovie appears in a folder of its own, which contains a Media folder. To delete video files you're *certain* you won't need again, throw away this Media folder.)

Naming, playing, and trimming clips

Once your clips are on the Shelf, you can do three things with them: rename them, play them, and trim them.

Renaming clips

As your clips show up on the Shelf, they take on such exciting names as Clip 01, Clip 02, and so on. Making a movie out of them is much easier if they're renamed Goober Smiles, Goober Falls Over, and so on. To do so, just click once on a clip's name, type the new name, and press the Return key.

Playing clips

To play a clip that's on the Shelf, click it once. You'll see the first frame show up in the Monitor. At this point, you can use any of the VCR-type buttons to play this clip, just as you used them to control your camcorder earlier in this lesson. You can use the same keyboard shortcuts, too, as shown in the previous figure.

Note, by the way, that pressing the Rewind or Fast-Forward buttons (or keystrokes) *repeatedly* makes iMovie play back faster and faster in the corresponding direction.

You can also drag the tiny box called the *playhead,* shown two illustrations ago, to view earlier or later parts of the clip.

Trimming clips

Even more important is *trimming* your clips. Like pro video editors, you'll quickly learn that it's always safest to capture, from your camcorder, more footage than you need — a few seconds before and after the main action, for example. Then, later, it's a snap to trim out the dead wood.

To trim a clip, click its picture in the Shelf (or in the timeline, if you've put it there). In the Monitor window, click just beneath the Monitor scroll bar, as shown here at left:

Two triangular handles appear. Drag these handles apart, as shown above at right. The scheme is simple: everything between them remains in the final clip; everything outside of them will be lost forever. If you find using the mouse too clunky for making fine, frame-by-frame movements of these handles, click one and then press the arrow keys on your keyboard to move it one frame at a time. (Add the Shift key to move one of these handles in *ten*-frame jumps.)

As you choose parts of a scene to crop out, keep this tip in mind: If you plan to use iMovie's cross-fades from one scene into another, leave a second or two of extra footage on the clip you're trimming. The iMovie program will do its cross-fading during this extra stuff, leaving the *really* important action un-faded.

Finally, when you've got just the good part isolated, choose Crop from the Edit menu. Everything outside your triangle handles gets chopped out. (See the little Trash can icon on the screen? Its megabyte count increases to hint at the stuff you've cropped out. You can't double-click this Trash icon to pull stuff out of it, as you can the real Trash icon on your desktop. But using the Edit menu's Undo command, you *can* undo the last 10 steps you took in iMovie — including cropping, deleting clips, and otherwise adding stuff to the iMovie Trash can.)

Step 2: Build the Movie

To assemble your clips into a movie, drag them out of the Shelf and into the timeline at the bottom of the screen. (Apple calls this timeline the *clip viewer.* That's a confusing name — you *actually* view clips in the Monitor window. So I'll call it the timeline.) Once there, each clip is an individual tile that you can drag left or right to make it play before or after the other clips.

As you work with your movie, what happens when you click the Play button (or press the space bar, which does the same thing) depends on what's high-lighted:

- ✔ If a clip is highlighted with a bright yellow border in the timeline, press-ing the space bar plays only that clip. To un-highlight all clips, choose None from the Edit menu, or just click above the timeline window.

- ✔ If nothing is highlighted, the whole movie you've built plays, starting at the location of the playhead under the Monitor. Press the Home key to start from the beginning.

When no clip is highlighted in the timeline, moreover, you can drag the play-head under the Monitor window to jump around in the whole movie under construction. As you do so (and while you play back a clip), you'll see the tiny cursor crawl across that clip's picture in the timeline. Once again, you can use the arrow keys to more precisely position the playhead.

Adding a cross-fade

Those slick-looking crossfades between scenes, as seen every night on TV news and in movies, are called *transitions.* iMovie offers several styles; click the Transitions button on the effects palette to make the list pop up.

Click the name of the transition you want. Use the slider above the transition palette to specify how many seconds long you want the crossfade to last. (One second is fairly standard.) Once you've done so, drag the name of the transition into the timeline window, between the two clips you want joined in this way. They'll scoot apart to make room for the new transition icon that appears.

The instant you do so, a tiny red progress line starts to crawl across the transition icon. Your iMac is now processing the crossfade — as the pros would say, *rendering it* — by melding the end of one clip and the beginning of the next. This rendering business is par for the course in video-editing programs; in most programs, however, you're supposed to sit there, staring dully at the progress indicator, until it's over. In iMovie, you can go right on building your movie; that little red line will keep quietly crunching its way across the transition icon in the background. When it's finished, click in your timeline just before the transition, press the space bar to play, and marvel in your new ability to make home movies look pro.

To delete a transition, click its icon in the timeline and then press Delete; to edit it (by changing its length, for example), double-click its icon, which returns you to the Transitions palette.

Adding titles

iMovie even lets you add rolling credits and opening titles to your little home flicks. It's not quite sophisticated enough to let you create "Long, long ago, in a galaxy far, far away"-type openings, but it beats block lettering on shirt cardboards.

Start by clicking the Titles button. A list of title-animation styles pops up. In the tiny text box underneath the list, type the text you'll want for the credits. Note that some of the effects, such as Rolling Credits, lets you type in *pairs* of text blobs, as shown below at left. After you've typed in a couple of pairs, click Add to tack on yet another pair to your credits. The program automatically adds the dots and lines up the names, as shown here at right:

Click the Preview button to see what this effect will look like. Adjust the timing slider above the list, exactly as with transitions, and then drag the name of the title into the timeline.

If you want to *insert* this title in front of a clip, so that the text appears on a black background, turn on the Over Black checkbox. If you'd rather have the text appear *on top of* your video, leave that box unchecked. You'll soon discover that superimposing a title on a clip usually breaks the clip in half — the part with the title superimposed is now one clip, and the unaffected part is separate.

Editing a title works exactly as it does with transitions: to eliminate one, double-click the title's icon in the timeline and then press Delete; to edit, double-click its icon. You jump back to the effects palette, where you can tweak the text, the amount of time it will stay on the screen, and so on.

Grabbing music from a CD

As though a movie with crossfades and credits weren't pro enough, you can also add a music soundtrack. If you're a technically savvy musician (you know who you are), great; save your work as an AIFF file (you know what that is) and import it into iMovie (you know how to do it).

If you're anyone else, you can rely on the kindness of your existing music CD collection, as long as nobody from the record company catches you. Insert a music CD into your iMac. In iMovie, click the Music button on the effects palette. A list of tracks from the CD appears. Click one, and then use the Play button on the effects palette to find an appropriate snippet.

See the Music tab of your timeline? Click it to view the audio tracks, as shown below. Drag a song from the Music list down onto the bottom audio track. There it shows up as a colored stripe, like this:

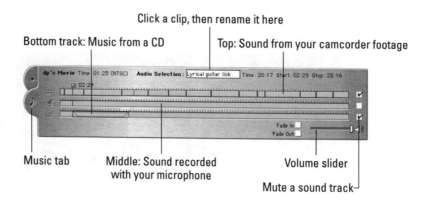

Click a clip, then rename it here

Bottom track: Music from a CD — Top: Sound from your camcorder footage

Music tab — Middle: Sound recorded with your microphone — Volume slider — Mute a sound track

Or, if you want to include only a part of the music, let the CD play; click the Record button once to start recording, and again to stop. The recorded music appears at the playhead point in the audio track.

You can, by the way, superimpose pieces of sound. Because there's only one "track" apiece for recorded narration and CD music, telling the overlapping colored stripes apart can be a challenge. But on that occasion when you want your background music to be a simultaneous playing of Carly Simon and Scott Joplin, you'll be ready.

Narration and sound FX

If you click the Sound button on the effects palette, you'll see that iMovie comes with a bunch of pre-recorded sound effects. Drag one onto your audio track to incorporate it into your film.

You can also record new sounds directly into your movie, thanks to the iMac's built-in microphone. Follow these steps:

1. **From your menu, choose Control Panels, and then slide out onto Sound.**

2. **Click Input, and from the pop-up menu, choose Built-in Microphone. Close the window.**

3. **In iMovie, click the music tab of the timeline. Click above the tracks to set the playhead where you want to begin your narration. On the effects palette, click Sounds.**

4. **Click Record Voice, lean close to the iMac microphone, and say what you've got to say. Click the Record button to stop recording.**

   The iMac microphone, if you were wondering, is the tiny slot on the iMac's forehead.

Your newly recorded sound appears in the sound track.

Editing sound in the timeline

Once you've laid a sound into the timeline, you can slide its colored ribbon right or left to align it better with the video. (You can play the video, drag the playhead, and so on, even when the music tab is selected — you just don't see the clips represented as pictures.) Drag a sound's ending handle to make it end sooner; click a sound, then drag the volume slider to change its loudness; or click one of the checkboxes, Fade In or Fade Out, to add a professional-sounding fade when the music begins or ends. And, of course, you can delete the sound completely by clicking it and then pressing the Delete key.

Step 3: Find an Audience

After you're happy with your movie, and you've waited for all the little red rendering lines to fulfill their destinies, check your movie. Press the Home key (to rewind to the beginning) and then the space bar (to play it one last time). For a delightful taste treat, click the Full Screen button (the round button just above the first picture in the timeline) to play the movie so that it fills your entire iMac screen.

If everything looks good, you're ready to show your filmless film to people. You can do so in one of two ways: by sending it back to the videotape, or by creating a QuickTime movie that other computers can play.

Sending your movie back to the camcorder

There's a lot to be said for sending your finished video back to the camcorder's tape. By connecting the camcorder to a TV, you'll be able to play your masterpiece for anyone. And by connecting the camcorder to a regular VCR, you can make and distribute VHS copies to anyone who's interested.

Begin by putting a cassette into your camcorder. *Don't record over something important!* Consider keeping a separate cassette just for your finished projects, for example, so you never risk recording over some important original footage.

Now, from the File menu, choose Export. The Export dialog box appears. Choose Camera from the pop-up menu, and then click Export.

If your camcorder is correctly connected to the iMac's FireWire jack, turned on, and in VTR mode, it now records your movie. When the recording is complete, you can prove that the transfer was successful; click the Camera button in iMovie, and then use iMovie's usual Play and Rewind buttons to control the camcorder, making it show your work one last time in its final form.

Saving your movie as a QuickTime file

A *QuickTime movie* is a single file on your hard drive that you can double-click to watch, mail to other people, put on the World Wide Web, save onto another disk, and so on. The one big QuickTime bummer, though, is that these movies take up enormous amounts of disk space. A standard, 600-megabyte CD-ROM disc, for example, holds less than two minutes of full-screen video. Obviously, that kind of movie would be lousy for e-mailing to somebody or posting on the Web; it would take 56 *hours* to transfer by modem.

The object of creating a QuickTime movie, therefore, is to reduce the size of the file. You can do that in three ways:

✔ **Make the "screen" smaller.** Instead of filling your screen, most QuickTime movies play in a small, three-inch-square window.

✔ **Make the color fidelity worse.** Using a conversion process called *compression,* you can make the iMac describe the color of each dot of the movie using less information. The result is a smaller (but grainier) file.

✔ **Make the frame rate lower.** A QuickTime movie, like a movie-theatre movie, simulates motion by flashing dozens of individual still photos in sequence. The more of these *frames* appear per second, the smoother the motion — and the bigger the QuickTime file. By telling your iMac to save the QuickTime movie with only, say, 12 frames per second instead of the usual 24, you create a file that's only half as big (but doesn't play back as smoothly).

After wrapping up your iMovie movie, then, here's how you save it: From the File menu, choose Export. When the dialog box appears, choose QuickTime Movie from the "Export to:" pop-up menu.

Now you have to decide how you want to compress your movie file. The dialog box offers you several canned settings:

✔ **E-mail, Small:** Shrinks your movie to a postage-stamp-sized "movie screen," showing only 10 frames per second — a file small enough to send someone by e-mail. Requires that the recipient have QuickTime 4.0 installed on their Mac. This version of the QuickTime extension (in the System Folder's Extensions folder) is available for free from *www.apple.com,* and comes already installed on every Mac since the summer of 1999.

✔ **Web Movie, Small:** Shrinks the movie to a three-inch window, shows 12 frames per second. This format, too, won't play unless the recipient has QuickTime 4.

✔ **Web Movie, Small (QT 3.0):** Your friends can play this kind of movie even if they don't have the latest QuickTime version. They'll get the same size and smoothness as Web Movie, but the audio isn't quite as good.

✔ **CD-ROM Movie, Medium:** Now we're talkin'. This option creates a movie that takes up nearly a quarter of the screen, playing a smooth 15 frames per second — with CD-quality sound. Don't try e-mailing *this* baby; it's too big to send. Play it off a hard drive, or (if you've bought a CD-ROM burner like those described in Appendix C) save it onto a blank CD.

✔ **CD-ROM Movie, Large:** Creates a QuickTime movie that's almost like TV. Plays in a huge window that nearly fills the screen, showing 30 frames per second (TV quality), with CD-quality sound. This kind of movie format takes up gigantic amounts of disk space, and probably won't even play back smoothly except on the fastest Power Macs. All that data is too much to handle for, say, an iMac.

✔ **Expert:** This command brings up a dialog box where Settings buttons let you specify *exactly* how your movie is compressed: how many frames per second you'd like, what size window it plays in, how much the colors should be compressed, and so on. *Hint:* Most of the time, you'll get the best results with Sorenson (for QuickTime 4.0 machines like yours) or Cinepak from the pop-up menu. These compression methods create movies that take up a lot less disk space, without rendering the colors too grainy.

When you finally name your movie, click the Desktop button, and click the Export button, iMovie begins the massive task of converting your movie into the compressed version. This conversion takes a *long* time — an hour to process a two-minute movie, for example.

Do not attempt to sit and watch it happen; let it run overnight. Find something useful to do — like watching a movie.

Your Free Built-In DVD Player

Making your own movies isn't the only way the iMac DV lets you get into digital video. It can also play *DVD discs.*

A DVD movie comes on a silvery disc that looks exactly like a compact disc. When you put it into a DVD player and press Play, it works exactly like a VCR — but with picture quality that's twice as sharp. And because it's not a tape, you can jump around in the movie without waiting to rewind or fast-forward. Today's video stores (or Web sites, such as *www.reel.com*) stock an ever-growing selection of movies on DVD — and not a single one has a sticker that says "Be kind — rewind."

One DVD came with your iMac — *A Bug's Life.* Just pop it into the CD slot at the front of the iMac. From the menu, choose Apple DVD Player. Now you can control the iMac like a VCR; use the Controller, shown below, as the "front panel." (If you don't see the Controller, choose Show Controller from the Window menu.) Use the Video menu to choose a "screen size" for the playback.

A B C D

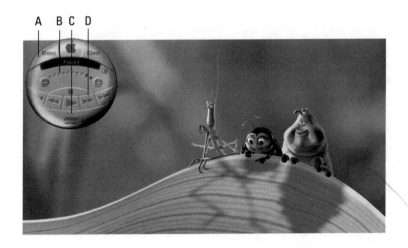

Once your DVD disc is playing, the Menu button (labeled A) brings up the disc's special features. They may include foreign-language sound tracks, director's narration, subtitles for the hearing impaired, and a list of "chapters" (scenes) in the movie. Use the controls marked B to adjust the volume. Click C to open a pull-out panel of advanced controls, including ones that let you play the movie in slow motion. Finally, D marks the standard VCR-style controls: Previous Chapter, Rewind (click twice for faster rewinding), Play/Stop (you can also press the space bar to play and stop), Fast Forward, and Next Chapter.

In Apple DVD Player, choose Apple DVD Player Help from the Help menu to read about even more fancy stuff you can do with DVDs. After a certain point, though, you'll probably decide that just *watching* Hollywood movies on your computer is fancy enough.

Chapter 11

Pix Tricks: Graphic Nonviolence

● ●

In This Chapter

▶ Scanning and digital cameras

▶ File formats and resolution

▶ Desktop pictures and startup screens

● ●

*Y*ou'll hear plenty of Windows bigots try to put down the Mac — it's only got 14 percent of the market, it's not what we use at work, blah blah blah — but when it comes to graphics, they'll shut right up. The Mac put computer graphics on the map, baby. The screen on your iMac is bright and gorgeous, and the software used to create and manipulate pictures is second to none in the business.

In this chapter, you'll find out what these formats are, how to make them, scan them, convert them, and put them to use.

Where Graphics Come From

If you're an artist, you can make terrific images in AppleWorks. But hand-made art isn't the same as *photos*. For photos, or if you're not artistically inclined, you can get electronic pictures from the Internet, digital cameras, and scanners.

The Web

When you see an image on the Internet that you'd like to preserve forever, try this: Hold the mouse button down on the picture. After a moment, you'll see a pop-up menu like this:

From this menu, choose Download Image to Disk (or Save Image As, depending on the Web browser you're using). In the Save As dialog box that appears, click Desktop, type a better name (to replace the picture's proposed name, which is usually something like *cgi-big.xref.83-22a.gif*), and then click Save.

When you quit your Web browser, you'll find, sitting there on your desktop, a new icon, named whatever you called it. What happens when you double-click this picture depends on which browser you used: if it's Internet Explorer, double-clicking a saved image file usually opens the picture in Picture Viewer, a tiny program included on every iMac.

If you double-click a graphic saved from Netscape Navigator or Communicator, you get this much more cryptic box:

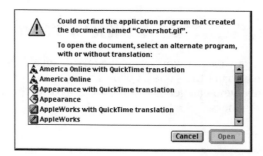

The remarkable question being asked here is: "I don't have the program that somebody used to *make* this picture. Which of the following programs would you like me to use to open the graphic?"

This may not seem like a very bright question to you. If the computer's so smart, let *it* figure out what program to use, right? But count your blessings: This dialog box is a vast improvement over the simple "Can't open this picture" message computers *used* to give you.

Anyway, almost always, the quick and clever answer is Picture Viewer (if you just want to look at the picture). If you want to make changes to the picture, choose AppleWorks instead. The image then opens up in the AppleWorks painting program, where you can edit the picture, resize it, draw a mustache on it, whatever.

Scanners

A scanner is a lot like a Xerox machine. You put a piece of paper on the glass, click a button, admire the bright alien glow and humming, and then watch a copy of the original pop up on your iMac screen. Scanners are fabulous for converting photos into graphics files, especially because scanners cost only around $90 these days. Umax, Microtek, and Agfa make them; Artec even makes one that matches the translucent look of the iMac. (Visit a Web site like *www.outpost.com* to view a selection.)

Most of these scanners come with a program called PhotoDeluxe. That's the software you're supposed to use for scanning. After you've installed PhotoDeluxe from its CD *and* the necessary software from the scanner's own CD, you're ready to proceed. Plug the scanner into one of your USB ports, turn it on, and do like this:

1. **Put your photo onto the scanner glass. Launch PhotoDeluxe. From the File menu, choose Acquire, and then click the brand of your scanner.**

   For example, in this picture, the scanner is a Umax Astra 1220.

2. **Click Preview.**

   The scanner lurches, hums, and then shows you what's on the glass at the moment:

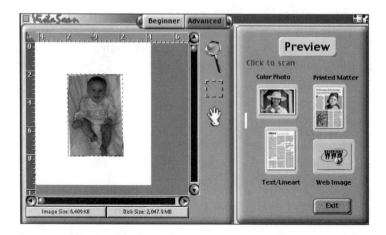

3. **Drag the edges of the dotted-line box until they neatly surround your photo. Then click the Color Photo button.**

   That's assuming you're scanning a photo. If you're scanning something that's black-and-white, like a magazine article or a black-and-white cartoon (known as *line art),* click Text/Lineart instead.

That's all there is to it. The photo shows up on your screen. Now, using the Guided Activities button in PhotoDeluxe, you can process or touch up your photo in about 100,000 different ways: make it brighter, smaller, fix dust specks, and so on. Some scanners even come with *OCR* (optical character-recognition) software, which attempts to turn a scanned image of book pages or other published material into an actual AppleWorks file that you can edit, copy, paste, and otherwise bend to your will.

Before e-mailing a scanned photo, by the way, be sure to reduce the thing to human scale, following the steps in "Mail them to someone," later in this chapter.

Digital cameras

A digital camera, like those described in Chapter 19, is another great (but much more expensive) method of getting pictures into your iMac. As noted in that chapter, you need one with a USB cable (or, if you have an iMac DV, a FireWire cable).

Because so many different companies sell digicams, I won't attempt a step-by-step tutorial here; in general, though, the procedure mirrors that of using a scanner: You launch a graphics program, choose an Import or Download command from the File menu, and wait while the camera sends its pictures to your computer.

Kodak PhotoCDs

If you want to convert your photos into electronic form only occasionally, you might prefer the Kodak PhotoCD plan. When you take a traditional roll of film to be developed, ask the camera shop to have them returned to you not just as prints, but also as a PhotoCD. When you pick up your photos, you'll also get a CD-ROM that contains those pictures, *gorgeously* scanned, each one in several different sizes. If you can afford the $1 extra per picture, this arrangement sure beats doing the scanning yourself.

What to Do with Graphics

So you've got some pix. What are they good for? Let us count the ways.

Mail them to someone

As noted in Chapter 8, it's easy to attach a photo to an e-mail message you're sending to someone. Remember, however, not to send a picture that's too big— nothing makes enemies of your recipients faster than having to sit there while some massive, 8-megabyte picture photo downloads. (A photo you've just scanned, for example, is probably enormous.)

Instead, use AppleWorks, PhotoDeluxe, or whatever other graphics program you have to scale down the image to a usable size. In AppleWorks, open the Format menu, choose Resolution and Depth, and set the photo to 72 dpi (dots per inch).

In PhotoDeluxe (the program that comes with most scanners), it's easy to convert a scan into something usable for e-mail:

1. **After scanning a picture, click Guided Activities, then Transform Photo, then the "Web Page or E-mail" button.**

   See the numbered tabs at the top of the screen? You're supposed to click them, one at a time, and process the photo using the controls on each screen. If you've already got a picture open in front of you (one you've scanned, for example), start with Step 3.

2. **Click Step 3. To crop the photo (trim out the excess borders), drag diagonally inside the photo. When the dotted-line box correctly identifies the part you want to keep, click inside the box.**

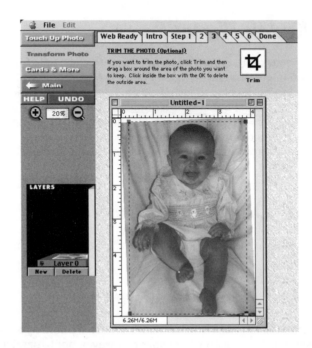

PhotoDeluxe automatically trims the photo.

3. **Click Step 4. Click the Photo Size button. In the dialog box that appears, specify the size you want the photo to wind up (in inches). Click OK.**

You've just re-sized the photo, making it bigger or smaller. Now comes the important part: you're about to make the picture smaller — not in dimensions, but in the file size, the number of megabytes you'll have to transmit by e-mail.

4. **Click Step 5. Click Reduce Resolution. Then click Step 6, and click JPEG format.**

You're asked to name and save the picture. Click Desktop, type a name, and then click Save. (To differentiate it from the original, gigantic scan, give it a name like "Baby Picture/Small.") Back in PhotoDeluxe, click Done.

On your desktop, awaiting your e-mailing or Web-page-posting pleasure, you'll find the newly cropped, scaled, compact graphic file. And if you ever need a job at *Life* magazine . . .

Put 'em on a Web page

In Chapter 9, you can read about the joys of hanging your own virtual shingle — a Web page — on the Internet, using the free iMac program called PageMill. There you'll learn how to incorporate photos into your Web pages.

Turns out your scanner, digital camera, or PhotoCD is ideal for creating such photos. If you've got a scanner, be sure to scale down the size and resolution of your scanned photos, as described in the previous section, before popping them onto your Web page. Big, screen-grubbing photos make Web-page visitors break out in hives.

Print it out

If you've just scanned a photo, and you've got a color printer like those described in Chapter 5, print away. Do *not* reduce the resolution, as described in "Mail them to someone" in the previous section. When printing — and only when printing — you *want* your scans to be gigantic. All that information means high resolution when you print, which means more attractive images.

Plaster your iMac desktop

Here it is, folks, the #1 use of photos on Macs today: using them as the backdrop of your entire computer screen. See "Hanging your own background wallpaper" in Chapter 13 for step-by-steps in replacing your colored desktop picture with a photo of your own.

What that chapter *doesn't* tell you is how to create a randomized desktop picture, one that changes every time you turn on the iMac. To do that, drag a whole *folder* full of photos into your Appearance control panel instead of just one photo. A different photo every day — isn't that what life's all about?

Chapter 12

System Folder: Trash Barge of the iMac

In This Chapter

▶ What the System Folder is for

▶ All the stuff in your Apple menu

▶ All the stuff in your Control Panels folder

▶ What junk you can throw out of your System Folder

*T*here it sits. Only one folder on your hard drive looks like it — or acts like it. It's the System Folder, which holds software that the iMac needs for itself. Every Mac has a System Folder. (Correction: Every *functioning* Mac has one.) Yours probably looks like any other folder, except that it's called System Folder and its icon has a tiny, special logo in the middle:

System Folder

Do it right now: Double-click your System Folder to open it. (Your System Folder is in your main hard-drive window.) Now click the zoom box, the tiny square in the inner top-right corner of the System Folder window, so you can see as much of the System Folder contents as possible. As a matter of fact, move your mouse up to the View menu and choose "as List." That should put everything into a neat list.

Just look at all that junk! *You* sure as heck didn't put it there — what's it doing there?

Who else would be utterly mad enough to say the following in public? *Half the stuff in your System Folder is worthless.* It's designed for power users, or people in big corporate networks, or superweenie jet-propulsion scientists and their Mensa-qualifying 8-year-old offspring. Meanwhile, these files are taking up room on your hard drive.

The System Folder Trashfest

Here's a wonderful, worth-the-price-of-the-book-right-there list of everything in your typical System Folder, item by item. I'll tell you which of these things you can safely trash or turn off.

Don't have a cow about eliminating stuff, either. The fewer items you have in your Control Panels and Extensions folders, the quicker your iMac starts up — and the less likely your machine is to crash. Besides, this is not like cleaning your attic, where if you toss that box of your drawings from elementary school, you've wounded your inner child forever. No, *this* stuff you can always get back again if you need it. It's all on the Software Install CD-ROM that came with your iMac.

As a bonus, as you go along, I'll try to point out some handy little treasures you didn't know you had. (Jeez, this is getting to be more like an attic-cleaning with every passing moment.)

Appearance, Application Support

The Appearance folder contains pictures you can use to decorate your desktop; Application Support is for your software's use only. It's where your favorite programs stash their own internal data files. Do your best to ignore both of these folders.

The Apple Menu Items folder

You'll recall that anything in this folder also appears in the menu at the left side of your screen.

(If you have Mac OS 9, by the way, many of the items described here are not, in fact, in the menu. Instead, they now come in one of two folders on your hard drive: the Applications folder or the Apple Extras folder. If you sort of miss seeing them in your menu, you can always move them there — see the instructions for adding things to your menu in Chapter 13.)

Most of the Apple menu items are also desk accessories like the ones you worked with in Chapter 3. So now you'll get to find out what exactly those things in your menu are . . . acquire a deep and abiding appreciation of their importance and value . . . and *then* throw them away.

Apple DVD Player — This command launches the program that you can use to watch DVD movies you've rented from Blockbuster. See Chapter 10.

Apple System Profiler — A neat little program that gives all kinds of mind-numbing technical details about your iMac. *You'll* probably never use it. But someday, when you're calling Apple in a desperate froth about some problem you're having, they may well ask you to consult the System Profiler to answer a couple of questions.

AppleCD Audio Player — It has Play, Stop, and Rewind controls for playing regular *music* compact discs in your CD-ROM drive; see Chapter 19 for instructions. (If you have Mac OS 9, your copy of this is in the Applications folder on your hard drive.)

Automated Tasks — Automated Tasks isn't a program at all. It's merely an alias, dropped by Apple into your menu for convenience. It lists several handy *AppleScripts* — mini-programs, each of which performs one simple timesaving step when opened. For example, Add Alias to Apple Menu puts an alias of a selected icon into your menu. Most of the others, such as Share a Folder and Start File Sharing, have to do with networking. (If you have Mac OS 9, your copy of this is in the Apple Extras folder on your hard drive, in the AppleScript folder.)

Calculator and **Note Pad** — You already know about these desk accessories (see Chapter 3). Leave them for now. (The Mac OS 9 copy of the Note Pad is in the Apple Extras folder of your hard drive.)

Chooser — You need this if you have a printer, as you can find out in Chapter 5.

Control Panels — This folder is simply a shortcut (an *alias*) to opening your real Control Panels folder. More on control panels later in this chapter.

Favorites — This command gives you quick access to files or folders you use a lot. See "More special folders," later in this chapter.

FaxStatus — Here's a little program that lets you monitor the status of faxes you're sending or receiving, as described in Chapter 19.

Graphing Calculator — Puts fancy moving 3-D graphs on your screen, so you can show your friends how high-tech and brilliant you've become. And if you're into math, it's actually pretty darned good at graphing little equations like $y = x - 1$. (Moved to a new address in Mac OS 9 — it's in your Applications folder.)

Internet Access — This set of handy Net-related commands includes:

> ✔ **Browse the Internet** — This command launches your Web browser, such as Netscape Navigator or Internet Explorer. And it opens to your preferred home page. (You use the Internet control panel to choose both which browser you prefer and which home page you like, as described later in this chapter.)

✔ **Connect To** — This tiny program-ette brings up a simple dialog box into which you can type an Internet or Web address. When you click Connect, your iMac dials and connects to that address, launching your e-mail program or Web browser. (See Chapter 6 for more on Internet connections. This little program is for people who have direct Internet accounts, not America Online.)

✔ **Internet Setup Assistant** — Walk through this series of screens while your Internet access company's tech-help agent is on the phone with you, and you'll save yourself a lot of grief in establishing an Internet account for the first time. (See Chapter 6 for details.)

✔ **Mail** — This command launches your e-mail program. (Applies to people with direct Internet accounts, not America Online.)

Key Caps — Another desk accessory. It helps you find out which combinations of keys you're supposed to press when you want to type wacky symbols like ¢ or ¥ or ™ (see Chapter 9).

Network Browser — For people with multiple Macs networked together, as described in Chapter 14. If that means you, use this program to see which other Macs are turned on and available. If that doesn't mean you, throw this thing out.

Quicken.com — An ad for the Quicken (checkbook software) Web site. Throw it away.

Recent Documents, Recent anything — A very handy shortcut! These submenus list the last few documents, applications (programs), and *servers* (other Macs in your office network) you've had open, so that you can get to them again conveniently.

If you're not on a network, you can do without Recent Servers. Open your Apple Menu Items control panel and put a zero where it says Servers; the Servers item will disappear from your menu.

Remote Access Status — This handy mini-program offers Connect and Disconnect buttons to help you get on and off the Internet (assuming you've signed up for a direct Internet account, as described in Chapter 6). And while you're connected, this window shows how long you've been tying up the phone.

Scrapbook — This desk accessory is worth keeping. Using Copy and Paste, you can put pictures, sounds, movie clips, or blocks of text into it for later use. For example, after you spend three weekends designing an absolutely gorgeous logo for yourself, paste it into the Scrapbook. Thereafter, whenever you need that logo again, open the Scrapbook and copy it, so that it'll be ready to paste into your memo or package design.

Sherlock or **Sherlock 2** — A turbocharged file-finding feature. Worth its weight in the precious metal of your choice. Just type in what you're looking for, and the iMac finds it . . . *fast*. (See the end of Chapters 4 and 7 for a complete demonstration.)

SimpleSound — A mini-program that lets you record sounds (using your iMac's built-in microphone). See Chapter 19 for details. (Mac OS 9 fans: Look for this one in your Applications folder, not your menu.)

Stickies — How did we *live* before Stickies? Sheer, purest genius. Stickies are electronic Post-It notes. That's all. Just choose New Note from the File menu, jot down what you want, and maybe pick a new pastel hue from the Color menu.

When you try to close Stickies (by choosing Quit from the File menu), you'll be asked nicely if you want the Stickies to reappear each time you turn on the iMac. Say yes, and you'll never forget another dog-grooming appointment.

The Contextual Menu Items folder

You can read about the fascinating *contextual pop-up menu* feature at the end of Chapter 2. For now, know ye that this feature provides shortcut menus when you click things (like icons and windows) while pressing the Control key.

It's technically possible to *add more* commands to these Control-key pop-up menus, and many Web-surfing power users do. If you become one of that special breed, this folder is where you put the additional commands (in the form of special icons).

The Control Strip Modules folder

You can read about the Control Strip in "The Control Panels folder" section to follow. There, you'll learn that the Control Strip is an ever-present floating strip of tiles that offer quick access to iMac settings (such as the speaker volume). This folder is where those tiles are stored.

The Control Panels folder

Control Panels is another folder inside your System Folder. As you can read in Chapter 3, a control panel is a tiny miniprogram that changes some aspect of the iMac's behavior.

Appearance — This beefy Appearance control panel lets you change the look and feel of your iMac's screen image in radical ways. For example:

- ✔ **Appearance** — These options let you choose a highlighting-pen color (for use when you drag your mouse across some text) and an accent color (for scroll bars and other tinted on-screen accessories).

- ✔ **Fonts** — Click the Fonts tab to view three pop-up menus that let you change the typefaces your iMac uses for menus, labels, and lists.

  Note especially the option called "Smooth all fonts on screen." When you turn it on, the edges of your on-screen type gets softer and smoother (or *antialiased,* as the geeks would say). See the Top 10 list at the end of Chapter 5 for an illustration.

- ✔ **Desktop** — By clicking the Desktop "tab," you can choose a photo or pattern with which to plaster the backdrop of your screen. (See "Hanging your own background wallpaper" in Chapter 13 for step-by-step instructions.)

- ✔ **Sound** — If you click the Sound tab and choose Platinum from the pop-up menu, you get crisp, cheerful little sound effects as you do anything on your iMac, like using scroll bars, menus, icons, the Trash, windows, disks, or almost anything else that requires mouse manipulation. (Health warning: Don't turn on sounds when using your iMac at the public library, at international chess matches, or during microsurgery on a relative.)

- ✔ **Options** — This panel offers a fascinating new option (on the Options tab) called Smart Scrolling. It puts both scroll-bar arrows to one end of the scroll bar, as shown here:

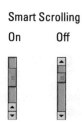

Smart Scrolling

On   Off

That option also makes the *scroll box* (the square handle you drag) larger or smaller to reflect the amount of the document that's visible in the window. That is, if the scroll bar handle is one-third the height of the scroll bar, you're seeing one-third of the document in your document window.

If you're splurting your Sprite, exclaiming, "Why, by gum, my iMac *always* does those things!", well, you're right. The iMac comes with Smart Scrolling turned on. If you turn it off, the scroll box is always small, and the arrows are at opposite ends of the scrollbar, as shown above at right.

✔ **Themes** — After you've visited all of the various tabs (Appearance, Desktop, Fonts, Sound, and Options) to get the iMac behaving just the way you like it, you can preserve the particular combination of settings you've just established as a *Theme*.

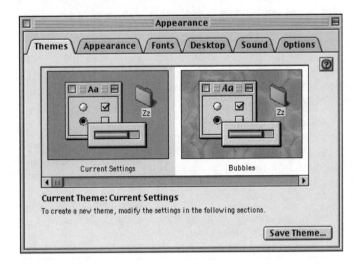

To do so, click the Themes tab, where you'll see a new entry called Current Settings. Click the Save Theme button, give your new "theme" a name, and call it a day. From now on, you can jump to your newly established theme (or any of the predefined ones) by clicking it whenever you feel the need for a change of scene.

Apple Menu Options — This little gizmo provides the submenus in your menu, so that you can (for example) open a specific control panel from the Control Panels command. It also creates, in your menu, folders that track the last bunch of documents and programs you used, which is handy.

AppleTalk — An important item *if* you're on a network. It lets you specify *how* your iMac is connected to other Macs (or laser printers); with Ethernet cables, LocalTalk wires, using the iMac's infrared transmitter, and so on. See Chapter 14 for more on hooking the iMac up to other Macs.

ATM — Adobe Type Manager. A control panel that makes certain fonts look smoother on the screen and in inkjet-printer printouts.

ColorSync — Software that tries to make colors consistent among scanners, monitors, and color printers. If you don't print in color and don't have a scanner, turn these off (see "How to ditch the crud you don't need" earlier in this chapter).

How to ditch the crud you don't need

In this chapter's blow-by-blow descriptions of your Control Panels and Extensions contents, you'll be reading about many items that serve no purpose on your iMac. In fact, they take up memory, may increase the likelihood of system crashes, and make the machine take longer to start up. Some people simply throw these away by dragging them to the trash.

It's safer, however, to simply *turn them off*. That way, if, God forbid, three months from now, you install some obscure program like Fridge Repairman Pro 3.4.2 that happens to require the software morsel you tossed, you'll be able to turn it back on and get on with life.

The key to turning off System Folder items is the Extensions Manager control panel. Open it like this: Click the menu; slide down to Control Panels; slide over to Extensions Manager. As you'll read in this chapter, Extensions Manager is nothing more than a list of almost every extension and control panel on your machine.

To turn something off, click the checkbox beside its name so that the X no longer appears. Then click the Restart button.

Now your iMac starts anew, without the memory-grubbing, speed-slowing software lint that you just turned off. This may seem like an intimidating procedure to you, but it's a healthy exercise that will leave you filled with feelings of technical prowess — and give you a faster, more stable iMac.

Control Strip — All this control panel does is hide or show the *Control Strip*. Trouble is, nobody ever bothers to explain the Control Strip to the average iMac fan — but it's a terrific time-saver that's worth meeting.

The Control Strip sometimes starts out as a tiny gray tab hugging the edge of your screen, like this:

Click that little tab (and let go) to make the Control Strip stretch out to its full length, like a python sunning itself on the beach. Here's what some of the typical tiles on the Control Strip do (your assortment may be slightly different):

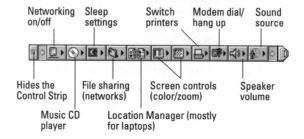

Networking on/off — Sleep settings — Switch printers — Modem dial/hang up — Sound source — Hides the Control Strip — File sharing (networks) — Screen controls (color/zoom) — Speaker volume — Music CD player — Location Manager (mostly for laptops)

Each tile, as you can see by the Speaker volume example in the picture, is a little pop-up menu; click a tile to view a menu of choices. You can muddle through life without ever using the Control Strip, of course — most of the tiles' functions are duplicated by the various gizmos in your Control Panels folder. But the Control Strip lets you adjust these settings much more conveniently.

If you click the little end tab, the Strip collapses so that only the tab appears, at the very edge of your screen. Another click expands it again. You can also shrink the Control Strip to any length by tugging — *dragging* — its little end tab.

Furthermore, if you press the Option key, you can drag the entire strip up or down the side of your screen, or across to the opposite edge. (You can't drag the Strip to the middle of the screen, however; it must hug the right or left side.) The Option key has another handy effect on the Control Strip: If you drag one of the little tiles while pressing Option, you can slide that tile horizontally to a new position.

If there's a tile you find yourself never using, feel free to get rid of it. While pressing the Option key, drag the tile to the Trash.

Date & Time — Lets you set the iMac's clock. Also controls whether the time appears at the top of your screen. If you have an Internet account, you can even make your iMac set its own clock by dialing into some high-tech atomic clock out in cyberspace somewhere. Now *that's* progress.

Dial Assist — Lets you create and store complicated dialing instructions for making calls with your modem. Unless you work at a company where somebody has told you otherwise, turn this off.

Energy Saver — This control panel is terrifically important on a computer like yours. It lets you set the iMac to shut itself down, or go to sleep, automatically after you haven't used it for, say, half an hour, to save electricity and make your screen last longer over the years. Pretty useful, really.

Extensions Manager — You can open this by choosing its name from the Control Panels command in your menu. You can also open it as the iMac is starting up by holding down your space bar. Either way, you'll be shown a list of almost *everything* listed in this chapter — all the control panels and extensions. By clicking their names, you can decide which of them you'd like to use during the work session that's about to begin. If you're a pack rat, for example, you could simply turn off the ones you don't need instead of throwing them away. *Great* for troubleshooting (see Chapter 16).

File Exchange — This little doodad gives your iMac two magical powers. First, if your iMac has a floppy drive, Zip drive, or SuperDisk drive, you can insert a disk from DOS or Windows computers and see its icon appear on the desktop, just as though it's a normal Macintosh disk. (Whether your programs can open the files *on* those disks is a topic for a book like *Macworld Mac Secrets* — but at least you'll be able to see their icons.)

Second, if there's one thing that frustrates novices and old iMac salts alike, it's seeing that infernal "Application not found" message when you double-click an icon. Thanks to File Exchange's second feature, when you double-click an icon, you don't get an error message — you get a dialog box that lists the programs you own that *can* open the mystery file.

File Sharing — The central control for *file sharing* (making your iMac's hard-drive contents available to other people on your office's network). If your iMac isn't on an office network, turn this sucker off.

File Synchronization — This fascinating doodad is, in effect, a backup pro-gram. It's designed to make the contents of one folder on your hard drive up-to-date with another folder (usually on a different disk or another com-puter on a network). Most people use it as a backup program that keeps a safety copy of, for example, a Documents folder on, say, a Zip disk (see Chapter 18). For step-by-step instructions, launch this program and then, from its Help menu, choose File Synchronization Help.

General Controls — A useful control panel. Sets your cursor-blinking speed, turns System Folder Protection on or off (which prevents marauding preteens from dragging anything out of your System Folder), and so on.

And have you ever noticed how, after a system crash and you turn the iMac on again, a message scolds you for not having shut down the machine cor-rectly (as though it's *your* fault)? Turn off the "Warn me if computer was shut down improperly" checkbox if you'd prefer the iMac not to rub it in your face. On second thought, don't; as you also may have noticed, after scolding you, the iMac automatically begins to *repair* any hard drive damage that may have occurred during the system crash. If you turn off the "Warn me" check-box, you also turn off this handy self-fixing feature.

The General Controls control panel offers a few other goodies, too; see the sidebar "Secrets of the General Controls" for a quick tour.

Internet — Shortly after you start hooking up to the Internet (see Chapter 6), you'll discover why only 35 percent of Americans are online: There are too many technical codes to type. In *each one* of your Internet programs (your Web browser, your e-mail program, and so on), you have to type your name, address, e-mail address, SMTP codes, social security number, junior-high math teacher's nickname, and so on.

The Internet control panel provides a central place to type in every conceiv-able shred of Internet-related information — right down to the signature at the bottom of your e-mails — *once*. Thereafter, each of your Internet-related programs can refer to *that* information (instead of making you retype it).

The Internet control panel is also the place where you indicate *which* e-mail program, and which Web browser, you like to use. You'll find this choice at the bottom of the E-mail and Web screens. After you've made your choice, double-clicking the Mail icon or Browse the Internet icon on your desktop launches the program you've selected.

Keyboard — Use this control panel to change how a key behaves when you keep it pressed. Does a held-down key start repeating like thissssssssssss? And how fast?

Many first-time iMac users fare better if they turn the repeating-key feature off. That way, if a book happens to lean on the spacebar while you're on the phone for 20 minutes, you won't hang up to find 536 pages of blank space in the letter you were working on.

This control panel also lets you change your keyboard's personality, making it type the correct funny symbols corresponding to Swedish, Italian, Dutch, and any of 18 other languages. People who can fluently speak 21 languages find this a handy feature, although they annoy the heck out of the rest of us.

Finally, the Keyboard control panel is the command center for programming your *function keys* (see "Fun with Function keys" in Chapter 13).

Keychain Access — The Keychain concept, new to Mac OS 9, is a good idea, but extremely complex. If your iMac is connected to a big sprawling office network, you might get tired of typing in your password every time you connect to another Mac on this network; the Keychain Access control panel lets you store your password for each remote Mac *once*. After that, you won't have to type passwords when you connect to those networked machines.

If such a central storage location for all networked-Mac passwords appeals to you, use your Mac Help command (in the Help menu). Search for "Keychain" to read all about it — or just ask the geek who set up your network to begin with.

Launcher — The Launcher displays a handy, in-your-face window containing jumbo icons for the programs and files you intend to use most often. For details, see "All about big fat Launcher buttons" in Chapter 4.

Location Manager — Using this complex control panel, you can change a slew of settings — the time zone, local Internet access phone number, speaker volume, choice of printer, and so on — with a single click of the mouse. I'd walk you through the 20-minute setup procedure, but Apple's already done a much better job. From your Help menu, choose Mac Help. Search for *Location Manager* and click the option called "Creating groups of settings (locations)."

Secrets of the General Controls

For many people, the purchase of an iMac is a primal attempt to get their lives, so full of traffic and turbulent relationships and scraps of paper, into some kind of order.

Little do they know what awaits them on the typical iMac: Their important documents get every bit as lost as their paper-based counterparts once did. Even the great Mac gurus of our time have, at one time or another, saved some document — and then found themselves unable to find it again because it got arbitrarily stashed in some hidden folder somewhere.

Enter the Documents folder — one of the features you can turn on in the General Controls panel. This special folder appears in your main hard drive window the first time you try to save a file, as shown below. Thereafter, the iMac shows you the Documents folder's contents every time you use a program's Open or Save command.

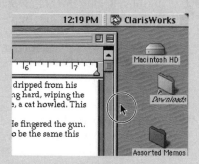

As you can see, a beginner — and we were all beginners once — might wind up accidentally clicking outside the word processor window, as shown above. Immediately, the desktop (Finder) jumps to the front, showing files and folders, and the word processor window gets shoved to the back, apparently vanishing, causing (in the beginner) distress, unhappiness, and occasionally hair loss.

Now then, suppose you open General Controls and turn *off* the "Show Desktop when in background" option. When you open a document *now*, the world of the Finder (icons, windows) *disappears,* as shown below. *Now,* if you click outside the word processor window, absolutely nothing happens. In fact, you *can't* return to the desktop without choosing Finder from the Application menu in the upper-right corner of your screen.

In theory, you'll never lose anything again; everything you do will always be in one place. (That feature makes backing up your work simple, too; you now have only one folder to copy to a different disk.)

The other great feature of General Controls is what I call self-hiding programs. To explain, let me show you what might happen when you reach for the scroll bar on a regular iMac:

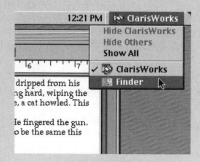

And if you don't quite need that additional complexity in your life, turn this thing off (see "How to ditch the crud you don't need" earlier in this chapter).

Map — This control panel is primarily useful for people who do business with people in different geographical locations. (In both Mac OS 8.6 and Mac OS 9, it's in the Apple Extras folder, not your Control Panels folder.) You type a major city's name and click Find, and the Map shows you where that city is. It also tells you how far away it is, and what the time difference is. (Want to see Apple's sense of humor at work? Type *MID* and press Return . . .)

Memory — As the French say, *Ne trashez pas!* You'll need this one. Details on memory, and Memory, in Chapter 16.

Modem — This simple control panel is where you specify the exact brand and model of the modem your iMac has. (***Hint:*** It should say "Apple Internal 56K Modem.") Pick the wrong one, and your ability to explore the Internet, send faxes, and attain Nirvana will be extremely limited.

Monitors — Use this control panel to switch between different color settings for your monitor (such as colors or grays) and different *resolutions* (degrees of magnification for the whole screen). If you want Internet photos to look half-decent, use the Thousands or Millions of Colors setting. And if you don't want blurry edges, use the 800 x 600 settings. (For details on this Resolution business, see "Zooming Into Your Screen" in Chapter 13.)

Monitors & Sound — On older iMacs, this single program contains the settings described in this chapter under separate entries: "Monitors" and "Sound." In late 1999, they got divorced.

Mouse — This control panel governs how quickly the cursor moves across the screen when you move the mouse quickly across the desk. It also lets you decide how fast two clicks must be to count as a double-click.

Multiple Users — This Mac OS 9 feature lets you set up a single iMac to accommodate different people who might be using it. For a tutorial, see Chapter 13.

Numbers — Lets you change the way the iMac punctuates numbers. For example, the French use periods in large numbers instead of commas. You'd say, "Bonjour! You owe moi $1.000.000, Monsieur." If you're satisfied with the comma way of doing things, throw this away.

QuickTime Settings — This control panel lets you adjust various settings pertaining to playing music CDs and CD-ROMs. You'll never need any of them except one: If you turn off the AutoPlay CD-ROM option, your iMac is protected against the AutoStart virus (see Chapter 16).

Remote Access — This control panel is where you specify your Internet name, password, and local phone number. No Internet account? Turn it off.

Software Update — OK, you're Apple Computer. You know that somehow, somewhere in the 9 million pieces of software in Mac OS Whatever, there's a bug — some little glitch left behind by a programmer. Don't you wish, now that 30 million people have installed your new system software, you could sneak into everyone's house and fix that bug?

Now you can. This control panel's "Update software automatically" checkbox makes your iMac dial the Internet according to a schedule that you specify (using the Set Schedule button). In about two seconds, it sends out a query to the huge humming master computers at Apple, seeking the answer to one question: "Have you fixed or updated anything?"

If the answer is Yes, your iMac begins receiving the fix automatically from the Internet (after asking your permission, of course). In just a few minutes, the huge humming master computers will have finished sending you the new goodies, and your iMac will be good as new. Scratch that — *better* than new.

(This feature works only for things like control panels and extensions — the things described in this chapter. It doesn't update your non-Apple software, such as Internet Explorer or Microsoft Word.)

Sound — At the left side of this window, which debuted on the late-1999 iMac models, lurk four control centers. The **Alerts** portion lets you choose which irritating sound effect you want to squawk at you when you make a mistake. **Input** lets you specify what sound source the iMac should use when making a recording (a delightful feature that's described in Chapter 19) — a microphone you've plugged in, for example, or your CD-ROM drive.

The **Output** section lets you set the volume for your speakers. And the **Speaker Setup,** the funnest one of all, affects your iMac's built-in stereo speakers. By dragging the little sliders, you control the relative balance between the two speakers; the iMac plays hissy sounds out of one speaker, then the other, as you tweak the controls, until they sound exactly right. (Hold down your mouse on one speaker image to freeze the hissing on that speaker alone.)

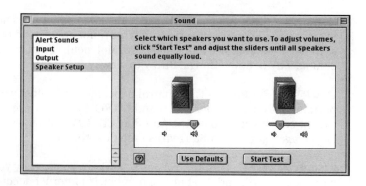

Speech — Extremely cool for at least 15 minutes. Lets your iMac read, out loud, what you have typed. Instructions in making it do so are in Chapter 19; in the Speech control panel, the primary activity is deciding whether or not you want the iMac to speak error messages that appear on the screen — and which voice you want it to use when it does so.

You haven't *lived* until your computer blurts out, in a nasal robotic voice during a sensitive job interview, "Your battery is completely empty. The computer will now go to sleep. Good night!"

Startup Disk — You have one hard drive inside the iMac. Some people purchase another one, or a removable-cartridge thing like a Zip drive, that plugs into your USB or (on iMac DV models) FireWire connector. Startup Disk lets you choose *which* hard drive's System Folder you want to run the show when you next turn on the computer. If the hard drive in your iMac is your only hard drive, open your Extensions Manager control panel and turn off Startup Disk.

TCP/IP — If you've signed up for an Internet account (see Chapter 6), this control panel stores the complex numbers that identify the company you've signed up with.

Text — Mr. Pointless. Would let you choose a language software kit other than English for your computer — if you had any installed. You don't. Throw this away.

Users & Groups — See Chapter 14 for details of setting up an office network, including what to do with this otherwise useless item.

Web Sharing — This control panel is primarily of interest to networked companies; it lets you make a particular folder on your hard drive available to anyone who dials into your iMac. If you don't have an office guru who explains how to use this, throw it away.

The Extensions folder

An *extension* is a little program that runs automatically when you turn on the iMac. It usually adds some little feature to your iMac that you want available at all times: the ability to connect to the Internet, for example, or play a CD-ROM disc.

Extensions aren't the only thing in your Extensions folder, however — oooooh, no; that would be far too logical. The Extensions folder also contains something called *shared libraries,* which are little blobs of computer instructions that your various programs call on when necessary. (Any file ending with *Lib* is one of these shared libraries. So don't go to a party and pronounce it "Open Transport Libb." It's "lybe," short for *library.*) Anyway, shared libraries are far less annoying than actual extensions, which make your iMac take longer to start up, use up memory, and contribute to freezes and crashes. Shared libraries don't do any of that.

About Apple Guide, anything-Guide — Remember, from Chapter 1, the electronic help desk we call the Help menu? These files contain the Help screens.

ActiveX Controls — Part of the Internet Explorer browser. You can throw it away.

AOL Link-anything — These files are required by America Online. If you're not an AOL member, turn these off.

Apple CD/DVD Driver, Foreign File Access, anything-Access — You need these for playing CD-ROMs on your iMac.

Apple Color SW Pro CMM, anything-SW, LaserWriter anything — SW stands for Apple StyleWriter, a discontinued printer. You'll find a whole bunch of these in your Extensions folder, and you should throw *all* of them away except the one that corresponds to the printer you actually use.

Apple Enet — You need this doodad only if you connect to other computers using your Ethernet jack, as described in Chapter 14.

Apple Monitor Plugins — Leave this. It adds useful options to your Monitors control panel.

Apple QD3D anything — Stands for QuickDraw 3D, a little-used technology for displaying 3-D images on the screen. A few games, however — notably Bugdom, which comes with the iMac — require these.

AppleScript, anything-Script — All components of a very technical feature intended for the kind of person who wouldn't be caught dead reading this book. However, even if you don't use these yourself, some of the iMac's best features depend on these extensions, so leave them in place.

AppleShare, Network anything, File Sharing anything — Still more doodads for networking Macs together. If you're not on a network, off they go.

Application Switcher — This extension makes possible the iMac's Program Switcher (see Chapter 13). It also lets you switch from one open program to the next by pressing ⌘-Tab. Try it — you'll like it!

ATI-anything — This software speeds up the appearance of images on your iMac screen, which you'll find especially useful if you play Mac games.

CarbonLib — You don't need this extension today. But maybe tomorrow, and for the rest of your life. Before you're through with this computer hobby, Mac OS X ("ten") will be on the market — and this doodad will let you run many Mac OS X programs on your humble, Mac OS 9 iMac.

Color Picker — The Color Picker is that dialog box that shows a big color wheel, allowing you to choose a particular color. It appears, for example, when you're in the Edit menu's Preferences command and you click a label color to change it. This extension adds a More Choices button to that dialog box, allowing you to choose some super-techie options.

ColorSync — See "ColorSync" in the Control Panels listing.

Contextual Menu Extension — Brings you the magical pop-up menus that appear when you hold down the Control key and click something. See Chapter 2 for the gory details.

Control Strip Extension — The Control Strip, described earlier in this chapter, is easy to modify. You can drag new tiles directly onto it (to install them) or Option-drag them to the Trash (to uninstall them). This extension makes it all possible.

Default Calibrator — This extension adjusts your screen at startup to ensure that it's colorifically perfect. If, by some fluke, you don't work in the professional color printing industry, toss this one.

Desktop Print anything — For people whose Macs are attached to *multiple* printers (perhaps in a big office, for example). Adds printer icons to your desktop, so that you can decide which one should print your latest masterpiece (see Chapter 5 for details). If you have but one printer, turn these off and have a happy life.

DNSPlugin — No joke: Apple describes this as an extension that "allows your computer to receive listings of network objects from DNS directory services." Turns out there's no such thing. Turn this off.

DrawSprocketLib — An extension used by certain games.

DVD Anything — On iMac DV models, these extensions make it possible for you to view videos on DVD discs. Don't leave Blockbuster without 'em.

EM Extension — See "Extensions Manager" in the Control Panels listing.

Epson Stylus — The software for an Epson inkjet printer. (More on printers in Chapter 5.)

FaxMonitor, Fax anything — Software that lets your iMac send and receive faxes (Chapter 19).

FBC Indexing Scheduler, Find, FindByContent — These extensions let you search for words *inside* your files using the Sherlock finding program. For details, read "Seeking wisdom in your own words — and on the Net" in Chapter 4.

FireWire anything — Required by the FireWire jacks on the side of an iMac DV (see Chapter 10).

Folder Actions — For programmers. Off it goes.

Font Manager Update — Fixes a bug pertaining to fonts. Leave alone.

HID Library, InputSprocket-anything — These files let the iMac accommodate the USB-attachable game devices — joysticks, gamepads, and so on — described in Appendix C. If you control the cursor only with your mouse, you can turn all this stuff off.

HTMLRenderingLib — Required by the Mac's Help command.

ICeTEe — This little gizmo makes possible a neat Internet feature almost nobody talks about. Suppose you run across a Web address (such as *http://www.apple.com*) in any document, even an e-mail or an AppleWorks memo. Just by ⌘-clicking it, you make your Web browser open and take you to the corresponding Web page. Neato!

Indeo Video — If you use Microsoft Internet Explorer (see Chapter 7), these extensions got dumped into your System Folder. They let your iMac see movies (which, presumably, you find on the Web) that have been prepared in Windows format (AVI).

Instant Palm Desktop — This item puts up the tiny green icon at the upper-right corner of your screen, as described in Chapter 9, that lists your schedule for the day.

Internal v.90 Modem, Internet Access — Software for your built-in modem and for connecting to the Internet, respectively.

Internet Config Extension — This extension goes with the Internet control panel, described earlier in this chapter.

Iomega driver — Lets your iMac work with Zip drives. If you didn't buy one, out this goes.

LDAP-anything — These doodads let Sherlock 2 look up people's names and phone numbers, as described at the end of Chapter 7.

Location Manager-anything — See "Location Manager," earlier in this chapter.

MacinTalk-anything — Lets your iMac *speak*. See Chapter 19.

Macromedia anything — Required by certain Web pages for special animated effects. Turn it off if you don't spend much time on the Web.

Microsoft-anything, MS-anything — All of this crud is required if you want to use Microsoft programs.

Modem Scripts — Before you go online (either with America Online or an Internet account), you're supposed to tell the iMac what kind of modem you own. You choose your model from a long list in the Modem control panel. For every corresponding modem name, a file sits here in your Modem Scripts folder.

Take a minute right now to *throw away* every modem-model file except the one you actually own: "Apple Internal 56K Modem (v.90)." You'll save RAM, hard-disk space, and time when you launch your modem programs.

MRJ Libraries — This folder (which stands for Macintosh Runtime for Java) contains the software necessary for your iMac to run Java programs — that is, animated ads and little games that you find on Web pages as you surf the Internet. You be the judge.

Multi-User Startup — Makes possible the Multiple Users feature described in Chapter 13.

Multiprocessing — This little guy awaits the day when Macs come with more than one processor chip. Yours doesn't. Turn this off.

NBP Plug-in, NSL UI Library — Used to access other networked computers over the Internet.

NetManage WinSock Lib — Probably the least helpful software name in the history of humanity. Anyway, this item was placed here by Quicken (see Chapter 9), and is required if you hope to pay your bills electronically. If you have no intention of using Quicken or going online with it, turn this off.

Open Transport, Open TPT-anything — This super-techie collection of System Folder lint (known as Open Transport technology) makes your iMac capable of connecting to the Internet, a network, or America Online.

OpenGL anything — These gadgets add speed to certain computer games. If you don't play 'em, you don't need 'em.

PalmConnect-anything — These modules let your calendar/phone book program (Palm Desktop, covered in Chapter 9) exchange information with a PalmPilot. If you don't have such a pocket organizer, turn these off.

Printer Descriptions — This folder contains one little file for each individual printer model. Open this folder and discard the icons for *all* printers you don't use.

Printer Share — Turn it off. Used to share StyleWriter printers (no longer sold) over a network.

PrintingLib — Makes laser printing faster. If you have an inkjet printer like an Epson, turn this off.

PrintMonitor — The genie that grants the miracle of *background printing*, described in Chapter 5.

QuickDraw 3D-anything — QD3D stands for *QuickDraw 3D*. This assortment of a half-dozen extensions lets your iMac show, create, and accelerate 3D graphics. These extensions are required primarily for a few games, including Nanosaur (see Chapter 9); if you don't play games, switch these babies off.

QuickTime-anything — You need these little jobbers for playing, or making, digital movies on the iMac. Many games and CD-ROM discs require these items.

Security-anything — Part of the Keychain password-storage mechanism described in the Control Panels listing of this chapter. If you don't share your iMac with other people, turn these off.

Serial (Built-in) — Still more Open Transport crud (see "Open TPT anything").

Shared Library anything — You need these to manage your *shared libraries*, described at the beginning of this section.

ShareWay IP Personal Bgnd — A very technical option for people who set up networks. If you're not on a network, turn it off.

SLPPlugin — Exactly like the delightful DNSPlugin described earlier in this section.

Software Updates-anything — Makes possible the Software Update feature described in the Control Panels listing of this chapter.

SOMobjects for Mac OS — Yet another shared library, as discussed at the beginning of this section. This one is required to make your *contextual menus* work.

Sound Manager — For sound recording and playback. Leave it for now.

Speech Manager — Makes possible the text-reading-out-loud feature described in Chapter 19. If you aren't regularly talking to your iMac — besides just arguing with it — off this goes.

STF anything — More stuff for your built-in fax modem.

StuffIt anything — Required by StuffIt, the program described in Chapter 6 that lets you open stuff you get from the Internet.

TCPack for AOL — Leave this on only if (a) you are an America Online member, and (b) you connect to it through a cable modem or other pricey high-speed connection. If you connect via built-in modem, off this goes.

Text Encoding Converter — All computers understand A through Z, but the wackier symbols (such as curly quotes, foreign diacritical markings, and so on) are internally summoned differently on each type of computer. Ever get an e-mail in which all the apostrophes appear as capital U's? Or in which all the quote marks have turned into weird boxes? Now you know the problem.

The Text Encoding Converter is designed to translate other computers' wacky alphabet references into the iMac's system, so that fewer nutty boxes and U's show up in your e-mail.

Time Synchronizer — The Date & Time control panel can set your iMac's clock *automatically* by dialing into the Internet. This extension makes that feature possible.

UDF Volume Access — Lets your iMac talk to certain specialized kinds of CD-ROMs, notably *DVD discs* (which are like CDs, but hold 14 times as much). ("Volume," in this case, doesn't mean "loudness;" it refers to a *disk*.) This extension is especially if you have an iMac DV model, which has a built-in DVD drive.

URL Access — Required by the Sherlock program (see the end of Chapter 7) to search the Internet.

USB-anything — Lets your iMac communicate with various USB devices (see Chapter 14).

Voices — Contains the "voice modules" for the different voices the Mac can use to speak (see Chapter 19).

Voice Verification — If you have Mac OS 9 *and* you've bought a microphone for your iMac *and* you're using the Multiple Users feature described in Chapter 13, this extension lets you *speak* your password to gain entry to your computer.

Web Sharing Extension — A companion to the equally useless Web Sharing control panel. Turn it off.

The Preferences folder

The Preferences folder is filled with information, and *none* of it's for you.

Every single file in this folder was put there by *another* piece of software. Let's say you change a setting in your word processor: You always want it to make your typing double-spaced, for example. Well, where do you suppose the computer stores your new setting? It jots it down in a *preferences file.* And this prefs file lives — wild guess — in the Preferences folder.

Prefs files are famous for frustrating beginners. Because they're for use by your programs, and not by you, virtually every one of them gives you a rude error message if you try to double-click it. You simply can't open a Prefs file; only your software can.

You really can only do one good thing with the Preferences files: throw them away. That is, throw away any that belong to programs you no longer use.

More special folders

In its noble (but hopeless) quest to neaten up your System Folder, Apple offers you several other, specially-iconed holding-tank folders. Such as:

- ✓ **Application Support:** Various Mac software companies wind up dumping all their programs' associated crud — dictionary files, file-conversion stuff, and so on — into this folder. The **Claris** folder is similar, but it's exclusively for housing pieces of programs from the former Claris Corporation (including AppleWorks).

- ✓ **ColorSync Profiles:** As you can read earlier in this chapter, ColorSync is a software scheme for ensuring that scanners, screens, and color printers all agree on what, for example, "red" is. This folder contains individual color-description lists for every model of Apple scanner, monitor, and printer. If color consistency is important to you, use the ColorSync control panel to specify which models you own.

- ✓ **Extensions (Disabled):** This explanation is tricky and techie, but I'll do my best. Remember Extensions Manager, described in the sidebar called "How to ditch the crud you don't need" earlier in this chapter? When you click some extension's checkbox to switch it off, Extensions Manager doesn't *delete* that extension; behind the scenes, it just *moves* it into this Extensions (Disabled) folder. When the iMac next starts up, it only "loads" the extensions that are in the actual Extensions folder.

To turn that particular extension on again, you can, of course, use Extensions Manager again — but you could also, in a pinch, move the file manually back into the regular Extensions folder. (Rival programs, like Conflict Catcher, work the same way.)

And if you turn off a *control panel,* sure enough, it winds up in a folder called **Control Panels (Disabled).**

✔ **Favorites:** "Favorites" means "icons I'd like quick access to from now on." To create a Favorite, click it and choose Add to Favorites from the File menu. It instantly appears in your Favorites command (in the menu), as shown here:

1. Choose Add to Favorites . . .

2. . . . and from now on, your favorite icons are available from the Apple menu.

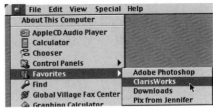

Behind the scenes, the iMac has simply placed an *alias* of that icon into the Favorites folder. (See Chapter 13 for a description of aliases.) In other words, to remove something from the Favorites menu, remove it from this folder.

✔ **Fonts folder:** This folder contains your fonts. (Did you guess?) See Chapter 5 for a detailed explanation of all this junk.

✔ **Help:** Apple puts its own help files (which create what you see when you use the Mac Help feature, for example) into this folder. Other software companies sometimes follow suit.

✔ **Internet Search Sites:** The Sherlock finding program is capable of searching the entire, vast Internet, not just your puny little hard drive. The files in this folder each teach the Find command how to talk to a different World Wide Web search page. (See Chapter 7 for more on Web search pages.)

✔ **Language & Region Support:** This folder contains files necessary to let your iMac show other languages on the screen. If you use your iMac only in one country, you can throw away all the other countries' files.

- **Launcher Items folder:** The purpose of this folder is to let you specify what jumbo icons you want to appear in your Launcher window, the iMac's one-click program-launching bay. See "All about big fat Launcher buttons" in Chapter 4.

- **Startup Items, Shutdown Items**: Fascinating, Captain. Anything you put into the Startup Items folder (a program, a document, a sound, a folder) gets opened with a mysterious automatic double-click whenever you turn on the iMac. If you don't do anything but word process, for example, drag the icon of your word processor into this folder. Thereafter, every time you power up for the day, your word processing program will be on the screen awaiting your brilliance.

  The Shutdown Items folder is the same deal, except anything in *here* gets run automatically when you *shut down* the computer. Automatic-backup programs come to mind. A sound that says "Th-th-th-th-th-that's all, folks!" also comes to mind.

- **Scripting Additions, Scripts Folder:** Places for programmers to stash their stuff.

Other files in the System Folder

Clipboard — Every time you use the Cut or Copy command in a program, the iMac, according to what you read earlier, socks the selected material away on an invisible Clipboard. Well, guess what: it's not actually invisible. Technically speaking, that info you copied has to be put *somewhere*. This is where: in the Clipboard file.

Little-known fact: You can double-click the Clipboard file to open a window that shows the last thing you cut or copied. (Another little-known fact: The last swallow of a can of soda is 69 percent saliva.)

Finder — This is the most important program on your iMac. Without it, a System Folder is just a folder, and your iMac won't even turn on. The Finder file is responsible for creating your basic desktop: the Trash, your disk icon, windows, and so on.

System — This is *also* the most important file on your iMac. It contains all kinds of other info necessary for the computer to run: reams and reams of instructions for the computer's own use. Without a System file, the iMac won't even turn on, either.

Desktop Printers — The icons for your various printers (*if* you have more than one). See the sidebar called "A shortcut for multiple-printer owners" in Chapter 5.

Scrapbook file, Note Pad file — When you paste something into the Scrapbook or Note Pad desk accessories, behind the scenes, the iMac actually stores it in these files.

Mac OS ROM — Whatever you do, don't fold, move, spindle, or mutilate this one. Throw it away, and you've got yourself a see-through, $1,200 doorstop. (Fortunately, a *clean install,* described in Chapter 16, can bring a thus-crippled iMac back to life.)

Part IV
Toward a New, Nerdier You

The 5th Wave By Rich Tennant

"Come here, quick! I've got a new iMac trick!"

In this part . . .

*E*nough about turning the computer off, e-mailing tribal members halfway around the world, and typing up mundane little bestsellers. Now it's time to interior-decorate your machine, do Option-key tricks, and perform other stunts described in the chapter appropriately titled, "Great Material that Didn't Quite Fit the Outline."

Then there's Chapter 14, which notes that the iMac is a particularly gregarious little machine. It likes nothing better than to sidle up to some other piece of machinery and talk to it.

Fortunately, this baby's got more connectors than I-95. Take USB, Ethernet, and wireless AirPort hookups, for example: You may not know what they are now, but you will a few pages from now.

Chapter 13

Great Material that Didn't Quite Fit the Outline

This chapter is filled with miniature iMac lessons. It reveals iMac features you'd be unlikely to discover on your own, unearths shortcuts and slick tricks, and shows you how to tailor your iMac so that it perfectly fits your personality.

In short, the following discussions are useful, surprising, delightful — but utterly random. They just didn't fit tidily into any other chapter. That's a syndrome we writers try to avoid, but greatly prefer to writer's block. May you find enlightenment even in randomness.

The Efficiency Nut's Guide to the Option Key

Yeah, yeah, everybody knows that you can close a window by clicking its close box. But you didn't fork over good money for this book to learn something that's on page 1 of the iMac manual (if, that is, there *were* an iMac manual).

No, these tips are much choicer. They show you how to unlock the power of that most overlooked of keys, the Option key. It's been placed closer to you than any letter key on the keyboard — and that's no accident.

Closing all windows at once

Suppose you've opened a gaggle of folders. Their windows are lying open all over the screen. And suppose that the niggling neatness ethic instilled in you by your mother compels you to clean up a bit.

You could, of course, click the close box of each window, one at a time. But it's far faster to click only *one* window's close box while pressing the Option key. Bam, bam, bam — they all close automatically, one after another.

The silence of the Trash

Let's review: You drag an icon on top of the Trash can and the icon disappears. The Trash can icon overflows. You smile gently at the zaniness of it all. Then you choose Empty Trash from the Special menu, and a little message appears on the screen, saying something like this.

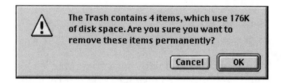

That's all very well and good, but busy people concerned with increasing their productivity may not always have time for such trivial information. Therefore, if you want to dump the trash, but you *don't* want that message to appear, press Mr. Option Key while you choose Empty Trash. (Option is also the key for emptying the trash when the iMac tells you something is "locked" in the Trash can.)

'Smatterafact, you can shut up the Trash's warning permanently, if you're so inclined. Click the Trash can. From the File menu, choose Get Info. Turn off "Warn before emptying." What an improvement!

Multitasking methods

As you discovered early on, the iMac lets you run more than one program simultaneously. (Remember when you tried some tricks with both the Note Pad and the Calculator open on the screen at once?) You can switch from one program to another by choosing the program's name from the Application menu at the top right of your screen, marked by the name and icon of whichever program is currently in front.

We haven't yet examined the other commands in this menu, such as Hide Others and Show All. These commands help keep your screen neat and clean. For example, suppose you're trying to use the Calculator, but so many other programs are running that your eyes cross.

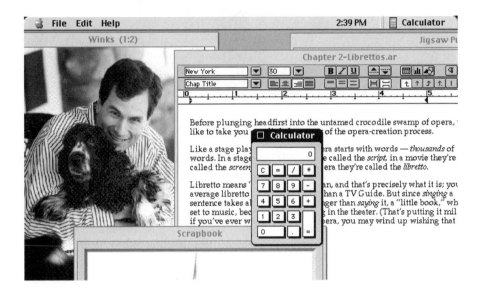

By choosing Hide Others from the Application menu, all windows that belong to other programs disappear, leaving the frontmost window all by itself.

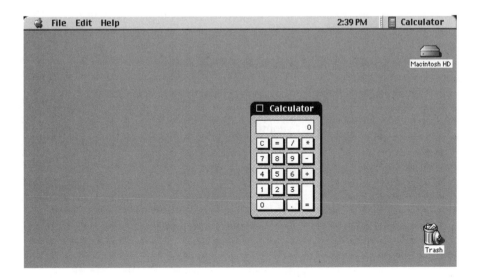

The other programs *are still running,* and they *do* still exist. But their windows are now hidden. You can verify this by checking the Application menu, where you'll see that their icons appear slightly dimmed.

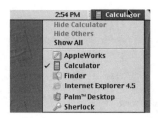

So how does the Option key play into all this? When you switch from one program to another, you can make the program you're *leaving* hide itself automatically. Just press Option while choosing the new program's name (or clicking in its window). That way, you always keep nonessential programs hidden.

You can even press Option as you click different tiles on your *Application Switcher palette* (described later in this chapter). Once again, the program you were just *in* gets hidden as you switch to the next program.

Buried Treasures

Did you enjoy those obscure, Option key tricks? Then you'll really love these equally scintillating techniques, not one of which requires the Option key.

Make an alias of a file

The File menu has a command called Make Alias. Although you might expect this command to generate names like One-Eyed Jake or "Teeth" McGuire, the term *alias* in the Macintosh world represents something slightly different — a duplicate of a file's *icon* (but not a duplicate of the file itself). You can identify the alias icon because its name is in italics, as shown here, and because a tiny arrow icon appears on the alias.

What's neat about aliases is that, when you double-click an alias icon, the iMac opens the _original_ file. If you're a true '90s kinda person, you might think of the alias as a beeper — when you call the _alias_, the _actual_ file responds.

So who on earth would need a feature like this? Well, there's more to the story. An alias, for one thing, requires only a tiny amount of disk space (a couple of K) — so it's not the same as making an actual copy of the full-sized, original file. (And you can make as many aliases of a file as you want.) Therefore, making an alias of something you use frequently is an excellent time-saver — it keeps the alias icon readily accessible, even if the real file is buried somewhere four folders deep.

Another very common trick: Place an alias of a program or a document into your menu, where you don't have to open _any_ folders to get at it.

Here's the drill:

1. **Click the real icon once.**

2. **From the File menu, choose Make Alias.**

3. **Open your System Folder.**

4. **Drag the alias into the folder called Apple Menu Items (within the System Folder).**

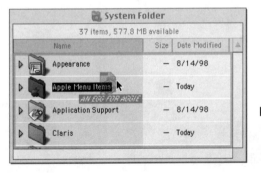

5. **Now look in your menu.**

Sure enough — there's your file! Choose it from the menu to open the original file.

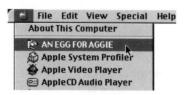

And yet, because you used an alias, the *real* file can be anywhere on your hard disk or on a different disk. You can move the real file from folder to folder or even rename it, and the alias still opens it correctly.

Spring-loaded folders

For years, people wanting to move an icon into a folder that's inside a folder that's inside *another* folder had to cancel all their meetings for the day and lock the door. They'd have to open the first folder into a window; open the folder inside it; drag the icon into place; and then close all the windows they've opened in the process.

On the iMac, however, you can simply drag an icon onto a folder (below, left) — *don't let go!* — and it will open *automatically* into a window (below, right).

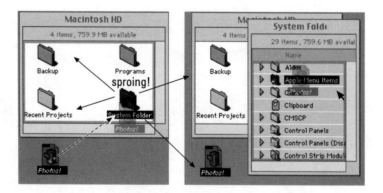

Drag that icon on top of the *next* folder, and it, too, will spring open — *don't let go!* — so that you can drop it on its final, target folder destination.

Now let go. All the windows that opened on your journey snap shut automatically. Using this technique, you can actually place an icon into a folder within a folder within a folder — with a single drag.

Trash, aliases, and a word of caution

If you trash an alias, you're deleting only the alias. The original file is still on your disk. If you delete the *original* file, however, the alias icons will remain uselessly on your disk, rebels without a cause, babies without a mother, days without sunshine. When you double-click an alias whose original file is gone, you'll just get an error message. (The error message offers you the chance to attach this orphaned alias to a *different* "real" file — but the original file is still gone forever.)

Likewise, if you copy your inauguration speech file's *alias* to a floppy disk, thinking that you'll just print it out when you get to Washington, think again. You've just copied the alias, but you *don't* actually have any text. That's all in the original file, still at home on your hard disk.

The iMac's Program Switcher

The *Application menu* is the menu in the upper-right corner of your screen — where you see the name of the program you're using at the moment. The Application *switcher* is a secret feature that appears only when you drag straight down the Application menu past the bottom and *tear it off* (below, left).

The menu turns into a small floating rectangle that lists your running programs (above, right); just click a program's name to switch to it.

And if you find this floating palette too wide for your tastes, click carefully just inside the right end of one of its buttons, as shown above — and drag to the left. You've just made the entire palette skinnier. And if you're out horseback riding, bouncing so severely that you can't manipulate your mouse, use the Application switcher shortcut: while holding down the ⌘ key, press the Tab key. This combo, ⌘-Tab, automatically lets you switch from one open program to the next — even if you haven't torn off the Application menu.

Isn't technology wonderful?

Zooming into your screen

As you've no doubt noticed, the iMac screen is gorgeous. It's bright, vibrant, and wide enough to show you two pages side by side. The propeller-heads would remark that it's an 800-by-600 screen, which means that it's composed of that many individual color dots across and down.

You're not locked into that setting, however. With a few judicious clicks, you can magnify the screen image, blowing up your work for a larger view. (When everything's bigger on the screen, of course, you see less overall area — you don't see two pages side by side anymore — the same way a more close-up map shows a smaller section of your town.) Or go the other way: reduce the image, so that you can see more pages at once, but smaller.

To try these settings for yourself, open the Control Strip by clicking the small gray tab that peeks out from the left edge of your screen, turning it into a horizontal tray full of useful gizmos. The one you want is the Screen Resolution icon, which is shown here:

Click the Screen Resolution icon to make the tiny pop-up menu appear; click the option called 640 x 480. Your screen instantly changes to show you the magnified view. If you choose 1024 x 768 instead, you zoom *out,* so that your iMac shows more real estate at a smaller size.

To restore the original setting, click the Screen Resolution tile again; choose the 800 x 600 command from the pop-up menu.

Making It Unmistakably Yours

The great thing about an iMac is that it's not some stamped-out clone made in Korea. It's one of a kind — or it will be after we get through with it. These tips illustrate some of the ways you can make the iMac match your personality, sensibility, or décor.

Have it your way — at Icon King

You don't have to accept those boring old icons for files, programs, and folders. If you want anything done around the iMac, heaven knows, you've got to do it yourself:

1. **Go into AppleWorks (the painting window) and make a funny little picture.**

   And I mean *little* — remember, you're drawing a replacement icon for some hapless file. Like this guy here, for example.

2. **Copy your creation to the Clipboard.**

3. **Go to the Finder and click the file whose icon you want to replace (as shown here at left).**

   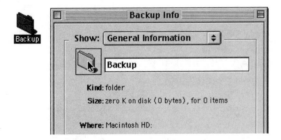

4. **From the File menu, choose Get Info, so that the Get Info box appears (previous picture, right).**

   (By the way: If you're in Simple Finder mode, which is described later in this chapter, then the Get Info command doesn't appear in the File menu. Turn off Simple Finder before taking this step.)

5. **See the folder icon in the upper left? Click that sucker — and then paste away!**

From now on, that little picture is the new icon for the file (or folder or disk). To restore the original icon, repeat the Get Info business, but this time, after you click the icon, press the Delete key.

Hanging your own background wallpaper

In the earliest days of computer technology, you could make a few feeble attempts at changing the way your Mac looked. You could, for example, fill your screen background with a wall of patterned teddy bears.

But the iMac says, "Teddy bears? — *Hah!*" Using the Appearance control panel, you can fill your desktop with not just a repeating pattern, but a *full-screen* picture file!

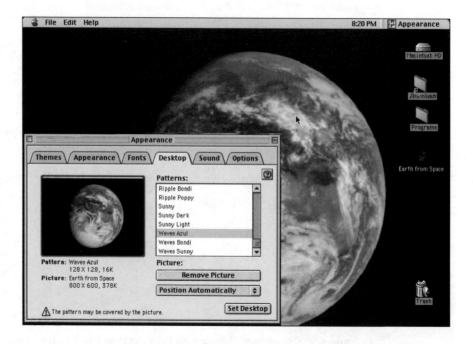

To do so, open the Appearance control panel. (From the menu, choose Control Panels, and then choose Appearance.) Click the Desktop tab, and then click the Select Picture button.

You're now asked to locate the graphic file you want to use as a backdrop. You're offered several folders filled with sample graphics files; double-click to open them, and then double-click to try out the different graphics. Most are spacey, bubbly artworks that look as though they were created by an air-brush artist listening to new-age music; none are actual photos.

But it's much more fun to slap your *own* picture on your desktop. As for *getting* such a picture file, well, that's up to you. America Online and the Internet are *teeming* with great pictures, from Planet Earth to Gwyneth Paltrow. It's also easy enough to make your own, using (a) software like AppleWorks or

Photoshop, (b) a digital camera like those described in Chapter 18, or (c) a scanner, also described in Chapter 18. (The photo of Earth from space shown above came from the NASA Web site at *http://photojournal.jpl.nasa.gov,* for example — your tax dollars at work!)

(Note to the hopelessly technical: You can use any JPEG, GIF, PICT, picture-clipping, or Photoshop file. Note to the frantically busy: Instead of clicking the Select Picture button, as described a couple paragraphs ago, you can also *drag* a graphics file directly onto the miniature desktop in the Appearance control panel. There it shows up in miniature form, as shown in the previous illustration.)

Color-coding your icons

Here's a pretty neat feature that hardly anyone uses but is still worth knowing about: color-coding. All you do is select an icon or a whole passel of them (below, left), and choose a color from a menu. The color choices are hidden in the File menu, as shown here (below, right).

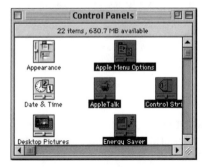
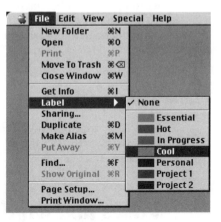

Two questions, then: (1) How do you change the colors and labels into something more useful, and (2) what's the point?

Well, most people never bother with labeling their icons. You could argue, though, that it makes life more convenient since you can use the Find command to search for a file that has a certain label. You might give one label to everything related to, say, a certain book project — *Saddam Hussein: The Sensitive Side* — and then, when it's time to back up your work, use the Find command to round up all files with the Hussein label so you can copy them all at once. (Or, when the project is over, you could happily *delete* them all at once.)

Anyway, if you *do* want to use this feature, you'll probably want to change the labels Apple suggests (Essential, Hot, In Progress, and so on) to something more useful. Here's how: From the Edit menu, choose Preferences. In the window that appears, click the Labels tab. You'll see a list of the label choices, something like this.

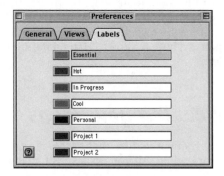

To change the wording of a label (remember that you're actually changing the wording of the Label *menu*), just double-click a label and type something new. To change the color, click the color swatch; a dialog box appears where you can select a new color by clicking.

Window-Mania

Your iMac doesn't run Windows; it runs the Mac OS. But that's ironic, because even though the iMac's operating system software isn't *called* Windows, it's really *good* at doing windows.

Views and window preferences

One famous aspect of the Mac is the degree to which you can tailor it to your tastes. You can make it look user-chummy and kid-friendly, or you can make it look high-tech and intimidating.

For starters, you can change the typeface used to display the names of your icons. If your vision is going — or you're trying to demonstrate the iMac to a crowd — make the font huge. If you want to fit as many icons as possible per square inch, pick a tiny, compact type style.

To adjust this typestyle, open the Control Panels (from your menu); open the one called Appearance. Click the Fonts tab. Now you get three pop-up menus, including one that controls the fonts for your menus and your icons.

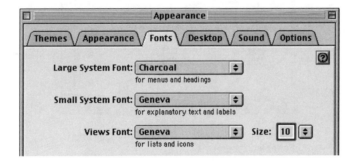

Go wild with these options. A couple of possibilities are shown here.

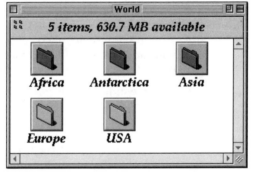

You might notice that the "look" in the second example is strikingly idiot-proof: big bold icons. If you could actually click the page of this book, you'd furthermore discover that *one* click on each of these "button" icons opens it, instead of the usual two.

That window got that way only after judicious tweaking — somebody chose the *as Buttons* command from the View menu.

Meet Mr. Window

Here's a map of a typical iMac window.

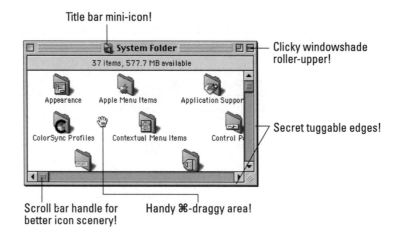

Title bar mini-icon!

Clicky windowshade roller-upper!

Secret tuggable edges!

Scroll bar handle for better icon scenery!

Handy ⌘-draggy area!

Now, since I'm not exactly sure that "Secret tuggable edges" and "Clicky windowshade roller-upper" are the actual official computer terms for these features, let me explain:

✔ **Secret tuggable edges:** In the olden days, you could move a window around the screen only by clicking its striped *title bar*. Today, however, you can actually hold your mouse button down on the thickened edges of each window — and move the window by dragging.

✔ **Clicky windowshade roller-upper:** Click this tiny square in the upper right of any window to make the window itself *disappear* — all except the striped title bar. The effect is like the Cheshire cat in *Alice in Wonderland* disappearing completely except for his smile, except that this is actually *useful*. By judiciously clicking the clicky windowshade roller-uppers, you can hide and unhide a bunch of windows with aplomb, easily burrowing your way around without losing sight of the big picture.

(If you press the Option key as you click this button, you roll up *all* of the windows in the current program — a great technique if you're in a hurry to hide what you're doing. Option-click again to restore them.)

✔ **Scroll bar handle for better icon scenery:** You may remember from Chapter 1 that the little square box inside a scroll bar lets you view what's hidden in a window — what's above or below what you're seeing, for example. (Man, I sure *hope* you remember — otherwise, you've been using your iMac all this time without ever writing a memo taller than three inches.)

But on the iMac, if you drag this handle slowly, you actually *see* the icons moving by, so you're much less likely to overshoot.

- **Handy ⌘-draggy area:** Scroll bars? You don't need no steenkin' scroll bars! You can move around inside a window just by holding down the ⌘ key while dragging anywhere inside. In other words, you can actually shift your view in a window *diagonally* (instead of having to use one scroll bar at a time).

- **Title-bar mini-icon:** See the tiny folder icon in the title bar (in the previous picture)? It's a *handle*. You can use it to drag the open window to another place, such as your backup disk or (in the case of perfectionist computer-book authors) directly to the trash.

- **Rearrangy columns 'n' things:** When you're looking at a window in a list view, you can make the columns of information bigger or smaller by dragging the tiny divider lines, indicated by A in this picture.

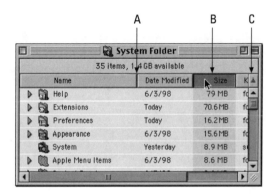

In fact, you can even *rearrange* the columns — putting the Kind column before the Size one, if that suits you — just by dragging the column headings around, such as B in the preceding picture.

Okay, while we're engaged in dead-horse beating, one more thing: You can click the tiny pyramid (marked C) to reverse the sorting order — from Z to A, for example, instead of A to Z.

Now we can all get a good night's sleep.

Poppin' fresh windows

Windows do something else funky, too: They *pop*. If you drag a window to the very bottom of the screen, something bizarre happens.

Drag to the bottom of the screen . . .

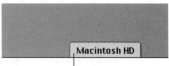

. . . and the window turns into a tab.

Sure enough, your little *window* turns into a *tab*. If you click this tab, the window shoots up like a strawberry Pop-Tart; click the tab on top again, and it crumbles back down into its former tab position. The point of this is that you can turn *several* windows that you use a lot into bottom-feeding tabs, like this.

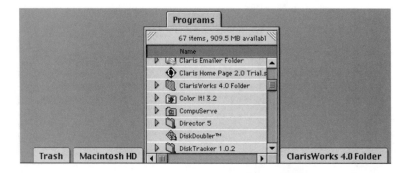

And then you can rapidly switch among them just by clicking tabs. (You don't have to collapse one popped-up windowette before popping up the next — the iMac automatically closes one when you click the next tab.) Try setting up frequently accessed windows this way, such as your Programs, Launcher, and Documents folders.

Oh, by the way: To turn a bottom-hugging tab *back* into a full-fledged window, just tug its tab way high up into the middle of the screen. No problem.

The iMac Keyboard: Not Your Father's Typewriter

If you've never used a computer before, you might be bewildered by the number of keyboard keys. After all, a typewriter has about 50 keys; your iMac has about 100.

Only some of the bizarro extra keys are particularly useful. Here's a list of the oddball extra keys and what they do.

- ✔ **Home:** On a normal computer keyboard, "Home" and "End" are ways of saying "jump to the top or bottom of the window." If you're word processing, the Home and End keys jump to the first word or last word of the file, respectively. If you're looking at a list-view window full of files in the Finder, they jump you to the top or bottom of the list.

  Peculiarly enough, the iMac keyboard doesn't have an End key — only a Home key. If that omission bothers you, visit *www.northcoast.com/ ~jvholder* to download, and install, the little control panel program called KeySwapper. It lets you designate a keystroke of your choice (Shift-Home, for example) to trigger the End key function. God bless software!

- ✔ **Pg Up, Pg Down:** These keys mean "Scroll up or down by one screenful." Once again, the idea is to let you scroll through word-processing documents, Web pages, and lists without having to use the mouse.

- ✔ **NumLock, Clear:** Clear means "get rid of this text I've highlighted, but don't put a copy on the invisible Clipboard, as the Cut command would do." In Microsoft Excel, the NumLock key actually does something obscure, but I'll let you nuzzle up to the manual for that.

- ✔ **Esc:** *Esc* stands for *Escape,* and it actually means "Click the Cancel button," such as the one found in most dialog boxes.

  Wanna try? From the View menu, choose View Options. Then press Esc, and marvel as the box goes away.

- ✔ **Delete:** This is the backspace key, as described in Chapter 3.

  If you're coming to the iMac with experience using Windows PCs, by the way, you may wonder where the Del, or *forward delete,* key went. The iMac doesn't have one. (Maybe that's why it was so inexpensive.) If you pine for that key, KeySwapper (mentioned six paragraphs ago) is once again the solution; it lets you designate a key of your choice to serve as the Forward Delete key.

- ✔ **Return** and **Enter:** In general, these keys do the same thing: wrap your typing to the next line. Be careful, though: Some programs distinguish between the two. In AppleWorks, for example, Return begins a new paragraph, but Enter makes a *page break,* forcing the next typing to begin on a fresh page.

- ✔ **Command (⌘):** This key triggers keyboard shortcuts for menu items, as described in Chapter 2.

- ✔ **Control, Option:** The Control key triggers *contextual menus,* as described in Chapter 2; the Option key lets you type special symbols (see Chapter 9) and access secret features (discussed earlier in this chapter).

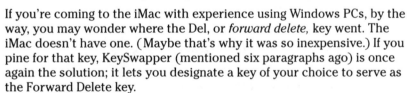

The "Just say no" keystroke

There's a wonderful keyboard shortcut that means no in iMac language. It could mean *No, I changed my mind about printing* (or copying or launching a program); stop right now. It could mean *No, I didn't mean to bring up this dialog box; make it go away.* Or: *No, I don't want to broadcast my personal diary over worldwide e-mail!* Best of all, it can mean *Stop asking for that CD! I've already taken it out! Be gone!*

And that magic keystroke is ⌘-period (.).

When you begin to print your Transcripts of Congress, 1952–2000, and you discover — after only two pages have printed — that you accidentally spelled it "Transcripts of Congrotesque" on every page, ⌘-period will

prevent the remaining 14 million pages from printing. Because the iMac has probably already sent the next couple of pages to the printer, the response won't be immediate — but it will be light-years quicker than waiting for Congress.

Or let's say you double-click an icon by mistake. If you press ⌘-period right away, you can halt the launching and return to the Finder. And if the iMac keeps saying, "Please insert the disk: Purple Puppychow" (or whatever your CD, floppy, or Zip disk was called), you can tell it to shut up by doing that ⌘-period thing over and over again until the iMac settles down with a whimper. Show it who's boss.

✔ **Help:** In most programs, this pint-sized key summons the software's built-in electronic help desk. Press it when you're in the Finder (at the desktop), for example, to make the Mac's Help Center appear. The Help button also works in AppleWorks, Microsoft programs, and most other popular software. (It may not work in lesser-known programs, or programs that don't have electronic help at all.)

Fun with Function keys

The keys across the iMac's top row, called *function keys,* are, shall we say, differently abled. Almost every keyboard has a row of function keys — but they generally don't *do* anything! On most computers, making them do anything useful requires programming them, which usually involves pliers and a couple of trips to Sears. You could write a whole book just about this complicated process. (*Function Keys For Dummies,* anyone?)

I'll do my best to explain their various talents with reassuring warmth. You'd do well, however, to cuddle up with your function keys some rainy Saturday afternoon and explore them yourself.

Older, CD tray-loading iMacs

Your first four function keys, F1 through F4, trigger the Undo, Cut, Copy, and Paste commands, respectively, in your Edit menu. The remaining keys don't do anything. If you feel like buying add-on software like QuicKeys, you can train these keys to launch your favorite programs, print, or whatever you dream up.

Newer, CD slot-loading iMacs

Your function keys are much smarter than on previous models. In about two minutes, you can teach them to launch your favorite programs and documents. You might rig it so that F1 opens AppleWorks; F2 takes you to America Online; and so on. Being able to jump to your favorite programs just by pressing function keys is a *glorious* time-saver.

Here's how to go about it:

1. **From the menu, choose Control Panels. Open the control panel called Keyboard. Click the Function Keys button.**

   This window appears:

2. **Click an F-key button (F1, for example).**

   Now you're shown a list of every file and program on your entire hard drive. You're about to use the navigational skills you absorbed so completely in Chapter 4.

3. **Navigate to the program you'd like this function key to launch, and double-click it.**

   Instead of doing all that, you can also just *drag* the icon of a file or program from your desktop directly onto the white blank that says "Nothing Assigned."

   Either way, the program's name now shows up next to its F-key designation.

4. **Click OK.**

Your newly programmed function key is ready to use! Pressing it opens the associated program or file. And if that program is *already* running, pressing the function key brings it to the front of whatever other programs you're using.

To de-assign a function key (so that pressing it does nothing), open that Keyboard control panel again, and click Function Keys again. Click the name of the program it's supposed to launch, and then click Clear. To associate the key to a different program or file, click the F-key button next to the slot you'd like to change.

When you're finished, click OK.

Multiple Personalities (Mac OS 9)

You can read about the vast, seething blob of software known as *Mac OS 9* in Chapter 17. If you're too weary to flip pages, here's the gist: An OS, or operating system, is the software inside your System Folder that controls your computer. Mac OS 9 is a modern, state-of-the-art new System Folder that adds several new features to your iMac. Original iMacs — those sold in 1998, for example — came with something called Mac OS 8.1, 8.5, or 8.6. You can get Mac OS 9 either by (a) upgrading, as described in Chapter 18, or (b) buying a new iMac after October 1999; these machines come with Mac OS 9 already on board. After all, you can never have too many iMacs.

Anyway, Mac OS 9 offers two dramatic improvements over its predecessor: Sherlock 2, described in Chapter 7, and the Multiple Users control panel. If you're the only one who uses your iMac, feel free to daydream during the following pages; the Multiple Users thing is exclusively for situations where several people might use the same iMac, such as in classrooms, families, or monasteries.

The big idea

The Multiple Users feature works like this: When you turn on the iMac, you see a list of everyone who uses the machine, like this:

Using the mouse, you click your own name. (If the system has been set up to require a password, you must enter it correctly before proceeding.) And now the iMac's ready to use — except that only *your* folders, programs, and documents show up on the screen. The stuff that belongs to the other students/children/monks is hidden from your eyes.

In every multiple-user setup, one person is the owner and administrator of the iMac master — for example, the teacher, parent, or monsignor. This person sees *all* the files and folders, as befits his or her exalted status. This is also the person who sets up the Multiple Users feature to begin with. In the following discussion, let's pretend that the master is *you*.

Setting up Multiple Users

Suppose three other people in your monastery share your iMac: the easily overwhelmed Brother Brian; Harold, the seven-year-old altar boy; and Giuseppe, the cybermonk who manages the group's Web site. Suppose you want to set up the iMac so that each person gets a perfect setup. Here's how you'd do it:

1. **From the menu, choose Control Panels. Open the control panel called Multiple Users.**

   A dialog box like this appears:

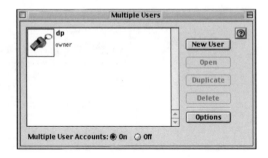

2. **Click New User.**

   Now this box appears:

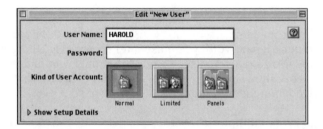

3. **Type** *Harold.* **(If you want to require a password before Harold can use the iMac, type a password into the appropriate blank, too.) Specify how much of the iMac world you want Harold to see by clicking Normal, Limited, or Panels.**

   This is a biggie. Not only can you specify which files and programs Brian, Harold, and Giuseppe can use, but you can also simplify their worlds. For Brother Giuseppe, the expert, you'll probably want to choose Normal mode, in which the iMac environment looks exactly as you see it every day, except that he can't change any of the Multiple User options, as you're doing now.

   For Brother Brian, you might prefer the Limited choice. Brian probably won't notice much difference between his world and the Normal one — except that no control panels show up in his menu. Furthermore, two folders show up on his desktop, one containing his documents and the other containing the *programs* he's allowed to use. (You'll specify these programs in Step 5.) This arrangement makes it easy for him to find his own files.

   For little altar boy Harold, on the other hand, you'll probably want the Panels option. When Harold turns on the iMac, he'll see nothing but two big windows — one containing his documents, the other his programs. It looks like this — his chosen programs listed in the left window, the documents he's created in the right:

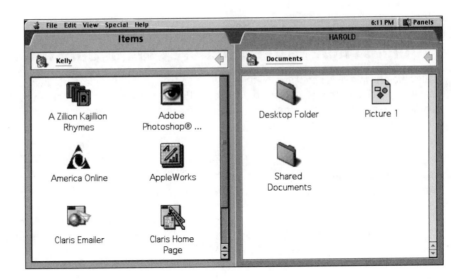

4. **Click the tiny triangle called Show User Details.**

   The window expands to reveal an army of additional options. If you click the User Info tab, for example, you can choose a small picture that will appear next to Harold's name on the sign-on screen. For help comprehending all these other options, use the built-in help screens (which appear when you click the question-mark symbol in the upper-right corner of the window).

   Now it's time to specify which programs little Harold will be permitted to use.

5. **Click the Applications tab. From the list of programs that appears, turn on the checkboxes of those you want available for the person whose account you're setting up.**

   If you think about it, this ability to include only Harold-appropriate programs can be a real blessing. He doesn't have to wade through a bunch of software he doesn't use, and your stuff is protected from accidental seven-year-old meddling.

6. **Close the window.**

   You return to the Users list. To create a similar setup for Brother Brian, click New User, and then start over from Step 3. (In Step 3, you'll probably want the Limited option.)

7. **Turn on the entire Multiple Users feature by clicking the On button at the bottom of the window.**

   (If Harold, Giuseppe, and Brother Brian go off on an evangelistic mission somewhere, by the way, you can turn off the entire Multiple Users apparatus by clicking the Off button here. When they return, you can turn the feature back on again; your settings and setup will be restored.)

Simple Finder: An easier way to simplify the iMac

All of the Multiple Users stuff is a useful way of setting up an iMac for a kid, student, or technophobe doesn't want to have, or shouldn't have, full access to all aspects of your iMac.

If that someone is *you,* however, there's an easier way to make the iMac easier. This option provides a streamlined, simpler Finder, where the menus are shortened to bare technophobe-friendly essentials, like Empty Trash and Shut Down. (Some of the missing commands: Make Alias, Close Window, Labels, Sleep, Get Info, and so on. Their keyboard equivalents, such as pressing ⌘-W to close a window, don't work, either.)

To try out this Simple Mac view, choose the Preferences command from the Edit menu; in the dialog box that appears, turn on Simple Finder. (Turn it off again the same way.) Even though the Sleep command is missing from the Special menu, you can still put the iMac to sleep just by closing it.

Once you've entered Simple Finder mode, please don't forget that you've done so. Because many standard iMac commands are hidden from the menus in Simple Finder mode, you won't be able to follow many of the lessons in this book when in Simple Finder.

Put another way, sometimes Simple Finder isn't so simple after all.

Using the Multiple Users feature

At last, you're ready to roll. From now on, whenever you turn on or wake up the iMac, you'll see the list of people with whom you share this iMac. Double-click your own name; type in your password, if you set one up in Step 3; and you're in your private, pre-established world.

People to whom you've turned on the Limited or Panels options will frequently encounter a message that mutters something about not having enough *access privileges.* For example, Brother Brian will get that whenever he tries to open a program that wasn't one of the ones you checked in Step 5. And little Harold will find that he can't save new documents he creates anywhere except in the Harold folder on the desktop. And *everyone* will see only his own files — even people to whom you've given Normal access — except you, the master. You see every file on the computer. The power — the *power!*

When you're finished working, by the way, don't shut the machine down; instead, mouse your way up to the Special menu and choose Log Off. The list of iMac-sharers returns, and the cycle begins anew!

Chapter 14

USB, Ethernet, AirPort, and Other Impressive Connections

In This Chapter

▶ Connecting your iMac to one other computer using Ethernet

▶ Plugging in add-on USB gadgetry

▶ Connecting your iMac to other Macs using a wireless AirPort Card

*T*he iMac doesn't have a floppy drive built in. But if the object of using floppy disks is to transfer files from your iMac to another computer, the lack of floppy drive is no big deal. The iMac can connect to other machines in several different ways:

✔ By attaching a file to an e-mail message, as described in Chapter 8.

✔ By sending files through the air, using the AirPort radio transmitter.

✔ By attaching a disk drive (such as a Zip drive, SuperDisk drive, or external hard drive) to the iMac's USB connectors.

✔ By connecting your iMac and another computer using an Ethernet cable.

This chapter shows you how to make connections using the last three methods.

USB Nimble, USB Quick

The 150 Macintosh models that came before 1998 had all different kinds of connectors: a printer jack, a modem port, a SCSI connector, an ADB port, and so on. They had all different shapes, and required all different cables. You were supposed to know what these jacks were for, what cable to use, what to plug into each one, and *when* to plug things in (that is, only when the computer is turned off, to avoid damage). Life was complicated — even more so than usual.

In the place of all those connectors, the iMac offers *one* kind of jack — called USB. (USB stands for Universal Serial Bus, but that won't be on the exam.) When compared to the older-style Macintosh jacks, USB offers a million advantages:

✔ You can safely plug and unplug USB gadgets from your iMac without turning off the computer first. (If you try that on a regular Mac's keyboard or SCSI jacks, the resulting electrical damage could turn your $3,000 computer into a $3 garage-sale item.)

✔ You don't have to know which jack gets which kind of gadget (printers, floppy drives, modems, joysticks, scanners, speakers, digital cameras, keyboards, microphones, mice, and so on). On the iMac, they *all* go into your USB jacks. (OK, only one at a time — but see "Attaching more USB doodads" in the next section.)

✔ Many USB gadgets draw power from the iMac itself, sparing you the ugliness and hassle of power cords and plugs for all your external equipment.

For a sampling of USB-ready gadgets, see Appendix C.

Where's the USB?

Your iMac actually has several USB jacks. Two are on the side of the computer. (On older iMac models, they lurk behind a plastic door.) Two more are on your keyboard itself. Each is marked by a three-pronged tree symbol (see Appendix A).

Of course, you're supposed to plug the *keyboard* into one of the iMac's USB jacks, and the *mouse* into one end of the keyboard. That leaves two free USB jacks for your choice of other appliances — one on the side of the iMac and the other at the free end of the keyboard.

Installing a new USB doodad

Like most computer add-ons, many USB gadgets come with special software to place on the iMac itself. You'll find this software, if it's necessary, on a CD that came with the USB gadget. Just insert the CD and look for an icon called Installer; double-click the icon and follow whatever instructions appear.

After you've installed the software, connect your gadget to the USB jack on the iMac. If the circuitry gods are smiling, your USB device should now work as advertised.

How to plug older Macintosh equipment into your iMac

The question always comes up: "I've got a favorite keyboard/mouse/printer/digital camera that's designed for a pre-USB Macintosh. How do I plug it into my iMac?"

Easy: By using USB *adapters,* little connectors that translate between the Macintosh gadgets you already own and the iMac's USB connectors. Appendix C lists a bunch of these.

Someday, however, no adapters will be necessary. All Mac models now include USB jacks, and therefore every kind of add-on gadget alive will eventually be available in a USB version.

Attaching more USB doodads

You may find only one problem with your USB connectors: After you hook up your keyboard and mouse, you've got only two USB jacks left. Maybe you've plugged in your printer and scanner — great — but now where are you supposed to plug your digital camera?

Easy: buy an adapter box that gives you more USB jacks. Those so-called *USB hubs* multiply your USB jack so that you wind up with four, eight, or even more jacks. Connect enough of these hubs to one another, in fact, and you can have up to 127 USB gadgets connected to your iMac all at once. (There's no need to fiddle with ID numbers, termination plugs, or cable flakiness, as there is with SCSI. And if you have no clue what those things are, thank your favorite deity — you missed a very unpleasant era.)

Appendix C lists a few of those hubs, along with their prices and photos.

Ethernet Made Eathy

Ethernet, a special kind of computer-to-computer connection, is fast, easy, and fun to pronounce. It lets you copy files between your iMac and another Mac just by dragging the files' icons, which comes in handy when you want to make backup copies, distribute your work to a co-worker, or copy files from your iMac to a desktop Mac.

Before you read on, grasp this: It's very, very easy to connect your iMac directly to another computer, requiring only a single $8 cable. It's much, much more complicated to set up an entire *network* of Macs in an office, requiring a $50 adapter box *and* a bunch of cables.

Nonetheless, you paid good money for this book (or visited a good library). I won't let you down. I'll lead you by the brain, step by step, through both scenarios.

Connecting to one other Mac

To connect your iMac to one other Mac (or even another iMac), you need an *Ethernet crossover* cable. (It's not the same as a regular Ethernet cable.) You can get such a cable for $10 or less at computer stores like CompUSA or from a mail-order joint such as Global Computer Supplies, at 310-635-8144.

Step 1: Get the cable

Plug your Ethernet crossover cable into each computer's Ethernet jack. That's the hole on the right side of your iMac that looks like an overweight telephone jack.

Step 2: Set up the iBook software

Next, turn your attention to the software on the Macs involved. The Mac's networking software is amazingly sophisticated. You could spend days setting up passwords, different degrees of access to different folders on each Mac, and so on — and many professionals do.

But if you're the only person who uses your iMac, all that rigmarole is overkill. If you have two Macs — an iMac and an iBook laptop, let's say — then you're probably more interested in some fast-and-easy system of transferring files between them.

For clarity, let's pretend that you're seated at an iMac and want to bring the *iBook's* icon onto the screen. (You could just as easily reverse the procedure.) Fortunately, you have to go through all of the following steps only one time! Thereafter, you'll be able to connect the computers with a quick double-click.

Follow these steps on the iBook:

1. **Open the AppleTalk control panel (from the Control Panels item in your menu), choose Ethernet from the pop-up menu, close the window, and save changes.**

   You may be asked if you want AppleTalk turned on; you do.

2. **Open the File Sharing control panel and, in the Owner Name and Computer Name blanks, type your name and a name for the iBook.**

   If you're the only one who uses this iBook, use a short, easy-to-type name for yourself, such as your initials or "me." (Leave the password blank for this security-free scenario.)

3. **Click the upper Start button, close the window, and save your changes; when you're warned that you haven't specified a password, just click OK and get on with your life.**

Step 3: Set up the iMac

Your iBook is ready for action. Here's how you bring its icon onto the iMac's screen (follow these steps on the *iMac:*)

1. **Open the AppleTalk control panel; make sure Ethernet is selected in the pop-up menu; close and save.**

   Again, let the machine turn on AppleTalk if it proposes doing so.

2. **Open the File Sharing control panel; type the *same* name that you used in Step 2 of "Set up the iBook software;" close the window, clicking OK if you're warned about the lack of password.**

3. **From the menu, choose Network Browser. In the window that appears (below, left), double-click the name of your iBook. Click Connect in the next dialog box (below, right).**

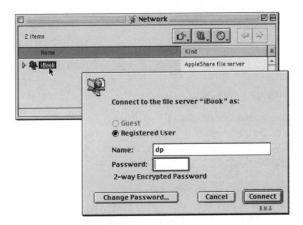

The iBook's hard-drive icon now appears in the Network Browser window. Double-click it to open the iBook's window — even though you're seated at a different computer!

You can use the iBook's contents as usual. To copy a folder, for example, just drag it from the iBook window into an iMac window, or vice versa.

To save time the next time, make an alias of the iBook drive icon, which is now on your iMac's screen. (See Chapter 13 for details on making aliases.) The *next* time you want to hook up, you won't have to bother with *any* of the steps you've just read. Instead, just double-click the alias you just made and click OK. The iBook's hard drive icon pops onto your screen.

Oh, and one more thing: If your machines aren't both turned on and connected by the Ethernet cable, you may see a mysterious message at startup. Just click OK; if necessary, restart one or both computers. (Next time the Macs are connected and turned on, no message will appear.)

Creating a real, live, full-office Ethernet network

You've been warned: The following setup isn't simple or inexpensive. It's not technically difficult, but you'll do a lot of muttering about the *number* of steps.

Suppose you have an iMac, an iBook, a Power Macintosh, and a laser printer — not to mention an office in which you'd like to wire all of this equipment together. Visit your local computer store (or computer-stuff Web site, such as those listed in Appendix B) and buy an *Ethernet hub,* which will set you back about $50, depending on the number of jacks it offers. (Ethernet hubs usually offer between 4 and 24 jacks, or *ports.* You need one port for every gadget you hope to connect.)

Also buy enough Ethernet (or "10BaseT," or "100BaseT") *cables,* in long enough lengths, to connect all your Macs and printers to the hub.

Big Step 1: Wire your office

Most people try to hide the hub and its ugly mass of wires by stashing it in a closet. Some even hire an electrician to snake the Ethernet cables through the walls, once again attempting to save themselves from the techno-ugliness of exposed wires.

When the dust settles, however, every computer and laser printer should be plugged directly into your hub box. The hub is the octopus body; the wires are its arms; your computers are its fingertips. (Don't plug any computer directly into any other machine.)

Big Step 2: Give each computer an identity

Sit down in front of one computer. Turn it on. Follow these setup steps:

1. **Open the AppleTalk control panel, choose Ethernet from the pop-up menu, close the window, and save changes.**

   You may be asked if you want AppleTalk turned on; you do.

2. **Open the control panel called Users & Groups. For each person who works in your office, click New User; type that person's name and chosen password; and close the New User window.**

If you're not worried about security — that is, if it's OK for everyone on the network to see what's on everyone else's computer — don't bother with that second part. Instead, just double-click the icon called Guest; from the Show pop-up menu, choose Sharing; and turn on the option called "Allow Guests to connect."

3. **Open the File Sharing control panel. In the Owner Name blank, type the name of the person who uses this computer. Also fill in the Password and Computer Name blanks. Click the upper Start button, close, and save.**

   The name and password should match what you typed in Step 2 for this computer. In other words, if this is the computer that Jesse Ventura will use, type that name exactly, and the same password you created for Jesse in Step 2.

4. **Highlight your hard drive icon (Macintosh HD). Click the File menu, slide down onto Get Info, and then click Sharing. Turn on the "Share this item and its contents" checkbox; close the window; click OK to save the changes.**

   Rather than making your *entire* hard drive available to other people on the network, you could instead begin this step by highlighting only one *folder*. Thereafter, your office mates would be able to access, over the network, only what's in the folder.

5. **Repeat Steps 1, 2, 3, and 4 for every computer.**

Now you're set up. Rent a video; you've earned it.

Big Step 3: Connect

The setup is complete! Now you're ready to try the network you've created.

1. **Invite your coworkers in to see your handiwork.**

   If it's just you, skip this step.

2. **From the menu, choose Network Browser.**

   If you've properly prayed to the Ethernet gods, the names of your other computers now show up in the list.

3. **Double-click the name of the computer to which you want to connect.**

   A window appears in which you're supposed to identify yourself.

4. **Click Guest, if that button is available. If not, type your name and password, as you've previously established them. Click OK.**

   The hard-drive icon of the computer you selected (or folder icon, if that's what you highlighted in Step 4 of Big Step 2) now appears in the Network Browser window. Double-click to open it and play with the files inside as usual.

You've made it through alive! If you had hired a consultant to set up your network, you'd have paid several hundred dollars.

As a reward, you're now free to enjoy any of the following activities:

- ✔ Open the distant computer's hard drive icon; you can open, trash, copy, rename, or reorganize the files of that computer, even though it's down the hall or across the room.

- ✔ Make an alias of that distant computer's hard drive icon, as described in Chapter 13. Put the alias on your desktop somewhere. Next time you want to access its contents, just double-click the alias, saving you several of the steps above.

- ✔ Shut down the computers, cancel your subscriptions, and move to an Amish community.

Wireless Networking: Your Ride to the AirPort

You young kids today — you don't know how lucky you are! Why, when I was your age, I used to have to dial the Internet by plugging a piece of *telephone wire* into the wall!

As you may have heard, however, the newer, CD slot-loading iMac models are considerably less restricted. Embedded in the plastic frame around the screen is a built-in *radio transmitter antenna* that gives these iMacs their wireless smarts. Using these antennas, you can perform any of these stunts:

- ✔ Surf the Internet without any wires attached to your computer. You can position the iMac even in a room with no telephone jack — as long as you're within 150 feet of one. This trick is especially useful if you're lucky enough to have had a *cable modem* or *DSL connection* (pricey, high-speed Internet cables) installed at your house. Now you can use the iMac anywhere in the house, even if it's not particularly near the cable modem or DSL cable.

- ✔ Play multiplayer Macintosh games with other AirPort-equipped Mac owners — without having to physically connect them.

- ✔ Copy files between your iMac and other Macs — again, without any wires.

- ✔ Let several other AirPort-equipped Macs surf the Internet simultaneously — over the single phone line that's plugged into your iMac.

All of these miraculous features come courtesy of an Apple gizmo called an *AirPort Card.* Once it's set up, this technology is simple to use. With time and patience, however, wirelessness shall be yours.

Installing an AirPort Card

Your iMac can't do *any* of those wireless stunts without an AirPort Card, which costs $100. An AirPort Card looks like a Visa card made of sheet metal. You can buy it from an Apple dealer, from the Apple Web site (*www.apple.com*), or from any of the mail-order joints listed in Appendix B. Once you have it in hand, you install it by opening the door on the belly of the iMac; turn the thumbscrew with a coin to do so. Then slip the card onto its card adapter and then into the slot, as shown in the illustrated instructions. Next, install the software that came on the AirPort CD-ROM — and get ready for the fun.

Going Online with a base station

The best-publicized benefit of installing an AirPort Card is that wireless Internet business. You cruise the Web and send e-mail — without being connected to anything. All the while, a tiny receiver somewhere else in your house does the actual dialing.

The name of that receiver is the *AirPort Base Station,* and it'll set you back another $300. The base station looks exactly like a shiny, chrome, six-inch flying saucer:

Instead of tiny aliens, however, the base station contains a built-in modem. Using a piece of telephone wire, connect the modem jack (not the Ethernet jack, which is slightly larger) on the base station to a telephone jack on the wall. Your iMac can then communicate with a base station from up to 150 feet away, even through walls and floors. (If you have a cable modem or DSL connection, plug it into the base station's Ethernet jack instead.)

Suppose your iMac is in the TV room, for example, and you launch your Web browser. Your base station, upstairs in your office, silently begins to dial. Now your iMac is on the Internet, fully connected at full speed, without actually being connected by wires to anything.

Note to teachers and small businesses: A single base station can accommodate *ten or more* AirPort-equipped Macs (iBook laptops, for example), all surfing the Web simultaneously. Just keep in mind that the more Macs are online simultaneously, the more slowdown you'll begin to notice.

Setting up your base station

The key to preparing a base station is the program called AirPort Setup Assistant. It's on your hard drive, in the Assistants folder. Run this program. One screen at a time, it will ask you for the answers it needs for the setup; for example, you'll be asked to give your base station a name and password.

Most people name the base station for its location: "Upstairs Base Station," or "Mr. Mullen's Math Class." As for the password, you'll have to type this password every single time you connect wirelessly to your base station. If that sounds like a drag, you can leave the password blank. (If you do so, however, there's a remote possibility that your next-door neighbor will be able to get onto the Internet using *your* base station. This scenario assumes that you live in a *very* tightly packed neighborhood, that your neighbor owns an iMac, and that he's smart enough to try logging onto your base station without a password.)

When it's all over, you'll have successfully configured your base station.

Connecting, and disconnecting, from the Internet

Haul your iMac over to some table from which you've never before surfed the Internet. Go online like this:

1. **From the AirPort tile of your Control Strip, choose the name of the base station with which you'd like to connect.**

   Most people have only one base station, so you'll see only one listed, like this:

2. **When the password box appears, type your password and then press the Return key.**

   If you didn't set up your base station to require a password, you won't be asked for one.

3. **Launch your favorite Internet program: Internet Explorer (for the Web) or Outlook Express (for e-mail) or whatever.**

   As soon as you try to connect, your base station dials the number. (The base station has no speaker, so you're spared the usual screeching, hissing, and so on. The outer two lights on the base station blink instead.) Once the connection is complete, you should notice no difference between Web surfing wirelessly and surfing . . . wirefully.

While you're connected, you can check the strength of your radio signal to the base station — either in the AirPort application in your Apple menu, or using the AirPort tile of your Control Strip. The five dots show you your signal strength. The farther away you go from your base station, the weaker the signal, and the slower your Internet surfing speed gets.

As advertised, the radio signal sent between the base station and your laptop isn't fazed by walls — much. Glass, paper, and wood are invisible to the signal, but concrete walls slow it down substantially. Solid metal is almost impenetrable, much to the disappointment of iMac fans on elevators, subway trains, and meat lockers.

When you're finished with your online session, you should probably hang up the base station, so that the phone line becomes available again for things like normal phone calls. You can hang up the base station in either of two ways:

✔ From the menu, choose AirPort. In the window that appears, Hang Up AirPort Base Station.

✔ Wait. After 10 minutes of your not doing anything, your base station hangs up automatically.

Using your iMac as a base station

You don't necessarily need to buy an AirPort base station to enjoy wireless Net surfing (although it's a very cool-looking gadget to have on your desk). Strange as this may sound, you can use your iMac *as* a base station for other Macs, such as iBook laptops. In other words, your iMac can remain tethered to the phone jack in your office to do the actual dialing, pretending to be a base station. You can then prance through the house with your iBook, merrily Web surfing.

If this arrangement appeals to you, run that AirPort Setup Assistant program on your iMac. (It's in your Assistants folder on your hard drive.) This time, however, select the Software Base Station option (if your version of the software offers it; the very first version didn't). Once again, you'll be asked to set up a name and password for this wireless network — a password you'll have to type each time you hook into this machine's invisible Internet connection.

When you reach the end of the series of Assistant screens, you're ready to begin. Pick up the iBook. Open the Control Strip. From the AirPort tile, choose the name you gave your deskbound computer, type the password, and then launch your e-mail or Web programs. The tethered iMac acts as the home base, doing all the dialing.

Communicating Mac-to-Mac

Web browsing and e-mail-sending aren't the only things your built-in antennae are good for. Without buying a base station, two iMacs can communicate with each *other* through the air. (Actually, any two AirPort-equipped Macs can do this: iMac, iMac, Power Mac G4, whatever have you.)

This arrangement makes two exciting features possible: first, you can transfer files back and forth among AirPort-equipped iMacs. Second, you can play games against your friends — a feat you'd ordinarily have to be connected (by network cables) to accomplish.

As it turns out, creating a wireless network between AirPortted computers is *exactly* like creating an Ethernet network, which is described earlier in this chapter (see "Ethernet Made Eathy"). There you'll discover how to set up a network in either of two ways.

The easy way, using just two computers

In this scenario, you own both computers, and don't care about security, because you're the only person with access to these machines. The instructions for creating a wireless connection between the two are almost exactly like those in "Ethernet Made Eathy." You'll make only a couple of changes to the steps listed there, like this:

1. **After installing the AirPort software on both computers, follow Steps 2, 3, and 5 of "Connecting to one other Mac" earlier in this chapter.**

   In other words, skip the two visits to the AppleTalk control panel.

2. **Open your Control Strip. From the AirPort tile, choose Computer to Computer.**

3. **Finish up with Step 6 of "Connecting to one other Mac."**

   The other computer's hard-drive icon now appears in the Network Browser window. Double-click it to see its contents, which you can now copy, delete, rearrange, or otherwise manipulate.

The full-scale, multiple-computer wireless network

Exactly as described in "Creating a real, live, full-office Ethernet network" earlier in this chapter, iMacs and other AirPort-equipped Macs can be connected more elaborately in classrooms, companies, and other multiple-computer situations.

1. **Install the AirPort software on each computer. Follow Steps 2, 3, and 4 of "Creating a real, live, full-office Ethernet network." Repeat for every computer.**

2. **Open your Control Strip. From the AirPort tile, choose Computer to Computer.**

3. **Finish up with Steps 7, 8, and 9 of "Creating a real, live, full-office Ethernet network."**

Once all of this is over, and you've had a good night's sleep, you'll be able to open the Network Browser program to see the names of all other AirPort-equipped computers within range (about 150 feet). You'll be able to bring the hard-drive icons of those other computers onto your own desktop, exactly as though they're CD-ROMs you've inserted into your own iMac, and play with their contents. Without stringing up a single wire. And Dick Tracy thought his video-phone watch was cool?

America Online vs. AirPort

Officially, you can't connect to America Online via your AirPort Card. AOL's special dialing software doesn't use the iMac's standard dialing system.

You can do so, however, if you *also* sign up for a standard Internet account through an ISP company like EarthLink (see Chapter 6). Make sure your iMac can connect to the Internet that way, and then set up your base station as described earlier in this chapter.

Now launch your America Online software. On the Welcome screen, click Setup; click the "Set up AOL to sign on from a new location" button; click Next; type a name like "AirPort connection"; click Next; click "Add a TCP connection"; click Next; and click OK. From now on, when you try to connect to America Online, you'll connect *via* your Internet account. Behind the scenes, your iMac actually dials your Internet company's local access phone number instead of

AOL's. As a result, you can now use your AirPort to connect to America Online.

Actually, once you've set this up, you can enjoy two more differences. First, you'll virtually never get busy signals, because behind the scenes, you're no longer dialing America Online directly. Second, you're entitled to a *huge* discount on America Online service. The company is so thrilled to have you connecting via somebody else's local access numbers that it's willing to cut your AOL bill from $22 per month down to $10 for unlimited service.

To receive the discounted rate, connect to America Online, use keyword *Billing,* and click "Change Your Billing Method." Specify the BYOA (Bring Your Own Access) plan, which is $10 per month.

That tip was worth this book's price right there, don't you think?

Part V
Troubleshooting Made Tolerable

The 5th Wave — By Rich Tennant

"Brad! That's not your modem we're hearing! It's Buddy!! He's out of his cage and in the iMac!!"

In this part . . .

Now it's time to take the bull by the horns, the sword by the hilt, the fish by the gills, and really take off. I bestow unto you the Mother of All Troubleshooting Guides, and then you'll find out where to go from there, with your trusty iMac ever by your side.

Chapter 15

When Bad Things Happen to Good iMacs

Introduction to Computer Hell

As a new computer owner, you probably aren't cheered up very much by the fact that this troubleshooting guide is one of the fattest parts of the book.

But let's face it: Computers are appliances. As such, they have minds of their own. And like other expensive appliances (cars, homes, pacemakers), they tend to get cranky at the worst possible times.

Now, when that happens, most beginners immediately suspect the circuitry. I understand the instinct. I mean, when VCRs, lawnmowers, or electric razors go on the fritz, you're right — you need a repair shop. But a computer's different; it has *software*. When your iMac starts behaving oddly, it's probably a software problem, not a mechanical one. That means that you can fix it yourself, for free. Almost always.

This chapter and the next show the steps you can take to restore your iMac's software to health. (By the way: Another excellent, if terse, source of troubleshooting information is the handbook that came with your iMac.)

About the cookbook

It turns out that about 90 percent of the things that go wrong with your iMac can be solved using the same handful of troubleshooting steps. To save you reading and me writing, I've consolidated them all into Chapter 16. As you read through this chapter's symptom-by-symptom listings, I'll refer you to one or another of those steps.

The iMac Freezes or Crashes

Two scary conditions are enough to make even pro iMac jockeys swallow hard. The first of these conditions, a *System crash,* occurs when the following message appears on the screen.

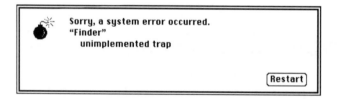

Your current work session is over, amigo; you need to restart the computer. (Safest way to restart is to use "The Restart Button," as described in the next chapter.) Anything that you've typed or drawn since the last time you saved your work is gone.

A System *freeze* is different — and, as horrific computer nightmares go, it's preferable. You get no message on the screen; instead, the mouse cursor freezes in place. You can't move the cursor, and nothing that you type changes anything. The iMac, as far as you can tell, has silicon lockjaw.

Escaping a System freeze right now

First resort: Try the amazing "Force Quit" keystroke. (See the section "The Amazing 'Force Quit' Keystroke," in the next chapter.) That should get you out of the locked program, at least.

Last resort: If the Magical Force-Quit Keystroke doesn't work — and sometimes it doesn't — you have to restart the iMac. This time, see "The Restart Button," in the next chapter.

The Amazing Self-Repairing iMac

A system crash on an iMac running Mac OS 8.5 or later (see Chapter 1) is just as emotionally wounding as it is on any computer. Yet the feeling doesn't last, thanks to what comes next. As soon as your computer starts up again after the crash, it gets to work *repairing itself*.

You'll see a big dialog box on the screen and a progress bar showing how long the self-surgery will take. In brief, your iMac is checking out its own hard drive to make sure nothing was damaged during the system crash. If it finds anything wrong, the iMac fixes it automatically. Since this is all taking place immediately following the crash, newborn problems get nipped in the bud, before they can grow up to be big, strong, meat-eating problems.

You *can* turn off this feature, if you like; open your General Controls control panel (see Chapter 12) and click to turn off the check box called "Warn me if computer was shut down improperly."

But don't.

Escaping repeated System freezes

Ninety percent of the time, freezes and crashes are related either to memory or to *extension conflicts*.

First resort: Increase the amount of memory allotted to the program that you were using, as described in the section "Giving More Memory to a Program," in the next chapter. Give the program 10 percent more, for example.

Second resort: Something, or *several* somethings, are clashing in your System Folder. See "Solving an Extension Conflict" in the next chapter. If you're in a hurry to get your work done and can't take the time, just restart your iMac while pressing the Shift key. That turns *all* extensions off. For this work session, of course, you won't be able to use your CD-ROM drive, send faxes, use America Online or the Internet, or use Microsoft programs, but at least you can get into your iMac and do basic stuff without the hassle of system crashes.

Third resort: Maybe one of your programs is either (a) buggy or (b) out-of-date. You can't do anything but contact the software company and hope for the best.

Last resort: If the crashes still haven't stopped, something in your System Folder may be gummed up. You're in for a 20-minute, but *very* effective, ritual known as a *clean reinstall* of your System Folder. For instructions, see the section "Performing a Clean System Reinstall," in the next chapter.

Problems in One Program

If your troubles seem to be confined to just one application, your troubleshooting task is much easier.

First resort: Give the program more memory, as described the section "Giving More Memory to a Program," in Chapter 16.

Second resort: First, some technical background: Whenever you launch a modern software program, it generally consults the *preferences file* in your Preferences folder. This preference file is where the program stores its little notes to itself about the way you like things set up: where you keep your toolbars on the screen (if it's Microsoft Word), what your favorite Web sites are (if it's Netscape Navigator or Internet Explorer), whether your prefer list views or icon views (if it's the Finder), and so on. If that file is damaged, so is your work session.

Now, what do we do when our government's malfunctioning? We throw out the components that aren't working and elect new ones. That's exactly the idea here: Open your System Folder, open your Preferences folder, and trash the program's preferences file. The very next time you launch that program, it will automatically create a new preferences file. Best of all — and here's where my political analogy breaks down — your new preference file is guaranteed to be uncorrupted.

This trick is especially useful in that most frequently used program of all, the Finder. The Finder Prefs file stores all kinds of settings important to your iMac work environment: the font and icon-layout settings used for Finder windows; window settings; whether or not the "Are you sure?" message appears when you empty the Trash; and so on.

Therefore, if you start noticing weird goings-on with your icons, windows, or Trash, try discarding the Finder Preferences file. Restart the iMac to generate a fresh, clean copy.

Last resort: If all else fails, try reinstalling the program in question — an updated version, if possible.

It's also conceivable that one of your extensions or control panels is causing trouble for this program. See "Solving an Extension Conflict" in the next chapter.

Error Messages

Let's start the troubleshooting session in earnest with a few good old American error messages. Yes, kids, these are the '90s equivalent of "DOES NOT COMPUTE." These are messages, appearing in an *alert box* like the fictional one shown here, that indicate that something's wrong.

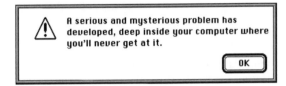

> ⚠ A serious and mysterious problem has developed, deep inside your computer where you'll never get at it.
>
> [OK]

"Application not found"

First resort: Not everything on the iMac is meant to be a plaything for you; the iMac reserves a few files for its own use. Certain items, especially in your System Folder, give you the "Application not found" message if double-clicked because they're there for your iMac's use, not for yours — such as icons in the Preferences folder, for example, or various other support-file icons for non-Apple stuff.

Second resort: In Chapter 3, you can read about programs and the documents that they produce (like parents and children). Sometimes, the "Application not found" message means that you're trying to open a document (child), but the iMac can't find its parent (the program used to create it).

So if you double-click an AppleWorks document, but the AppleWorks program itself isn't on your hard disk, the iMac shrugs and asks, in effect, "Yo — how am I s'posed to open this?" To remedy the situation, reinstall the missing program on the hard disk.

More often, though, you're double-clicking something you downloaded from the Internet or America Online — something created by *someone else,* using a program you don't have. For example, let's say I send you a word processor file, but you don't have the same word processor program I do.

To read such files, launch *your* word processor *first* and then choose the Open command from the File menu (next figure, left).

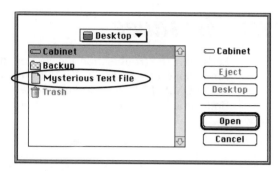

The usual list box appears, and you'll see the text file listed there (above, right). Double-click to open it.

The same applies to generic *graphics* documents. These files, in technical-sounding formats like PICT, JPEG, and GIF, can be opened by almost any program. (America Online or Netscape Navigator, for example, can open all three.) Yet if you try to *double-click* a generic graphics file, you'll be told, "Application not found." (That's because graphics files can be opened by *so many* different programs that the iMac doesn't know which one you want to use.) Again, the solution is to launch your graphics program *first* (America Online or Netscape Navigator or ClarisWorks or Photoshop, for example) and *then* open the file via the Open command.

Third resort: Are you, by chance, trying to open a file that you received via America Online e-mail — from somebody *not* on America Online? In that case, you may be out of luck. AOL has this unfortunate habit of garbling e-mail attachments that originate from the Internet itself. (See Chapter 8 for more on e-mail, and the end of Chapter 6 for more on opening downloaded goodies.)

Last resort: Sometimes you get the "Application not found" message even if you're sure that the document's parent program *is* on the disk. (You double-click an AppleWorks document, for example, and you're told that the application — AppleWorks — can't be found, even though it's *sitting right there* on the disk in plain sight!)

In a situation like this, the iMac's genealogical gnomes have become confused: The computer has lost track of which program is associated with which kinds of documents. In the words of Mac gurus everywhere, "You gotta rebuild the desktop." For instructions, see the "Rebuilding the Desktop File" in the next chapter.

The only virus worth worrying about

There are plenty of reasons to be glad you use a Macintosh. Consider computer viruses (software written by some sociopath to gum up the works of any computer it encounters): while 10,000 different computer viruses attack Windows-compatible computers, until 1998, there was not a *single virus* that could destroy Macintosh files.

Nowadays, there is one Mac virus — called AutoStart. If your iMac "catches" this virus, you'll notice three odd symptoms: first, the iMac restarts itself just after you insert a disk of some kind. (That's your iMac coming down with the virus.) Second, your hard drive starts thrashing and making noise about every half hour. Third, some of the files on your hard drive may become corrupted and un-openable.

Fortunately, it's easy to protect your iMac against this virus: From the   menu, choose Control Panels and open the control panel called QuickTime Settings. Turn off the CD-ROM Auto-Play option. That's it — you're protected. (It's perfectly okay to leave "Enable *Audio CD* AutoPlay" turned on. That option makes music CDs start playing when you insert them into your iMac, and it's completely safe.)

"You do not have enough access privileges"

First resort: Open the General Controls control panel. If "Protect System Folder" or "Protect Applications Folder" is turned on, then you get the "access privileges" message whenever you try to move an icon into, or out of, the System Folder or Applications folder.

Last resort: Could it be you're using Mac OS 9, and somebody has turned on the Multiple Users feature described in Chapter 13? In such a case, you get the "access privileges" message when you try to open *anything* that you haven't been explicitly permitted to use by the person who set up the iMac.

"DNS Entry not found" or "Error 404"

You get these messages when using your Web browser (see Chapter 7). It says that the Web page you're trying to visit doesn't exist. Usually this means you've made a typo as you typed the Web address (sometimes called a *URL*), or the page's address has changed and you don't know it, or the computer the Web page is on has been taken off the Internet (for maintenance, for example).

"You are running low on memory"

Believe it or not, this message appears even on iMacs with *boatloads* of memory. It doesn't mean that your *iMac* is running low on memory; it means that your *program* is gasping for air, even though the computer itself has gallons and gallons of memory just sitting around.

Each program, when it comes from the factory, has been given a memory *limit*. It's not allowed to use more memory than its limit, even if there's lots available on the iMac.

Fortunately, you can *change* this limit; if a program you use often is acting flaky, crashing, or giving "running low on memory" messages, you should raise the program's memory limit. Complete instructions are under "Giving More Memory to a Program," in the next chapter.

"Application has unexpectedly quit"

Your program has probably run out of memory. Again, see the section in the next chapter called "Giving More Memory to a Program."

Numbered error messages

This may strike you as hard to believe, but the numbers in some error messages (Type 11, Type 3, Error 49, and so on) are *no help at all*. They're valuable only to programmers — and even then, not very. A few examples:

Error code	Message	Meaning
–1	qErr	Queue element not found during deletion.
–2	vTypErr	Invalid queue element.
–3	corErr	Core routine number out of range.
–4	unimpErr	Unimplemented core routine.

As an Apple programmer once explained it, it's like finding a car smashed into a tree with its tires still spinning. All you can say for sure is that something went wrong. But you have no idea what *led up* to the crash. Maybe the guy was drunk, or distracted, or asleep. You'll never know.

Same thing with your iMac. The machine knows that *something* happened, but it's way too late to tell you what. Restart it and get back to business.

Out of Memory

As a service to you, the Tremulous Novice, I've gone this entire book without even a word about memory management, which is a whole new ball of wax. I hoped that you'd never need to think about it. Memory becomes an issue only when you get the message "There is not enough memory to open Word" (or whatever program you're trying to open), and that's why you're reading about memory in a troubleshooting chapter.

Your iMac has a fixed amount of memory. Think of the iMac as a station wagon. You can pack it with camping gear, or you can pack it with your kid's birthday-party friends — but probably not with both. Even if you manage to cram in the kids *and* the gear, if you *then* try to cram in the dog, somebody in the family is going to say, "There is not enough room to take Bowser."

That's what the "not enough memory" message is trying to tell you.

Each program that you open consumes a chunk of the iMac's limited memory. You're entitled to run as many programs as you want simultaneously — the Note Pad, the Calculator, your word processor, and so on — *provided* that they all fit into the amount of memory your iMac has. If you try to open one too many programs, you'll get that message about the dog. (*You know what I mean.*)

Before we begin, remember that there are two different kinds of memory shortages. First, there's the "You are running low on memory" type, which indicates that a *program* doesn't have enough memory; see "Giving More Memory to a Program" in the next chapter.

Second, there's the "Not enough memory to *open* this program" problem, which means that your *iMac's* memory is all used up. The following discussion applies to this second scenario.

First resort: Quit programs

If you're told that you're out of memory, the easiest way out of the situation is to *quit* one of the programs you're already running. (You quit a program by choosing Quit from the File menu.) So if you're running Word and you try to open AppleWorks, and you're told that there's not enough unused (free) memory, you'll just have to quit Word first.

Often, you may have programs running and not even know it. Remember that just because a program has no *windows* open doesn't mean it isn't running. When you're done working on something, did you just close the window, or did you actually *choose Quit* from the File menu? If you didn't actually Quit, then the program is still running and still using up memory.

To get rid of that program, choose its name from the Application menu (in the very upper-right corner of the screen). Then choose Quit from the File menu.

Second resort: Defragment your RAM

Imagine an obnoxious driver who parks on the divider line, thus occupying two parking spaces. Half a parking space is wasted on either side. Those two wasted gaps, when added up, equal one whole parking space — but that's of no help when you want to park your *whole* car.

In the same way, your iMac's memory can get broken up into pieces as you launch and quit various programs during the day. Suppose your System Folder is using 12, then there's an empty block of 4, then America Online is using 8, then there's an empty block of 4, and so on. You might try to launch, say, AppleWorks — but even though your calculations show that you *should* have enough memory to do so, you get the "out of memory" message. Your iMac, it turns out, doesn't have enough *continuous,* unbroken memory to run that latest program.

The solution to this problem (which is called, geekily enough, *memory fragmentation*) is to *quit* all your programs, and *then* launch all the programs that are supposed to fit in your iMac's memory. This time, you won't leave holes in your memory setup, and you'll be able to use all the memory you deserve. (Restarting the iMac achieves the same purpose.)

Third resort: Get RAM Doubler

Here's a fascinating possibility for the RAM-shy iMac fan: Buy a $60 program called *RAM Doubler*.

RAM Doubler uses several potent, deeply technical tricks to make your iMac *behave* as though it has twice or three times as much memory as it really does. The only fundamental understanding of RAM Doubler that you need is this: It lets you run *more small programs at the same time.* It doesn't let you run one *big* program that requires more real memory than you have.

So Billy Bob, who has a 32-meg iMac and who wants to run AppleWorks, Quicken, Photo Soap, and America Online at the same time, is made in the shade. He no longer has to quit one of those programs just to free enough memory to launch another. RAM Doubler lets him keep all of those programs going.

Jenny Sue, however, wants very much to run MindReader Pro, which requires 36 megs of RAM, on her 32-meg iMac. She's out of luck. RAM Doubler's double-memory tactics don't let you run any *big* programs that you couldn't run before.

Fourth resort: Use virtual memory

As with RAM Doubler, virtual memory (a free, built-in feature) lets you run programs whose combined memory requirements add up to much more than your iMac should be able to handle.

Although you may not have realized it, the virtual memory feature has been turned on since the day you bought your iMac. In times of memory shortage, however, here's how to crank its level higher, thus letting you run even more programs simultaneously:

1. **From the ₡ menu, choose Control Panels; in the resulting window, double-click Memory.**

   The Memory control panel appears, like this.

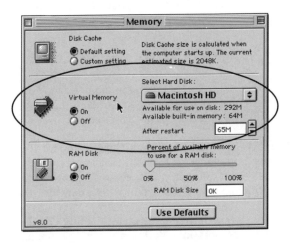

2. **Make sure the Virtual Memory switch is On.**

   On an iMac, virtual memory should *always* be on, at least a little bit (see Step 3). The technical details would curl your nose hairs, but let's just say that having virtual memory turned on makes these models run faster and use memory more efficiently.

   (*Geek disclaimer:* The only time virtual memory should be off is if you've bought RAM Doubler, described in the previous section. It replaces virtual memory.)

3. **Using the little up- and-down-arrow buttons next to the words "After restart," specify how much total memory you'd like to wind up with.**

   Virtual memory works by using a chunk of your *hard disk* to simulate additional RAM.

For some mysterious technical reason, however, you can't just use the Memory control panel to dial in the amount of *additional* memory you'd like. The iMac must reserve hard-disk space equal to *all* the memory, real and "virtual." (That's why you won't be allowed to turn on virtual memory if your hard drive is full.)

Now, the iMac should, at the very least, have virtual memory set *1MB* higher than its actual installed RAM. If your iMac has 32 megs of RAM (consult this book's Cheat Sheet), virtual memory should be set to at least 33MB.

It's safe to crank your total memory, using the virtual memory controls, up to *double* your real memory. But be careful: the higher you set this number, the slower your iMac may run. If you have 32MB of RAM, your total memory (including virtual) shouldn't exceed 64MB; things will get so slow as to be unworkable.

4. **When you're done with your virtual-memory setup, restart the iMac.**

Last resort: Buy more

After a certain point, knocking yourself out to solve out-of-memory problems reaches a point of diminishing returns. You get so worn out from workarounds that they're not worth doing.

At that point (or much sooner), just spring for the $50 or $75 and *buy more memory*. You can get it from any mail-order company (see Appendix B). When you call, tell them that you have an iMac; they'll tell you what kind of memory chips you need and in what quantities they're available.

If you have one of the recent, "slot-loading CD" iMac models, you've got a neat little memory-installation door on the machine's underbelly. Installing memory is especially easy, even if you've never done computer surgery before. For instructions, choose Mac Help from your Help menu. Look up "memory."

If you have an older iMac model, install the new memory chips yourself only if you've got a knowledgeable buddy looking over your shoulder. Otherwise, get an Apple dealer to do it for you.

Having lots of memory to kick around in is a joy. Your iMac runs faster, has fewer crashes and glitches, and acts like a new machine. It's a situation I heartily recommend.

Startup Problems

Problems that you encounter when you turn on the iMac are especially disheartening when you're a new Mac user. It does wonders for your self-esteem to think that you can't even turn the thing *on* without problems.

No chime, no picture

First resort: Chances are very, very, very good that your iMac simply isn't getting electricity. It's probably not plugged in. Or it's plugged into a power strip whose On/Off switch is currently set to Off.

Second resort: You're supposed to turn the machine on by pressing the round key at the upper-right of your keyboard. Maybe the keyboard isn't plugged in. Try the identical power button on the front of the iMac.

Last resort: If those steps don't solve the problem, your iMac is as dead as Elvis. Get it in for repair. But that's virtually never the actual problem.

Picture, no ding

Every iMac makes a sound when you turn it on. The speaker-volume slider (in the Sound control panel, or the Monitors & Sound control panel) controls the sound of the startup chime.

First resort: Open the Monitors & Sound control panel and make sure that the volume slider isn't all the way down. Make sure the Mute check box isn't turned on.

Last resort: When headphones are plugged into the iMac, no sound can come out of the iMac speakers. Unplug the headphones, in that case.

A question mark blinks on the screen

The blinking question mark, superimposed on a System Folder icon, is the iMac's international symbol for "I've looked everywhere, and I can't find a System Folder."

The blinking question mark means that your hard drive's not working right — or that it's working fine, but your System Folder got screwed up somehow. In either case, here's what to do:

First resort: After ten seconds of panic, turn the iMac off and try starting again or just restart it. (See "The Restart Button" in the next chapter.)

Second resort: Find the Software Install CD that came with your iMac. Put it in the CD drive. Restart the iMac (see "The Restart Button" in the next chapter) while pressing the letter C key until the smiling Mac appears.

Once you're running, find the program called Disk First Aid. Run it and use the Repair button. Most of the time, Disk First Aid can repair your hard drive.

Third resort: If the hard-drive icon still doesn't appear, perhaps the System Folder is calling in sick. Reinstall the System Folder from your Software Install CD, as described in the section "Performing a Clean System Reinstall," in Chapter 16.

Fourth resort: Try *zapping the PRAM* (pronounced PEA-ram). See the section "Zapping the PRAM" in Chapter 16.

Last resort: If nothing has worked and you still can't make your hard-drive icon appear on the screen, your hard drive is sick. Call your local dealer or Mac guru, and do *not* freak out — chances are very good that all your files are still intact. (Just because the platters aren't spinning doesn't mean that they've been wiped out, just as your Walkman tapes don't get erased when the Walkman runs out of batteries.)

In fact, if you've purchased an add-on disk drive (see Chapter 18), you may be able to rescue the data from your disk yourself. Buy a disk-recovery program, such as Norton Utilities or TechTool Pro. That'll let you grab anything useful off the disk and may even help heal what's wrong with it.

The power button on the keyboard doesn't work

If pressing the power button at the upper-right corner of the iMac keyboard doesn't turn on the machine — but the identical power button on the *front* of the iMac *does* turn it on — then you may be witnessing a peculiarity of the iMac keyboard. This keyboard does not, in fact, turn on the iMac unless it's plugged directly into the side of the iMac — not when it's plugged into a *USB hub* (see Chapter 14).

Either turn on your iMac by pressing the front-panel power button, or plug your keyboard directly into the iMac.

Some crazy program launches itself every time you start up

In the words of programmers everywhere, "It's a feature, not a bug."

Inside the System Folder, there's a folder called Startup Items. Look inside it. Somebody put a program or document in there.

Anything in the Startup Items folder automatically opens when you turn on the iMac. This feature is supposed to be a time-saver for people who work on the same documents every day. Open the Startup Items folder and remove whatever's bothering you.

General printing problems

If you're using an inkjet printer from, for example, Epson or HP, your first thought in times of printing trouble is to call the company (or visit the company's Web site). Such printers are famous for requiring periodic software upgrades, which are available at no charge from the company or its Web site. Such printers are also famous for being backed by companies that actually answer the phone and help you troubleshoot at no charge.

Inkjet printers: Blank pages come out

It's your cartridge.

First resort: If you haven't used the printer in a while, try your printer's "clean nozzle" command. (You'll need to consult the manual to find out exactly how you invoke it.)

Last resort: Your cartridge is probably empty. Replace it.

Finder Foul-Ups

The Finder, you'll recall, is your home base. It's the desktop. It's the Trash can and icons and all that stuff. It's where you manage your files, rename them, copy them — and sometimes have problems with them.

You can't rename a file

The file is probably locked. Click it, choose Get Info from the File menu, and deselect the Locked check box. Or maybe the file is on a locked *disk,* such as a CD-ROM disc. You *can't* rename anything on a locked disk.

You can't rename or eject a disk

Well, you can't rename a CD, ever. A CD is permanently locked.

But suppose you've equipped your iMac with one of the add-on disk drives (such as a floppy-disk drive or SuperDisk) described in Chapter 18. I'm gonna take a wild shot at this one. I'll bet you've got File Sharing turned on (in the File Sharing control panel). Right?

It's true: If you're using this feature (known as *file sharing*), you're not allowed to change your hard drive's name. You'd wreak havoc with the other people on the network, who are trying to keep straight who you are.

If you really want to bother, open your File Sharing control panel and turn *off* File Sharing. Now you can rename your disk. (You're often not allowed to eject CDs or Zip disks when File Sharing is on, either.)

All your icons show up blank

If you get zapped by the "generic icons" problem, where every document looks like a boring blank sheet of paper, your invisible Desktop file has become corrupted. See "Rebuilding the Desktop File" in the next chapter.

It's January 1, 1904

Ever wonder how your iMac always manages to know what time it is — even when it's been *unplugged?*

Turns out the iMac has a battery — a built-in, five- to seven-year battery that maintains the clock even when the computer is off. When this battery dies, your iMac's clock resets itself to January 1, 1904 (or January 1, 1956)! All your new or modified files get stamped with that date, too. And no matter how many times you reset your clock, it stubbornly jumps back to that date in antiquity.

Because this book was published only a year after the iMac was invented, the dead-battery problem is pretty unlikely to strike you, the new iMac owner, for quite a while. Therefore, if your iMac's clock keeps setting itself to 1904 or 1956, you must be reading this chapter several years *after* the iMac's debut. In that case, I have three questions. First: Just how old *is* your copy of this book, anyway? Second: Aren't you glad that Macs are exempt from the "Year 2000 Glitch"? Third: Who won the World Series in 2003?

I'd love to tell you which Eveready battery to pick up at your local drugstore, but no such luck. Your iMac's internal battery must generally be replaced by an Apple technician, usually at a cost of about $25.

Disk Disasters (Floppies, CDs, and Co.)

Disks are cheap and handy and make excellent coasters. But when they start giving you attitude, read on. (Some of these problems, of course, arise only if you've bought an add-on disk drive — for floppies or Zip disks, for example — for your iMac.)

Your CD vibrates scarily

A CD-ROM disc in the iMac can spin so fast that, believe it or not, it can occasionally start spinning lopsidedly — like an out-of-balance washing-machine load — from the infinitesimal weight of unevenly applied *paint on the CD label.*

Actually, this noisy syndrome is nothing to worry about. Still, Apple solved the issue with a software patch just after the iMac debuted. If you have Mac OS 8.6 or later on your iMac, you've already got the patch. Obviously, therefore, you don't have the problem, and so you're not even reading this.

If you're running any earlier system software, however, and the noise bugs you, visit the World Wide Web, as described in Chapter 7. Go to *www.apple.com/support/imac*. There you'll find an Updates command that lists something called the iMac CD Firmware. Download and install it by following the included instructions; it should help the loud, vibrating CD-ROM syndrome.

You can't install a new program from your SuperDisk

If you've equipped your iMac with a SuperDisk drive (as described in Chapter 18), you may run into this peculiar problem. Although most software these days comes on a CD, a few older programs still come on a stack of floppy disks. During the installation of such programs, a normal Macintosh floppy-disk drive automatically spits out Disk 1 when it's time for you to insert Disk 2 — but not the SuperDisk. The *screen* says "Please insert Disk 2," but Disk 1 remains happily nestled in your SuperDisk drive. Weird, huh?

The solution is a software update, called 2.0 (or something higher), which you can download from *www.superdisk.com/sc/sc_dl.html.*

The CD Drawer Won't Open

This note is only for people whose iMac model *has* a CD drawer (not for owners of slot-loading iMac models): If the CD drawer is empty, it should open when you press the capsule-shaped button. If there's a CD in it, the disc's icon should appear on the screen; drag the icon onto the Trash can to open the drawer and eject the disc.

But if the drawer won't open when you press the button *and* no icon shows up on the screen, something's jammed.

First resort: Insert a paper clip into the tiny hole on the CD front panel, as described on page 82.

Second resort: If the paper-clip trick doesn't work, get a butter knife. Gently pry the drawer until it pops open. You'll generally discover that somebody put a CD in without snapping it down over the center hub.

(***Note:*** Apple definitely doesn't recommend this technique, but it works well and saves you an expensive trip to the repair center.)

Everything's Slow

If the iMac has begun acting slower since you've owned it, something may indeed be wrong.

First resort: After several months of using an iMac, it actually *does* slow down. The problem is a bloated Desktop file; the solution is described in the section "Rebuilding the Desktop File" in Chapter 16.

Last resort: If your hard drive is rather full, perhaps it needs to be *defragmented*. See "Defragmenting Your Hard Drive" in the next chapter.

Hardware Headaches

These glitches aren't as common as software problems, but they're just as frustrating.

Your mouse is jerky or sticky

Like children, mops, and mimes, a mouse does its work by rolling around on the ground. It's bound to get dirty.

To clean it, turn it upside down in your hand. Very firmly rotate the donut-shaped plastic bottom of the mouse counterclockwise so that you can remove the cute little two-colored ball. Dump the ball into your hand, wash it off under the faucet, and let it air-dry completely.

In the meantime, go to work inside the socket where the ball usually is. With tweezers or something, pull out any obvious dust bunnies and hairballs. The main thing, though, is those little rollers inside the cavity: You'll probably see stripes of accumulated gunk around them. With patience, a scissors blade (or a wad of sticky-side-out Scotch tape), and a good light, lift off that stuff, preferably making an effort not to let it fall inside the cavity. Keep turning the mouse right side up and tapping it on the table to dislodge stuff.

When you put everything back together, both you and your mouse will be much happier.

Double-clicking doesn't work

You're probably double-clicking too slowly, or you're moving the mouse a little bit during the double-click process.

Your monitor's too small

"Your monitor's too small" could mean almost anything. Maybe you're happy with *how much* screen area you have, but you wish you could enlarge it, decreasing the band of empty black space around the screen. Maybe you're having trouble reading text on the screen, and wish you could magnify the whole thing. Or maybe you actually wish you had a larger screen — both magnified *and* more screen area.

First resort: Try zooming your screen in or out, as described in Chapter 13 (see "Zooming into your screen").

Second resort: Open the Monitors & Sound control panel. Click the Geometry button, as shown here:

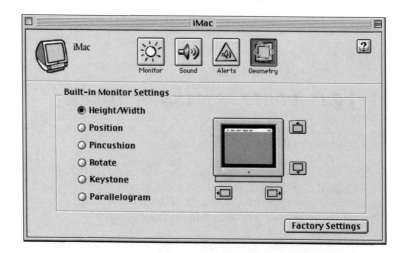

Click the Height/Width button. Now, by clicking the tiny adjustment buttons on the right side of the window, you can gradually enlarge the entire picture until it fills the plastic border of your screen. (Actually, you can even blow it up *bigger* than that, chopping off the edges of the picture, if you're in one of those moods.) This process doesn't affect how much area you can see; it just enlarges what you're already seeing.

Last resort: If you have one of the recent DV-model iMacs, you can attach a second monitor to your iMac. It shows the same picture as the built-in iMac screen, but (if the monitor is bigger) can show that image at a larger size. At least you won't have to squint anymore.

Your monitor shimmers

Of course, I don't mean that your monitor *itself* jiggles; I mean the picture.

First resort: Your iMac's being subjected to some kind of electrical interference, such as a lamp, a fan, or an air conditioner running on the same circuit. Try a different plug, a different monitor location, or a different career.

Last resort: You live in an earthquake zone. Move to the Midwest.

Chapter 16

The Problem-Solving Cookbook

In This Chapter

▶ Repairing your own iMac

▶ Solving extension tussles

▶ Clean heart, clean installations

*I*f you've read the previous chapter, you've now heard about everything that can possibly go wrong, and you're thoroughly depressed.

Here, then, is therapy: a chapter containing everything you can possibly do to *fix* the problem. Remember, you'll almost never find out what caused the problem to begin with; just be happy that the following techniques are almost magical in their ability to cure things.

Rebuilding the Desktop File

The Desktop file is a very important file on your disk. How come you've never seen it? Because the Desktop file is *invisible*. (Yes, iMac icons can be invisible. Remember that fact if you ever get involved in antiterrorist espionage activity.) The file is something that the iMac maintains for its own use.

The iMac stores two kinds of information in the Desktop file: the actual *pictures* used as icons for all your files; and information about the parent-child (program-document) *relationships* that you're having trouble with.

If the Desktop file becomes confused, two symptoms let you know: the "generic icon" problem, where all your icons show up blank white, and the "Application not found" message that appears when you try to double-click something.

Another desktop-related problem: over time, this invisible file gets bigger and bigger. Remember, it's having to store the pictures of every little icon that crosses your iMac's path. And just because you throw some icon away after using it doesn't mean that its image gets cleared from the Desktop file — it doesn't. And the bigger your Desktop file gets, the slower your iMac becomes in its efforts to open windows, display icons, and start up in the morning.

Resetting your Desktop file, therefore, has two delightful benefits. First, it cures the generic-icon syndrome and the "Application not found" problem (because it re-learns the relationships between files and their pictures). Second, it makes your iMac faster (because it purges all the unnecessary left-over icon images from its invisible database).

Here's how you do it:

1. **From the Special menu, choose Restart.**

2. **As the iMac starts gearing up, press and hold the Option and ⌘ keys.**

    Don't let go. Keep them down until the iMac explicitly asks you whether you want to "rebuild the desktop." Click OK.

After that's done, your document double-clicking will work, your icons will return, and your iMac, having been cleansed of all obsolete icons, will run faster and more smoothly.

Zapping the PRAM

The PRAM ("PEA-ram") is a tiny piece of special memory that's kept alive by your iMac's built-in battery. The PRAM stores the settings you make in your control panels, such as the sound volume, mouse speed, memory, network, and screen settings.

Rarely, rarely (but still sometimes), this tiny bit of memory gets corrupted somehow. Typical symptoms: Your control panels don't retain their settings; you can't print; or you have strange networking problems.

To reset the PRAM, turn off the iMac. When you turn it on again, hold down the ⌘, Option, letter P, and letter R keys until you hear the second or third startup chord. Release the keys.

Afterward, you may have to reset your iMac's mouse-tracking speed, desktop pattern, speaker volume level, clock, network connections, and so on. Still, it's but the work of a moment to reset them using your control panels.

The Amazing "Force Quit" Keystroke

Here's the amazing keystroke for escaping a frozen program: ⌘-Option-Esc. (This is about the only time that you'll ever use the Esc key.)

You get a dialog box that says, "Force [this program] to quit?" and warns you that any work you've done since the last time you used the Save command will be gone forever. Click Force Quit, and — when this trick works — you exit the program you were working in.

So what's the big whoop? Well, if you had several programs running, this technique dumps only the *one* that you were working in — the one that crashed. You now have a chance to enter each of the other programs that are still running and save your work (if you haven't done so). Then, to be on the safe side, restart the iMac.

The Restart Button

To restart your iMac when it's frozen or crashed, press the power button on the front of the iMac. Hold it in for six seconds, or until the machine restarts.

If that doesn't either restart the computer or display a message that *offers* to do so, then you're probably (a) using one of the early iMac models or (b) experiencing a particularly nasty system crash. In either case, proceed like this:

- ✔ **Slot-loading iMac models:** Examine the right side of the computer, where all the jacks are. Find the Restart button. It's marked by a tiny left-pointing triangle; the picture in Appendix A shows you where it is. Push this button to restart a frozen computer.

- ✔ **Earlier iMac models:** Open the plastic door on the right side of the iMac. Locate the tiny hole between the phone jack and the USB connectors (as shown in Appendix A) — and push a straightened paper clip into it until the computer restarts.

And if *that* doesn't work, unplug the iMac from the wall. Plug it back in and turn the machine on. (That always works.)

Solving an Extension Conflict

Okay, here it is — the long-awaited extension-conflict discussion.

See, each *extension* (a self-loading background program, such as a screen saver, that you install in your System Folder) was written by a programmer who had no clue what *other* extensions you'd be using. As a result, two extensions may fight, resulting in that polite disclaimer "Sorry, a System error has occurred."

These things are easy to fix, once you know the secret. Shut off your iMac (choose Shut Down from the Special menu), and then turn it on again. But as the iMac is starting up, *hold down the Shift key* and keep it down until (1) you see the message "Extensions off" or (2) you arrive at the desktop, whichever you notice first.

Your iMac probably won't give you any more trouble — but now, of course, you're running without any of your cute little extension programs. No CD-ROMs, no fax software, no Internet access, and so on.

If the point of this exercise is to pinpoint *which* extensions aren't getting along, you have two choices. One is free but takes a lot of time. The other way costs $70 but works automatically.

✔ **The hard way:** Turn off the iMac and then turn it on again. While the iMac is starting up, press and hold the space bar down. Eventually, you'll be shown a complete list of your extensions, like this:

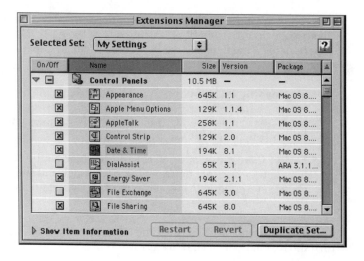

The point here is that you can *turn off* selected extensions and control panels just by clicking their checkboxes. (The little X means *on*.)

Special bonus feature! In the previous picture, see the tiny triangle where it says Show Item Information? Click that to see a top-secret panel that tells you what each extension is for. Click an extension's name in the list, and you'll be shown a little caption for it, such as "Warranty Minder Pro: This extension keeps track of how long it's been since you bought your iMac, and it makes sure nothing goes wrong until after the warranty period is over."

But I digress. Using your Extensions Manager list, turn off the first few extensions and control panels. Then restart the computer (click the Restart button at the bottom of the window).

If the iMac doesn't exhibit whatever unpleasant behavior you've been having, you can pretty much bet that one of the extensions you turned off was the guilty party. If the iMac *does* crash or act balky again, repeat the whole process, but this time turn some more extensions off.

Through trial and error, you eventually should be able to figure out which pair of extensions doesn't get along.

✔ ***The easy way:*** Buy a program called Conflict Catcher. This program does many useful things for managing your extensions, but its main virtue is catching conflicts. It can figure out, all by itself, which extension (or extensions) caused your iMac's problems. All you have to do is sit there, restarting the iMac over and over, each time telling Conflict Catcher whether or not the problem has been solved yet. By the time the process is over, the program will emblazon the name of the errant extensions on your screen; you then can dismember, disembowel, or trash them as you see fit.

(You can get a free, seven-day Conflict Catcher demo version from America Online or on the Internet at *www.casadyg.com*. It lasts just long enough for you to figure out which extensions were driving you crazy.)

Giving More Memory to a Program

When you turn on your iMac, several megabytes of its available RAM (memory) get used up by your System Folder's contents — your operating system. Then, every time you launch a program, a little bit of the leftover free RAM gets used up.

Here's how to find out where your memory is going at any particular moment:

Go to the Finder. From the menu, choose About This Computer. This helpful dialog box appears, showing several important numbers about your use of memory:

This is how much real memory your Mac has, not counting "fake" memory contributed by RAM Doubler or virtual memory.

This is the largest chunk of memory you have left, into which you can open more programs. (There may be smaller chunks available, too.)

In the bottom part of the box, you can see what's already taking up memory and how *much* memory each program is taking up (see those bars?).

You may find it useful, however, to change the amount of memory that each of your programs uses. If you're experiencing a lot of System crashes, for example, the program may need a bigger memory allotment. If memory is at a premium, you may occasionally be able to give a program *less* memory, freeing some for other purposes.

Here's how:

1. **Quit the program whose memory appetite you want to change and then click its icon.**

   This step frequently confuses beginners; for help in quitting a program, see Chapter 15. And don't be fooled into clicking the *folder* a program's in, either — open the folder and click the program icon itself. (Classic example: America Online. If you highlight its *folder,* these steps won't work. Instead, *open* that folder and click actual, triangular, America Online *program* icon.)

   Don't be fooled into clicking a program's *alias,* either. An alias is a file whose name appears in *italics, like this;* see Chapter 13 for details. If your program's name does appear in italics, open the File menu and choose Show Original. Now you can proceed to Step 2.

2. **From the File menu, choose Get Info.**

If you don't see the Get Info command, then you may be in Simple Finder mode, or you may be using the Multiple Users feature. Both are described in Chapter 13; exit Simple Finder mode, or turn off Multiple Users, before proceeding.

When you choose Get Info, a dialog box appears.

3. **From the Show: pop-up menu, choose Memory.**

   If you don't see a Memory command, see Step 1: You're probably trying to Get Info on a folder or an alias, as described in Step 2.

   In any case, you now see a window like this:

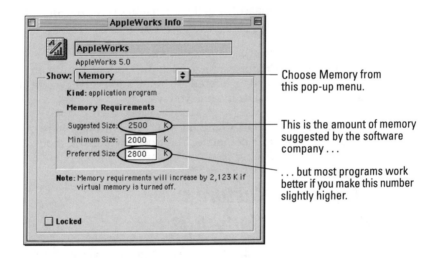

4. **Change the number in the Preferred size box.**

   This number is the amount of memory that the program will actually consume when you run it. If your aim is to make this program stabler or faster, try increasing this number by, for example, 10 percent.

   Unless System crashes make your life more interesting, don't set the Preferred size *below* the Suggested size, though.

Performing a Clean System Reinstall

This procedure is just a wee bit technical. But it's amazing how many problems it solves. Font problems, crash problems, freeze problems, glitch problems, weird bad vibes that you can't even describe very well — all of them go away when you do a *clean install*.

As the gears of your System Folder grind away day after day, little corruptions and rough edges can develop. The following procedure replaces your old, corroded System Folder with a brand-spanking-new one. It's nearly guaranteed to wipe out any erratic, bizarre crashes or freezes that you've been having; after all, it restores the iMac to the exact condition it was in the day it left the factory.

This process requires the Software Install CD that came with your iMac.

Step one: Install the fresh software

Turn on the iMac. Insert the Software Install CD (or the Mac OS 9 CD, if you bought Mac OS 9 since buying your iMac).

Double-click the Mac OS Install icon. After you've clicked the Start button on the Software Installations screen, click the Options button on the regular Installer screen. You'll be offered a "Create additional System Folder (clean install)" option — that's the one you want.

Then click whatever OK, Continue, or Install buttons you're offered, until the installation process is complete. The whole deal takes about 10 minutes.

Step two: Restore your personal belongings

The result of all these shenanigans is a virgin, clean System Folder, free of any corruptions. Your iMac will run smoothly, fast, and trouble-free — I guarantee it.

Unfortunately, all your customized fonts, control panels, preferences, Web bookmarks, and menu items are stranded back in your *old* System Folder! That includes the settings necessary for you to get onto the Internet, by the way.

Ideally, you should install each of these items from their original, store-bought disks, and manually enter your preference settings anew. If that's too much hassle, set up your old System Folder and your new System Folder side-by-side in tall, skinny, list-view windows. Now copy anything that's not in your *new* System Folder, item by item, from your old System Folder to your new System Folder. (Key folders to compare with their newer counterparts: the Preferences; Extensions; Control Panels; Apple Menu Items; and Fonts folders.) Do so with care, however, so that you don't simply reinstate whatever problems you were having.

To restore your Internet settings, open the Preferences folders of your Previous System Folder (left) and new System Folder (right), side-by-side, like this:

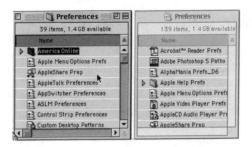

While pressing the Option key, drag the following preference files from the left window (the old System Folder) into the right window. (The Option key tells the iMac to *copy,* not just move, each item. Moving them would be fine, too, but copying them leaves your old System Folder intact — just in case.)

- ✔ America Online (a folder)
- ✔ Explorer (a folder)
- ✔ Internet Preferences
- ✔ Modem Preferences
- ✔ Remote Access (folder)
- ✔ TCP/IP Preferences

With each item, you'll be asked if you're sure you want to replace the newer item with the older; yes, you do. The Remote Access folder, by the way, will tell you that it can't be replaced "because it is in use." Outsmart it by throwing away the Remote Access folder from the *right-side* window before dragging the Remote Access folder again from the *left-side* window. (That sentence really does make sense; you may have to read it slowly.)

(P.S. — If you bought Conflict Catcher, as described earlier in this chapter, you don't have to do this comparison manually. Use its Clean-Install System Merge command to compare your old and new System Folders automatically — and, at your option, to copy any of your personal belongings into the new System Folder.)

Going back in time

Suppose you've just done a clean system install. In the unlikely event that your iMac behaves even worse with the new System Folder than with the old one, you can always go *back* to using the old System Folder. Do so by *throwing* *away* the new System Folder; opening and closing the Previous System Folder; and then restarting the iMac. (You can take the word Previous off the System Folder's name, if you like.)

Other ways to restore your iMac

In addition to the CD called Software Install (described in the previous steps), your iMac also came with a CD called Software Restore. This second CD is useful in more dramatic circumstances, such as your deciding to erase your iMac's hard drive and start over (which might be useful if you plan to sell the iMac or when the FBI bursts through your door).

To use this CD, try this. While the iMac is on, put in the Software Restore CD and close the tray. Now restart the iMac while pressing the letter C key continuously. Release the C key only after you see the message "Welcome to Macintosh" on the screen.

The Apple Software Restore icon (in this Software Restore CD's main window) can perform two kinds of surgery on your System Folder: one called a *Restore in Place,* the other called *Erase "Macintosh HD" Before Restoring.*

The "Restore in Place" option

This procedure gives you fresh, clean copies of everything that came with your iMac — including the System Folder and all the free programs — without touching any of the stuff *you've* added, such as your hard-won AppleWorks documents, e-mail, and so on.

Unfortunately, Restore in Place also replaces a few useful files in your System Folder: the ones that tell your iMac how to connect to the Internet, and the ones that store your bookmarks for Web browsing. To avoid losing them, follow these awkward but necessary steps:

1. **Open the System Folder. Open the Preferences folder. Drag the following items out of the Preferences window and onto the desktop: the America Online, Explorer, and Remote Access folders; and the Internet, Modem, and TCP/IP Preferences files.**

   If you like, close all the windows you've just opened.

2. **Open the Software Restore CD. Double-click the Apple Software Restore icon. Choose the Restore in Place option.**

   The Software Restore program goes about its business; when it's finished, you'll be asked to restart the iMac.

3. **When the iMac restarts, open the hard drive, then the System Folder, then the Preferences folder. Throw away the Remote Access folder. Finally, drag the six items from Step 1 from your desktop back into the Preferences folder.**

   When you're asked if you want to replace newer items with older ones, click OK each time.

You've just given yourself a spotless, fully functioning System Folder and new copies of all the pre-installed iMac software, while preserving your Internet settings at the same time.

The "Erase before restoring" option

When you double-click the Apple Software Restore icon, the second option, "Erase 'Macintosh HD' before restoring," is extremely extreme. It *wipes out* everything you've ever created on your iMac, erasing the hard drive completely and restoring the iMac (and its pre-installed software) to the way it was the day you opened its box. *All of the work you've done is deleted.*

Use this trick only under dire circumstances.

Defragmenting Your Hard Drive

Your hard drive, if you'll indulge me, is like a closet maintained by a guy who's always in a hurry. When guests are coming over, he cleans up the living room by throwing everything into the closet, not particularly neatly. Every now and then, when he gets time, he unpacks the closet and repacks it neatly, putting everything in a tidy, organized place.

The hard drive, too, is in a hurry. When you ask it to save a file, it doesn't wait around: It shoves that file wherever it can find space. Sometimes, that even means sticking the file in *two* places, splitting it as necessary. Over time, more and more files are stored on your hard disk in pieces. It's no big deal: When you need that file again, the hard drive remembers where all the pieces are and is perfectly able to bring the file back to the screen.

But all this hunting for pieces slows the drive down, especially when your drive gets 80 percent full and stays that way for awhile. And like our busy closet keeper, you'll find it very satisfying, every six months or so, to reorganize the files on your disk so that they're each in one piece, neatly placed end to end on the hard-drive surface.

You can *defragment* your drive (which is the term for it) in two ways. First, you can copy everything onto other disks (such as SuperDisks or Zip disks, if you've bought one of those add-on drives), erase the hard drive, and copy the files back onto it. Second, you can buy a program just for defragmenting your drive. These programs are called things like Norton Utilities and DiskExpress. (Back up your work before using these programs, however; if you're into living dangerously, go skydiving.)

Chapter 17

Beyond the iMac: Where to Go from Here

The first 16 chapters of this book are the crash course. Now, Grasshoppa, it's time for you to venture forth into the world by yourself. Go for the gold. Do the right thing. Use the Force.

But first, a few parting words of wisdom.

Where to Turn in Times of Trouble

You own the world's most forgiving, self-explanatory computer. But things will go wrong. And not even this astoundingly complete book can anticipate the problems you may encounter while running BeeKeeper Pro or No Namo Scanner Doodad Plus. Fortunately, the world is crawling with help possibilities.

Your 15 minutes of free help

For example, during the first three months you've owned your iMac, you can call Apple's delightful toll-free hotline at (800) 500-7078 and ask your questions of the gurus there. (Hint for the budget-conscious: Apple doesn't know when you bought your iMac. They measure your 90 days, therefore, from your first *call*, not really from the day you bought your machine.)

Beyond those 90 days, Apple charges you nosebleed-inducing fees for your use of their experts (unless the computer actually turns out to need fixing, in which case the fee is waived). The number for this service is (888) 275-8258 (toll-free again), and you can choose to have your wallet milked in either of two quantities: One problem solved for $50; ten for $290.

The bottom line: Try to have all your problems in the first 90 days.

$150 for three years

If you anticipate needing phone help at least three times, you're far better off buying AppleCare. It's an extended-warranty program that covers all iMac troubles for three years, including mechanical problems. During that time, you can call Apple's help line all you want at no extra charge. Keep in mind, however, that you must sign up for this program during the first year you own your iMac.

Free help sources

If spending money isn't your way of problem solving, consider these all-expenses-paid avenues:

- **www.apple.com/support/iMac:** Part of Apple's Web site (see Chapters 6 and 7). You can get software updates, ask questions in electronic bulletin-board discussion areas, and access the Technical Information Library — a searchable electronic encyclopedia of all things Macintosh. All kinds of common iMac questions and answers are listed there for your perusal pleasure.

- **AppleFax:** Call 800-505-0171 by telephone, listen to the instructions, punch in your own fax number when you're asked for it, put in a fresh roll of fax paper, and stand back. They'll fax you a list of pretyped answers to common questions.

- **800-SOS-APPL:** This phone number brings you to a voicemail labyrinth that would freak out Theseus. Dig deep enough into the maze and you can find automated, prerecorded tips, tricks, and troubleshooting techniques.

- **No Wonder Web page:** Visit this page for free, 24-hour, personal computer help at *www.nowonder.com*. Did you get that? *Free, personal* help from a live human being. If you got rich from the Internet stock boom of the 1990s, go ahead and call Apple for $50 a shot — but otherwise, you'd be crazy not to try the No Wonder service.

- **MacFixIt Web page:** You get hundreds of discussions of little tweaky specific iMac problems at *www.macfixit.pair.com*.

Otherwise, your next resort should be a local user group, if you're lucky enough to live in a pseudometropolitan area. A user group, of course, doesn't exist to answer *your* personal questions; you still have to do some phoning and hobnobbing and research. But a user group *is* a source of sources. You can call up and find out who will know the answer to your question. (To find the nearest user group, call Apple's referral service at (800) 538-9696.)

The other great source of help is an electronic meeting place like America Online, where you may get your question answered instantly — and if not, you can post your question on a bulletin board for somebody to answer overnight. Try keyword **MOS**, for example. (See Chapter 6 for details on keywords.) If you're Internet savvy, you can visit a *newsgroup* called *comp.sys.mac* for similar assistance. (See Chapter 6 for information on newsgroups.)

As for your continuing education — after you spend a month's salary on a computer, I'll bet you can afford $20 more for a subscription to *Macworld*, *MacAddict*, or *MacHome Journal* magazine. Agreed, huge chunks of these rags may go right over your head. But in every single issue, you'll find at least one really useful item. You can learn all kinds of things just by reading the ads. And if you're not in touch with the computer nerd world at least by that tenuous thread — via magazine — then you might miss stuff like free offers, recall notices, warnings, and other consumer-oriented jazz.

Upgrading to Mac OS 9 — and Beyond

If you bought your iMac before November 1999, it came with the System Folder version called Mac OS 8.1, 8.5, or 8.6 — splendid operating systems, without a doubt. Subsequent iMacs, however, come with the newer Mac OS 9. You can read about Mac OS 9's most attractive new features in this book — see Chapter 7 for details on Sherlock, and Chapter 13 for info on the Multiple Users feature. Many other, much smaller features lurk, all designed to make the iMac faster, easier, and trouble-freer.

If your iMac didn't come with Mac OS 9 on board, you can buy it for $90 or less from any of the mail-order outfits listed in Appendix B. Fortunately, installing it onto your iMac isn't terribly complicated:

1. **Insert the Mac OS 9 CD-ROM. Double-click the Install Mac OS 9 icon.**

   A welcome screen appears.

2. **Click Continue; OK; Install; and wait until the process is done.**

When the process is complete, you'll be asked to click a Restart button to turn your iMac off and then on again. When it comes to, Mac OS 9 will be running your machine.

Whenever you upgrade your operating system in this way, however, you run the risk that any *add-on* programs — that is, software that didn't come from Apple — might develop quirks and tics. Your big, everyday, came-with-the-iMac programs like AppleWorks and Outlook Express probably won't be affected. But stuff you've bought, or downloaded from the Internet, may occasionally behave oddly after a system-software upgrade.

In that event, you have three choices:

✔ Contact whoever made the software in question — or visit the corresponding Web page. Check to see if an upgrade is available. (It almost always is.)

✔ Do without the software.

✔ If you can't live without the software in question, and there's no fixed version in sight, you can always go back to your old system-software version. To do that, grab the system-software CD-ROM that came with your iMac and do a *clean install,* as described in Chapter 16.

Save Changes Before Closing?

If you decide to get more into this Macintosh thing, I've listed major magazines, Web sites, and mail-order businesses in Appendix B.

But wait a minute — the point of this book wasn't to convert you into a full-time iMac rabbit. It was to get you off the ground. To give you just enough background so you'll know why the computer's beeping at you. To show you the basics and help you figure out what the beanie heads are talking about.

Don't let them intimidate you. So *what* if you don't know the lingo or have the circuitry memorized? If you can turn the thing on, get something written up and printed, and get out in time to enjoy the sunshine, you qualify as a real iMac user.

Any dummy knows that.

Part VI
The Part of Tens

The 5th Wave   By Rich Tennant

In this part . . .

Here's what we *For Dummies* book authors often refer to as "the chapters we can write in one day apiece" — a trio of top ten lists, for your infotainment pleasure.

Chapter 18

Ten More Gadgets to Buy and Plug In

• •

*I*n this chapter, you'll find out about several impressive high-tech gadgets you can spend money on — yes, it's Credit Card Workout #4. These devices give the iMac eyes and ears, turn it into a national network, and turn it into an orchestra. You're not obligated to purchase any of them, of course. But knowing about some of the amazing things your computer can do will help you understand why the iMac is such a big deal.

A Scanner

If the point of a printer is to take something on the screen and reproduce it on *paper,* a scanner, then, is the opposite — its function is to scan an image on paper and throw it up on the iMac *screen.* After the image has been scanned and converted into bits and bytes that the iMac understands (meaning that it's been *digitized*), you can manipulate the image any way that you want. Erase unwanted parts, make the background darker, give Uncle Ed a mustache, shorten your brother's neck — whatever. The more dignified use for a scanner is grabbing real-world images that you then paste into your own documents, particularly in the realm of page layout and graphic design. Got a potato-industry newsletter to crank out? Scan in a photo of some fine-lookin' spuds, and you've got yourself a graphic for page one.

So how much is all this gonna cost you? A middle-of-the-line color scanner, such as the Umax Astra pictured here, costs around $130 — including software that can do a decent job of converting scanned articles into typed-out, editable word processor documents. (When shopping, be sure to request an iMac-compatible scanner — one with a *USB connector,* such as a Umax Astra 1220U or Agfa SnapScan 1212u.) (See Chapter 11 for a scanning crash course.)

A Digital Camera

Ordinarily, the concept of paying $500 for a camera that lacks any way to insert film would seem spectacularly brain-dead. Yet that's exactly the point of *digital cameras,* like those from Kodak, Casio, Olympus, Sony, and others. They store between 10 and 150 photos without film — actually, in *RAM,* now that you know what that is — and when you get home, you can dump the images into your iMac (after connecting a cable), thereby freeing your camera's RAM for another round of happy-go-lucky shooting.

For people who need instant, no-cost developing (doctors, people needing pictures for World Wide Web pages, real-estate hounds, fraternity party animals, and so on), these cameras are a godsend. As a matter of fact, just to prove the point, I took the photos in this book using a little Olympus jobber. The results aren't pro quality — you'll have to pay $5,000 or more for digital cameras that take magazine-quality photos — but they're great for, say, illustrating computer books.

Incidentally: Be sure to buy a camera with a *USB connector* or, if you have an iMac DV model, a *FireWire connector.* If you buy one that has a *serial cable,* you'll have to buy a serial-to-USB adapter, such as those listed in Appendix C.

A Mouse

The iMac's mouse is much more amazing than most mice. For example, it's see-through — and the little rubber ball inside is two-toned so that you can see it rolling as it moves.

Unfortunately, the iMac's mouse is also a royal pain. Unlike every other mouse in the world, it's perfectly round, so you can't rest the butt of your hand on it. If you bought your iMac recently, only the subtle groove on the mouse button lets you tell by touch when you've got it pointed straight — and the original iMacs don't even have that groove.

If you're fine with the iMac mouse, great. Otherwise, getting a replacement is extremely easy and inexpensive. The iMac mice sold by Ariston, Macally, Belkin, or iMaccessories, for example, are translucent, just like the iMac's mouse — but they're oval-shaped like real mice, and they are therefore more comfortable and easier to position without looking.

Surprisingly enough, you can even get USB mice that are generally sold for *non*-Macintosh computers and plug them right into the iMac (or the iMac's keyboard). These mice have multiple buttons, instead of the iMac's one, but never mind — all three buttons do the same thing.

A Joystick

The iMac, with its high-speed G3 chip inside and superb graphics, makes a great game-playing machine. But how can you get the feeling of soaring over the fields of France in a fighter plane using a *mouse* to control the action? You can't. You need a joystick. It works just like a real airplane joystick, controlling your movement in flight simulation, driving simulators, shoot-'em-ups, and other games. They cost between $20 and $50, and they're listed by the dozens in the Internet at *www.imacintouch.com.*

Speakers or Headphones

Oh, yes indeedy: The iMac is more than hi-tech — it's hi-*fi,* capable of churning out gorgeous stereo sound. If you're used to the tinny two-inch built-in speakers that came built into the 1998/early 1999 iMac models, though, there's very little chance you'll mistake your living room for Carnegie Hall.

But if you get a pair of miniature speakers designed for the purpose, you're in for a tintinnabulating treat. If you play iMac games, particularly CD-ROM discs, you won't believe what you've been missing; the sounds are suddenly much richer and deeper.

If you don't do much more with sound than listen to your iMac's startup chord, don't bother buying external speakers. And if you *do* want speakers, not just any old speakers will work. They must be *self-powered,* and they must be *shielded;* the magnets inside normal stereo speakers are enough to distort the image on your monitor like the Sunday comics on Silly Putty. In other words, buy speakers designed for the purpose; Apple, Yamaha, Sony, and many other companies make lines of iMac-ready speakers.

You may also have noticed, by the way, that the iMac's front panel offers *two* headphone jacks — ideal for music listening with a loved one or battle games with a not-so-loved one. If add-on speakers are too involved for your taste, you'll get the same extremely rich sound by popping a pair of Walkman headphones into one of these front-panel jacks. (When you do so, the iMac's built-in speakers automatically shut up.)

The Harmon/Kardon Subwoofer

If your iMac has a CD slot (instead of the older CD door), then you've got one of the upgraded iMac models of late 1999. *Your* machine's built-in speakers are *not* tiny and tinny. In fact, they're fairly amazing for a personal computer — they're made by Harmon/Kardon, a premiere stereo-equipment company. In fact, to quote Apple's brochure:

> The Harman/Kardon Odyssey audio system's design innovations include high bandwidth (100Hz to 20,000Hz usable frequency response), an ultra-high neodymium magnet (for improved bass and higher efficiency), a lightweight aluminum diaphragm (for maximum bandwidth, high sensitivity and smooth frequency response), a voice coil that uses copper-clad aluminum wire to reduce moving mass and improve high-frequency response, and a magnetically-shielded motor design that allows distortion-free use in close proximity to sensitive devices.

I don't know what that means, but it sure *sounds* like it should sound good.

You're missing, however, a third piece of the dream sound system imagined by the Harmon/Kardon engineers: a *subwoofer.* The term may suggest an underwater dog, but it's actually a transparent, bubble-like, separate module that fills in the lower range of musical notes. It looks like this:

If you're much of a stereo or home theatre nut, you already know that a sub-woofer adds subsonic thudding and power to any music. If you use your iMac's CD drive to listen to music CDs, or (if you have an iMac DV model) its DVD drive to watch movies on disc, this additional item makes the sound system second to none (on computers, anyway). You can get the subwoofer from *www.apple.com,* among other places. (Note to the wary: You need Mac OS 9 or later to use the iSub.)

Music and MIDI

MIDI, pronounced like the short skirt, stands for Musical Instrument Digital Interface. What it *means* is "hookup to a synthesizer." What it *does* is let your iMac record and play back your musical performances using a synthesizer attached to it. When you record, the iMac makes a metronome sound — a steady click track — and you play to the beat. Then, when you play back the music, your keyboard plays *exactly* what you recorded, complete with feeling, expression, and fudged notes; you'd think that Elvis's ghost was playing the instrument, except that the keys don't move up and down. Then you can edit your fudged mistakes and wind up sounding like [insert your favorite musician here].

All you need is a little box called a MIDI interface (about $50) that connects your iMac to the synthesizer. (Be sure to buy a *USB* version of it, such as those described in Appendix C.) You also need a program that can record and play back the music, called a *sequencing program.* Some easy-to-use and inexpensive ones are MusicShop and Freestyle. And, of course, you need to get your hands on a synthesizer. Or, for making sheet music, investigate Encore, Overture, or Finale. Check out a music store and get jammin'.

A Projector

If you use your iMac to give slide shows or classroom lectures, you may sometimes wish you could project images onto a TV or movie screen. With the addition of a *video-output adapter,* such as the USB Presenter (*www.aver.com*), you can hook your iMac up to a TV or LCD projector so that all the world may enjoy your creativity.

In fact, if you have an iMac DV, you don't even need such an adapter; see "Attaching a Second Monitor" in Appendix A.

Zip, SuperDisk, & Co.

As I'm sure you're aware by now, the iMac comes without a floppy-disk drive. In truth, that's no big deal; floppies are embarrassingly old, slow, and low-capacity.

On the other hand, many people need *some* kind of disk to store stuff on; backing up your work on the Internet (see Chapter 7) or onto another Mac on the network (see Chapter 14) isn't for everybody.

So what are you supposed to do? Go back to writing on Post-it notes? Well, you could always buy an add-on disk drive for your iMac — one that plugs into the iMac's USB jacks. Your choices are:

- ✓ **A floppy drive:** For $80 or less, you can equip your iMac with the missing limb it's always dreamed of: a true-blue, bona fide floppy disk.

- ✓ **A SuperDisk drive:** Spend a little more; get a little more. The $140, translucent, iMac-colored SuperDrive accepts *both* floppy disks *and* SuperDisks, which look, smell, and act exactly like floppies — except that they hold about 83 times as much. Additional SuperDisk disks cost about $10 each, and they hold 120 megabytes each. A handy double-duty solution.

- ✓ **A Zip drive:** Here's yet another add-on disk-drive attachment. This one comes in translucent blue. It accepts Zip disks, which look like floppy disks that have been hitting the Ben & Jerry's a bit too often. Each holds 250MB and costs about $15; the Zip drive, the player, costs $200 or $100, depending on whether you get the 250-meg or 100-meg versions. Zip disks, like SuperDisks, are convenient, sturdy, and easy to work with; the advantage here is that hundreds of thousands of people already own Zip drives. You can carry your project around on a Zip disk in your pocket, for example, confident that your friendly neighborhood Kinko's, corporate office, or print shop is likely to have a Zip drive that can accept it (the disk, not your pocket).

- ✓ **A rewritable CD-ROM drive:** Yes, Virginia, the impossible has become possible: You can now make (or *burn,* as the geeks like to say) your own CD-ROMs. You attach one of these special CD drives (about $350) to your iMac's USB jack; you insert a blank CD (they cost about $2 each); and you specify what you'd like preserved forever by dragging it off of your hard drive.

For details on all of this stuff, see Appendix C.

A Movie Camera

By "a movie camera," I don't mean a $600 digital camcorder (although you can buy and plug *that* in, too, if you have an iMac DV model; see Chapter 10). I have something smaller and cheaper in mind.

The QuickCam (see Appendix C) is a golf-ball-sized movie camera. It plugs into your iMac's USB jack and lets you make smallish — but genuine — digital movies, recording whatever you point it at. There's no less expensive way to try your hand at filmmaking.

Chapter 19

Ten Cool Things You Didn't Know Your iMac Could Do

• •

*I*t's fast, it's hip, and it complements any décor. But the iMac does more — much more. Try *these* some lazy Saturday afternoon.

Play Music CDs

Yup, it's true. Pop your favorite music CD — Carly Simon, 10,000 Maniacs, Smashing Pumpkins, the soundtrack to *Lethal Weapon XIV* — into the iMac's CD-ROM drive. Some iMacs are set up to begin playing such music CDs automatically; others you have to command to begin playing.

Either way, if you'd like to control your music CDs the way you would on a $300 CD player, use the "front panel" in your menu called AppleCD Audio Player. It should look familiar.

Hunt around long enough, and you'll figure out how to make your CD play, stop, skip randomly among the songs, play louder or softer, and so on.

In fact, if you click the tiny down-pointing triangle (below the NORMAL button), you'll expand the panel so that you can view the names of the individual songs on the CD. Unfortunately, they start out being called "Track 1," "Track 2," and so on — it's up to you to click such names and type the correct song titles. (Press Return after each title to move down to the next blank or Shift-Return to move upward. While you're at it, click the words *Audio CD*, just above the track list, and type the name of the disc, too.) After you do all this, the Player will automatically remember the album and song titles the next time you insert the disc.

But here's the best part: Click the PROG button. Now you can drag any title on the left side to any slot on the right side. (Drag it back to the left if you change your mind.) You also can drag titles up or down on the right side. What's great about this feature is that you can drag your favorite songs into the "playlist" on the right side *more than once* — and leave the annoying songs out of the playlist completely.

And oh, by the way: if you bought an iMac DV, it can also play DVD *movies,* such as the ones available for rental at your local video store. Details in Chapter 10.

Talk

It's been said that we spend the first year of a child's life trying to get it to talk, and the next 18 years trying to get it to shut up. Well, with the iMac, getting it to talk is fantastically easy.

Lots of programs are capable of talking. Word 98, AppleWorks, America Online, and WordPerfect are some examples. But the program that requires by far the least manual-reading (when it comes to talking) is the delightful, bargain-basement word processor known as *SimpleText.*

Find one of your copies of SimpleText (use your Find command). Launch it and then type up something you've always wanted to have said to you, such as, "You are *such* a god! Holy smokes — *everything* you do turns out fantastically! I'd give anything to be more like you."

Then move that mouse on up to your Sound menu and choose Speak All. Aren't computers great?

Now: For added hilarity, go back to the Sound menu. There you'll find a Voices command that lists as many as 18 different voices to choose from. They're great: male, female, kids, deep voices, shaky voices, whispered voices. You'll spend hours, I predict, making up funny sentences for each character voice to say.

Of course, Apple didn't create a talking iMac just for you to fool around making up silly sentences. This technology has some actual, useful uses. For example, there's no better way to proofread something important than to listen to it being read to you.

Sing

Although it's a little humbling that your iMac may be more talented than you are, it does indeed sing. It has a somewhat limited repertoire — in fact, it knows only four songs — but it can use any lyrics you want, and it never even stops to take a breath.

To make your iMac sing, you simply need to get it talking, as described in the preceding section. Then choose one of these voices from the Voices menu:

- ✔ **Pipe Organ:** Sings to the tune of the Alfred Hitchcock theme.
- ✔ **Good News:** Sings to the tune of "Pomp & Circumstance," otherwise known as the graduation march.
- ✔ **Bad News:** Sings to the tune of the funeral march.
- ✔ **Cellos:** Sings to the tune of "In the Hall of the Mountain King," from *Peer Gynt,* by Edvard Grieg. Such culture!

Punctuation marks make the iMac start over from the beginning of the melody. Sample lyrics for the Good News graduation-march melody, for example, should look like this:

You just won the jackpot good luck and God bless

Too bad you owe half to good old IRS!

Play Movies

Your iMac is quite handy with movies. It can make them, record them, and show them.

The cornerstone to all this is a technology bundle called *QuickTime,* which takes the form of some files that are probably sitting in your System Folder at this very moment (in your Extensions folder).

Getting movies to play on your screen is simple: Just double-click a movie file's icon to open it. It opens a program called Movie Player or QuickTime Player, as shown here.

Drag this doodad to
jump around in the
movie

Click here to start
or stop playback

To play the flick, click the little "play" triangle to make it play back. (Or press the space bar.) You'll quickly discover a few disappointing facts about digital movies: They often play in a small window, and they're generally short. That's because QuickTime movie files take up obscene amounts of hard drive space for each minute of footage.

The bigger challenge, therefore, is simply *getting* a movie you want to watch. Several sources spring to mind: You can download movies from the Internet or America Online (see Chapter 6), although these enormous files take enormous amounts of time to transfer to you by modem. The CD-ROM that comes with each issue of MacAddict magazine, and the newsstand issues of *Macworld* magazine, also contains QuickTime movies each month.

If you bought an iMac DV model, you can also make your *own* movies — big, full-screen, smooth ones, as described in Chapter 10. If you didn't buy that model, you can still make movies on a smaller scale, using a little golf-ball-sized doodad called a QuickCam. It captures digital videos onto the iMac with color and sound. Then you can edit them, play them backward, edit out the embarrassing parts, or whatever.

Send Faxes

Because your iMac has a built-in fax modem, you're in for a delicious treat. Faxes sent by an iMac come out looking twice as crisp and clean when a real fax machine receives them. And sending faxes couldn't be more convenient for you — no printout to throw away, no paper involved at all. Your iMac sends the thing directly to another fax machine's brain.

Here's what you do. Begin by typing (or opening) whatever it is you want to fax. Usually, this means a letter you've written in, say, AppleWorks. Make sure it's in front of you on the screen.

Now take a look at your File menu and notice where it says Print. Got it?

Okay, let go of the mouse now. With one hand, press and hold down the *Option and ⌘ keys* on your keyboard. With the other, go back up to the File menu and look at the word Print. If all went well, that word Print has now changed to *Fax!*

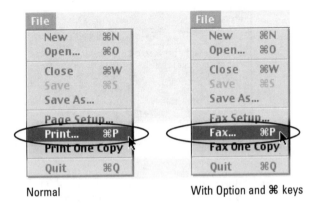

Normal   With Option and ⌘ keys

If you choose the Fax command, you'll be shown a window like this.

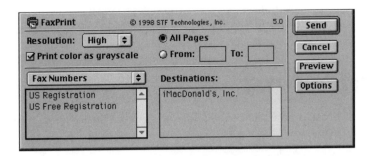

From the Fax Numbers pop-up menu, choose Temporary Address to specify your lucky recipient's fax number. When you're finished, you'll see that person's name on the right side of the window; click Send to send the fax.

If, by the way, you plan to send faxes to the same person more than once in your lifetime — a distinct possibility — you may wonder how to avoid having to use the Temporary Address feature every time you fax.

Easy. Find the program called Fax Browser on your hard drive (in a folder called FAXstf, in your Applications folder). Launch it. From the Window menu, choose Fax Numbers; in the next window, click the New Contact button and then type your correspondent's name, fax number, and other info (pressing Tab to jump from blank to blank). Repeat until you've input all your fax numbers.

From now on, whenever you send a fax, specifying the recipient is as easy as dragging the recipient's name from the left-side list to the right-side list, as shown here.

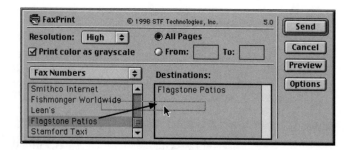

Oh, and one more thing. Suppose you fax a *lot*, and you find it a royal pain in the sacrum to have to launch the Fax Browser program every time you want to add a fax number to your permanent list. Wouldn't it be easier, you're thinking, to be able to add a fax number to your permanent fax book when you *send* the fax, right in the FaxPrint box (as shown in the previous picture)?

If so, a few dollars buys you the full, professional version of FAXstf. See the upgrade information in the FAXstf folder.

Receive Faxes

If you promise not to tell anyone, here's a little secret: Your iMac can *receive* faxes, too.

Now, if you want to be able to get faxes, you must treat your iMac like a fax machine: that is, dedicate a second phone line to it — or live with having to plug it into your phone jack (thus blocking normal voice calls) every time you're expecting a fax.

Here's how to do it: First, find the folder on your hard drive called FAXstf. In there is a program called Fax Browser.

Launch Fax Browser. From the Edit menu, choose Settings. On the left, scroll until you see the icon for Fax Modem; click it. You'll see a pop-up menu that lets you make the fax/modem answer the phone when it rings (and how many rings). If it says Never, then yours won't answer the phone.

When the fax comes in, your Apple menu blinks. Launch Fax Browser to read and, if you like, print the fax.

There. I just saved you $200.

Fit in Your Pocket

It happens to the best of us: You've truly integrated your iMac into your life. It's got your calendar, your phone numbers, your to-do list — everything you need. And now you need to leave the house. What's an iMac fan to do?

Your options are:

- ✔ Stuff your iMac into your pocket before each trip. Shred your clothes and look like an imbecile as you walk into business meetings with unsightly bulges.
- ✔ Get a PalmPilot.

A PalmPilot is one of those amazing handheld computers, about the size of an audio cassette. You can buy various models from various companies, from the Handspring Visor ($180) to the Palm V ($400). Except for their looks, they're all basically alike. Each comes with a little stand that plugs into your iMac and sucks out a copy all your critical information: your calendar, phone book, to-do list, memos, and even e-mail. (The Handspring Visor plugs straight into your iMac's USB jack and comes with all the software you need; the Palm devices require a $40 USB adapter, as described in Appendix C.)

The really great part is that, when you return home from your trip, you plug the PalmPilot back into your iMac — and any changes you made while on the road are automatically sent *back* to the calendar and address book on the iMac.

You can't run iMac *programs* on a PalmPilot, but you *can* keep your life's critical information with you without buying a second computer or new wardrobe. If, as suggested in Chapter 9, you keep your appointments and phone book in the Palm Desktop program that came with your iMac, you have no further steps to make. Suppose you return from a meeting with several new phone numbers you've written into your PalmPilot. You just place it in the cradle, press the Sync button, and your PalmPilot and your copy of Palm Desktop (on the iMac) automatically update each other. (Now you know why it's called *Palm* Desktop.)

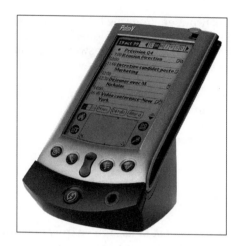

Record Sounds

The iMac has a microphone built right into the front. It's not exactly the same one Madonna licks in her videos, but it's good enough for what we're about to do. And that is to change the little beep/ding sound the iMac makes (when you make a mistake) into some other sound, like "Oops!" or a game-show buzzer or a burp or something.

How to record a sound

Here's how it works:

1. **From the menu, choose SimpleSound.**
2. **Click the Add button.**
3. **To record, just click Record and speak into the microphone.**

   Be ready to click Stop when you're done, or else you'll accidentally include a bunch of silence and fumbling at the end of your sound.

You can play back your new sound in a plethora of ways. You could, mnemonically enough, click the Play button. Then again, you could click Save and give the sound a title so that you'll be able to preserve it for your grandchildren. When you return to the list of sounds in the Sound control panel, click your new sound's name to play it. If you leave it selected in the list, though, you've just selected it to be your new error beep.

A sound-playing fact for the detail-obsessed

Here's a way to play a sound that doesn't even involve opening a control panel: If you're a double-clicking kinda person, open your System Folder and then double-click the System *file*. It opens into a window showing all your fonts and all your sounds. Just double-click any sound's icon to hear it played.

How to adjust your iMac's speaker volume

While we're on the subject of sound, now would be as good a time as any to show you how to adjust your iMac's sound volume.

The easy way, of course, is to use the Control Strip, described and illustrated in Chapter 12.

The macho way (*translation:* long way) is to choose Control Panels from your menu. Open the one called Monitors & Sound or just Sound. You'll see the master volume sliders for all the various sound-makers attached to your iMac.

This is also, by the way, where to tell the iMac *what* it should be recording: the sounds from your microphone, for example, or the sounds from a music CD you've put into your CD drive. Use the Sound Input pop-up menu to switch between them.

Run Windows Programs

It's true: Never again must you feel game-deprived. The iMac can run almost any Windows program alive. All you need is a program like SoftWindows or Virtual PC. Your Windows programs won't run quite as fast as they would on the fastest actual Windows *computers* — but they'll run.

Print Photos

Armed with a digital camera (see Chapter 18) and a color printer (see Chapter 5), there's no reason for you to spend money and time waiting for your photographs to get developed. Now you can spend money and time printing them from your iMac, instead.

The bad news: The glossy photo paper costs $1 per letter-sized sheet. You can't make enlargements — if you try to enlarge your digital photos, they start to look grainy. The digital camera (but not the printer) is expensive.

The good news: The printing is fairly fast. It looks amazing, especially on the $1-a-sheet glossy paper. And you can edit your photos before you print them, correcting the color tint, adding or removing bushes, adding or removing unwanted family members.

Part VII
Appendixes

The 5th Wave   By Rich Tennant

In this part . . .

Here they are: The appendixes you've been waiting for. How to set up your computer, what stuff you can buy for it, and where to get it.

Appendix A

How to Set Up an iMac

· ·

Setting up the iMac should take less than five minutes; all you have to do is plug in a few cables. (See Chapter 5 for instructions on plugging in your printer.)

I Took Off the Shrink Wrap! Now What?

When it comes to setting up your iMac, a few pointers:

✔ When you lift the computer, use the handle on top, sure — but support the bottom front edge with your other hand. (The handle-like thing on the *bottom* isn't actually a handle, and it won't support the weight of the iMac. So don't carry it upside down.)

✔ Figure out where you're going to put the thing. Unless you're into pain, don't put it on a desk where the keyboard will be higher than your elbows.

✔ Decide whether or not it's worth flipping out the "foot" bar at the bottom of the iMac's front edge. Try the viewing angle with and without the foot.

Once you've nestled the iMac into its new home, here's how to set up the rest of it:

1. **Plug the mouse into one end of the keyboard.**

   It makes no difference which side — if you're left-handed, you can plug the mouse into the left end of the keyboard.

2. **Observe the jacks on the right side of the iMac, as shown on the next page:**

   On older iMac models, these jacks (also called ports) are hidden behind the plastic door on the right side of the machine. Open this door by sticking your finger into the big hole and pulling; the door opens downward.

   On newer models, there's no plastic door. The ports are staring you in the face 24 hours a day.

3. **Plug the keyboard into one of the two small rectangular USB jacks on the right side of the iMac, as shown here:**

Orignal (CD tray) iMacs

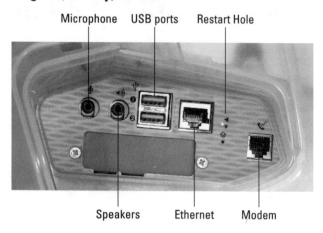

Current (CD slot) iMacs

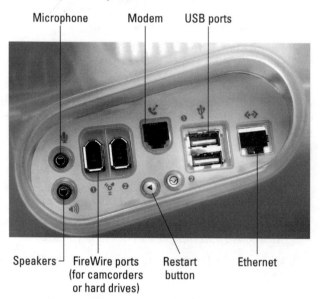

4. **Plug the iMac's power cord into the wall.**

The shocking truth about the iMac's side panel

All of the iMac's jacks are neatly tucked on the right side of the machine.

Surprisingly enough, however, the *cables* aren't supposed to snake out through the big round hole in the middle of the plastic door (if your iMac model even *has* a door). Instead, they're supposed to emerge through the two gaps at the *bottom* of this side-panel door, on either side

of the hinge. (The big round hole in the middle is for your finger, so that you can pull the door open.)

On the other hand, hundreds of thousands of people mistakenly trail their cables through the round finger hole, and nobody's yet been arrested.

---

5. **If you plan to sign up for the Internet or America Online, plug the included piece of telephone wire into the modem jack on the side of the iMac.**

Don't plug the phone wire into the wrong jack! The modem (correct) and Ethernet (wrong) jacks look almost identical. You want the one marked with the tiny telephone picture. On older iMacs, the modem port is on the far right. On iMac models with slot-loading CD-ROM drives, the modem port is dead center.

The other end of the phone wire, meanwhile, goes into a telephone jack in the wall, as described in Chapter 6.

Switching the iMac on

Quick! Flip to Chapter 1!

What You've Got Here

You'll hear all kinds of numbers and specifications tossed around when you go computer shopping. But the only four that matter are (1) how big its hard drive is, (2) how much memory it has, (3) what processor chip is inside, and (4) how fast it runs. I thought you might be interested in knowing how your iMac rates.

✔ **Hard-disk space.** The first number that matters is the size of the hard disk inside the iMac. The size is measured in *gigabytes*. (If you're at a cocktail party, you can say *gigs* for short.)

The stuff that you'll be creating — letters, manuscripts, whatever — is pretty small. This entire book would take up about *2* megabytes of the thousands available on your hard disk. But if you plan to work with graphics or digital movies, your hard drive could actually fill up over time.

The iMac's hard drive size depends on the model you bought. Original iMac models had hard drives that hold 4 or 6 gigs. (There are 1,000 megabytes in 1 gigabyte.) The late-1999 models' hard drives hold 6, 10, or (in the Special Edition model) 13 gigs. *That* ought to keep you busy for awhile.

✔ **Memory.** As described in Chapter 1½, *memory* is where your work resides while you're actually working on it (as opposed to the hard drive, where your work hangs out when the computer is off). But memory is much more expensive than disk space, so you get a lot less of it.

The 1998 iMacs came with 32 megs of memory; today's models come with 64 or (in the Special Edition model) even 128 megs. The more memory you have, the more you can do with your computer simultaneously (type in one window, surf the Web in another, and so on).

Newspaper ads often give you both critical numbers (memory and disk space) separated by a slash. You may read, for example, "iMac 64/10G." In your newfound savvy, you know that this model has 64 megs of memory and a 10 gig hard drive for permanent storage.

✔ **Processor chip model.** The third important number is the name of the primary processor chip. The heart of an iMac is the famous *PowerPC G3* chip.

✔ **Processor chip speed.** A chip's speed is something like blood pressure; it's how fast the data moves through the machine's circuits. The range of speeds, measured (get this) in *megahertz,* is 8 (on the original 1984 iMac) to 500 or more (the latest Power Macs). Your original iMac runs at 233, 266, or 333 MHz; the models introduced in late 1999 run at 350 or 400. Faster ones become available about every six months.

(*Caution:* You can't compare megahertz ratings among different chips or different kinds of computers. For example, you might think that a 400 MHz iMac would be just as fast as a 400 MHz "Intel inside" clone. Nope! The iMac would be much faster.)

Mastering Your Monitor

The iMac's screen is adjustable. You can zoom in or out, magnifying or shrinking everything on the screen (see "Zooming into your screen" in Chapter 13). Technically speaking, your iMac has a 15-inch monitor — but when you zoom out to its highest resolution, those 15 inches cram in as much as you'd see on a traditional *17*-inch screen — just smaller.

As you go through life with your awesome new iMac, keep this fact in mind — and feel free to adjust the monitor setting depending on the kind of work you're doing.

Attaching a second monitor

It's worth noting, by the way, that if you have an iMac "DV" model, you can hook up a second, *bigger* monitor. You'll see precisely the same image on both screens (the built-in screen and the external one). But if you find that the most "zoomed out" setting of the iMac's built-in screen (1024 x 768) makes the picture too small, attaching a big fat 17-inch (or larger) external screen may be just the ticket. The ability to attach a big external monitor is useful if you use your iMac to make presentations, too; you can connect the iMac to, for example, a projector in an auditorium.

Here's how you set up a second monitor:

1. **Turn off the iMac. Replace the vented cover on the iMac's back panel with the special, "VGA" vented cover provided in the accessory kit that came with your iMac.**

   For step-by-step instructions, choose Mac Help from your Help menu. Search for "external monitor."

2. **Attach the cable from the second monitor to the monitor port on the back of the iMac, like this:**

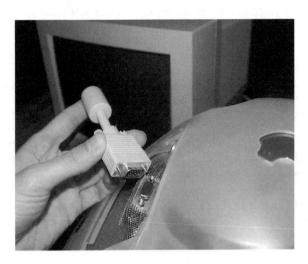

For the record, the back of the iMac has what's called a *VGA connector.* That's the same kind of monitor jack found on every Windows PC on earth, and all Mac models since 1996. If you have an even older Mac monitor, you can get an inexpensive adapter for it; visit an electronics shop, a CompUSA, or an appropriate Web site, for example, *www. griffintechnology.com.*

3. **Turn on the iMac.**

   Both screens light up.

4. **Use the Control Strip to choose a degree of magnification for both screens, as shown here:**

You can choose among three settings: 640 x 480 (very large), 800 x 600 (sort of large), or 1024 x 768 (perfect for a 17-inch monitor).

A bit about color bits

Your iMac can show three degrees of color richness. That is, you can switch your screen from showing a total of 256 different colors (which makes photos look kind of blotchy), thousands of colors (which makes photos look great), or *millions* of colors (which makes photos look unbelievable).

To switch among these different settings, use your Control Strip, as shown in the previous illustration. This time, however, click the tile that looks like a rainbow. You'll be offered several choices — "256 Colors," "Thousands of Colors," and so on. Use "Thousands" or higher when you're editing photos or movies. (The original iMac's circuitry can't manage the "Millions" setting when you've selected the 1024 x 768 magnification mode, as described two paragraphs ago. The revised iMac, released in November 1998, can.)

Aren't you glad you asked?

The Resource Resource

Magazines

MacHome Journal
For beginners, students, at-home Mac users. Visit the Web site, sample the articles, to judge the tone.
800-800-6542
415-957-1911
www.machome.com

Macworld
News, reviews, analysis; more advanced. You can always read the articles and reviews, for free, at the Web site, so that you can try before subscribing.
800-288-6848
303-447-9330
www.macworld.com

MacAddict
Fun, irreverent, lots of games and gadgets; every issue comes with a CD-ROM filled with goodies. The articles aren't on the Web site, however.
800-666-6889
415-468-2500
www.macaddict.com

User Groups

Apple User-Group Info Line
800-538-9696 ext. 500
Call to get the number of the nearest Mac club.

Deep-Discount Mail-Order Joints

Contact these outfits when you're interested in buying any of the programs or add-ons described in this book.

MacConnection
www.macconnection.com
800-800-4444

MacWarehouse
www.macwarehouse.com
800-255-6227

Mac Zone
www.maczone.com
800-248-0800

Cyberian Outpost
www.outpost.com
(800) 856-9800
(860) 927-2050

Shopper.com
www.shopper.com
A Web site that compares prices of computer add-ons and software from every mail-order firm on the Web. You'd be crazy not to comparison shop here before buying anything; you can save major money on everything you buy.

Great iMac Web Pages

MacSurfer
www.macsurfer.com
A daily roundup of articles about the Mac from newspapers and magazines around the country. Click a listing to read that article.

iMacintouch
www.imacintouch.com

TheiMac.com
www.theimac.com

iMacworld.com
www.imacworld.com

iMacCentral
www.imaccentral.com
News, updates, tricks, and
product announcements —
all about the iMac.

SiteLink
www.sitelink.net
A Web page that links to
other Web pages about
the Mac (and the iMac).
You'll be on the Web until
you're 90.

MacOS Rumors
www.macosrumors.com
The *National Enquirer* of the
Macintosh world — wild,
juicy, sometimes erroneous
rumors about Apple's
secret plans for the future.

Lots of Homegrown Web sites
The Web is full of additional
iMac-related Web sites.
Generally, they're unproof-
read but entertaining, each
run by one or two people.
You might scope out, for
example, iMac2day,
iMacOnline, Daily iMac,
Everything iMac, and so on.
(The Web address is
always the same:
www.___.com, where the
Web page name goes in the
blank. No spaces allowed.)

Appendix C

The Ultimate iMac Buyer's Guide

*T*his appendix lists dozens of gadgets and accessories. Most plug into the iMac's USB jack, and many match the iMac's striking translucent looks. Get out your Visa card, read the details using the Web-page addresses I've included here, and go wild.

As for the prices here — consider them rough guides. Not only do they rise and fall like John Travolta's career, but some companies list "street" prices (what you'll actually pay) and others list *list* prices, which nobody actually pays.

One more thing: Unless you mail me your front-door key, it's going to be a little tough for me to keep the following pages updated. On the Web, however, various lists of iMac-compatible products are updated constantly. Try, for example, these two authoritative lists of Mac- and iMac add-ons:

- ✔ Apple's list of USB-compatible products at *http://guide.apple.com/ uscategories/usb.html*. Includes clickable links to the Web pages of every company listed here.

- ✔ iMacintouch, which is at *www.Macintouch.com/imacusb.html*. It's a similarly up-to-date listing of add-ons for Macs and iMacs.

Printers & Printer Adapters

With the proper cables, you can plug your iMac into any of — get this — over 1,500 different printer models. For example, the following companies make iMac-ready printers:

Alps MD-1300 — Chapter 5 describes the most common kind of printers: inkjets and laser printers. There's a third kind, though: *dye sublimation,* which is less common because it's usually astronomically expensive. This photo-quality dyesub printer, however, is only $400 — and unlike inkjets, the color printouts from *this* baby don't smear or fade.

Alps also makes an even higher-res photo printer, the $600 MD-5000 Desk Top Print Shop, shown here, which lays down a staggering number of dots per inch (2,400 dpi). A $99 USB adapter cable is required for both printers. Alps, *www.alps.com.*

Epson — The Stylus Color line of inkjet printers are incredibly popular with Mac and iMac fans. They're inexpensive, yet produce gorgeous color printouts; the bestselling model, the 740, even comes with a translucent blueberry plastic cover to match your iMac (you can order a replacement to match your iMac's color). The 740 prints five pages per minute up to 1,440 dots per inch, and costs about $240; models 750, 900, and 1,200 are faster and higher-quality. A few older models (440, 600, 640, EX, 700, 800, 850, 1520, or 3000) can work, too, but only if you also buy the $50 USB/Parallel Printer Adapter Kit. *www.epson.com/printer.*

GCC Technologies — Inkjet, schminkjet: if you're in business for yourself, you really should have a laser printer for top-quality, smudgeproof, black-and-white printouts. GCC makes several under $1,000, which you can attach to your iMac either with a USB cable or an Ethernet cable (see Chapter 14). *www.gcctech.com.*

Hewlett-Packard — HP has been making great printers for decades; the color inkjets in the DeskJet series, such as the 810C, 812C, 880C, 895Cse, and 895Cxi all connect directly to the iMac's USB jack. (Remember, the USB cable is almost never included with printers.) HP makes nice laser printers, too, that connect to your Ethernet jack (see Chapter 14). *www.hp.com/ cgibin/peripherals/pandi.pl.*

iPrint and **Asanté** — Farallon makes two $110 adapters that accommodate pre-USB Macintosh printers. One, the iPrint LT, is for *LocalTalk* printers (usually laser printers); also requires a PhoneNet connector (see Chapter 5) for the printer. This device's less expensive rival is the AsantéTalk adapter (around $90; *www.asante.com*).

Farallon's other adapter, the iPrint SL, is for injket printers like Apple StyleWriters (models I, II, 1200, 1500, 2200, 2400, and 2500). Each iPrint plugs into your iMac's Ethernet jack. *www.farallon.com.*

Lexmark Optra E310 — Lexmark, the printer division of IBM, designed this very inexpensive ($400) compact laser printer (8 pages per minute, 600 dots per inch) to connect to the iMac's USB port. (If you're planning to set up an Ethernet network, as described in Chapter 14, you can also consider any of Lexmark's other laser printers, which connect to the Ethernet jack instead.) *www.lexmark.com/printers/laser/index.html*

PowerPrint USB to Parallel — Talk about mind-blowing choices: This $100 adapter kit lets your iMac hook up to any of 1,500 different *IBM-compatible* printers — every conceivable kind, price, and model. Comes with software and a cable that hooks up to one of your USB jacks. Infowave, *www.infowave.com.*

Multifunction Printers

These machines combine several functions in a single gadget — ideal if you work out of a *very* small office. Canon, for example, makes the $380 MultiPass C635, which includes a scanner, fax machine, color copier, and color printer (*www.ccsi.canon.com/prodfact/c635.html*).

Epson, meanwhile, makes the Stylus Scan 2000, Stylus Scan 2500, and Stylus Scan 2500 Pro — $350, $500, and $700, respectively — which vary by scanning quality and features. Each is primarily a scanner, copier, and printer; however, these machines don't include a fax modem. Your iMac, however, does. *www.epsonamerica.com.*

Adapters for Older Mac Gadgets

Serial, ADB, and *SCSI* are three kinds of jacks not found on the iMac. (*Serial* means "modem or printer jack," *ADB* means "keyboard or mouse jack," and *SCSI* means "external hard drive, Zip drive, or scanner jack.") But because all 150 previous Macintosh models had them, thousands of older, pre-iMac add-on gadgets are alive, well, and kicking around the offices of the world. Fortunately, they can connect to an iMac with one of these adapters.

Serial adapters

A *serial* port is the small round connector on old Macs — where you used to plug in your modem, printer, PalmPilot, digital camera, or digital drawing tablet. The following adapters hook into your iMac's USB port; you plug your old Mac gadget into the adapter.

USB Serial adapters

This kind of adapter box accommodates many StyleWriter, Epson, or HP printer models; the PalmPilot cradle; certain digital cameras; and even Wacom drawing tablets. Read the compatibility lists on the corresponding Web sites before buying, however; this kind of adapter doesn't work with MIDI, GeoPort, LocalTalk, or some printer models. Keyspan's USB Twin Serial Adapter is $80, offers two serial ports, works with all StyleWriter models, and is pictured here (*www.keyspan.com*); Entrega's is made of translucent plastic, costs $80, and is called the CON-USB-D8 (*www.entrega.com*).

ADB (mouse and keyboard) adapters

The iMate is a little translucent adapter that lets you plug old-style (ADB) Macintosh keyboards and mice into the iMac's USB jack. $40 from Griffin Technology, *www.griffintechnology.com*.

Microphone adapters

The iMic adapter lets you plug any microphone or RCA-jack line input into your iMac's USB jack. $25 from Griffin Technology, *www.griffintechnology.com*.

SCSI adapters

SCSI (pronounced "scuzzy") technology can be a royal headache, sometimes requiring much fiddling and experimenting. It's a type of connector and fat cabling found on all pre-iMac Macintosh models. But if you've got some aging SCSI gadget (such as a Zip drive, Jaz drive, hard drive, or scanner) that you want to mate with your iMac, a USB-to-SCSI adapter will fit the bill.

You can choose the $80 USB SCSI Converter from Entrega (*www.entrega.com*), the $80 ScUSBee from Second Wave (*www.2ndwave.com*), the $80 USB XpressSCSI from Microtech (*www.microtechint.com*), the $80 iSCSI from Ariston (*www.ariston.com*), or the $80 uSCSI from Newer Technology (*www.newertech.com*).

Digital Cameras

As you can read in Chapter 18, as expensive gadgetry goes, these babies are pretty wonderful.

QuickCam VC — This $80 golf-ball-sized USB-jack camera can take still pictures (352 x 288 dots, which is pretty small) and even digital movies (at about 15 frames per second). It's got an adjustable focus lens and a six-foot cable. (The QuickCam itself is sold for Windows computers only. But with the addition of the free software located at *www.logitech.com/Cameras/ quickcamvcmac.html,* it'll work with your iMac, too.) Logitech, *www.logitech.com.*

iSee Camera — This archrival to the QuickCam looks nearly identical: It's a two-inch gray sphere. But its picture-taking quality is better (640 x 480 resolution), and the price ($110) isn't bad. iSee plugs directly into your iMac's USB jack, and it can even make low-res digital movies. From Ariston, *www.ariston.com.*

Digital Cameras — These digital cameras don't use film. Instead, you get a TV-style display built into the camera to see your pictures. You can delete the ones that didn't turn out and try again; when the camera's memory is full, you dump the pictures onto your iMac for viewing, editing, and sending over the Internet. All of these cameras plug directly into your iMac's USB jack. The average cost is around $700. Kodak's line of cameras (such as the DC220, DC280, DC290, and so on), is pictured here, and is described at *www.kodak.com/US/en/nav/digital.shtml;* for Toshiba's line, try *www.toshiba.com/taisisd/dsc/products/cameras/index3.htm.*

ImageMate — Many digital cameras use, as "film," a removable memory card called a CompactFlash card. This $90 gadget is an external reader/writer of such cards, so that you can rapidly transfer pictures from thus-equipped digital cameras to your iMac. From SanDisk, *http://www.sandisk.com/ cons/imagemate-USB.htm.*

PC Card Reader or **CameraMate USB** — These machines accept *PC cards,* yet another form of "electronic film" used by today's digital cameras (including the abovementioned Kodak models). Fill up a PC card with pictures, slip it into a PC Card Reader, and it's transferred to your iMac. $150 for Ariston's card, *www.ariston.com,* or $90 for the Microtech CameraMate, *www.microtechint.com.*

Disk Drives

The iMac doesn't come with a built-in floppy drive. Although there are plenty of ways to back up your work without disks, most people prefer to be able to carry their stuff around on a disk. These gadgets plug into your USB jack.

External floppy drives — Buy one of these, and now your iMac has a floppy drive that you can detach and leave behind when you're traveling. Compare the styling and features of, for example, the $100 uDrive (Newer Technologies, *www.newertech.com*), the $80 iFloppy (iDrives, *www.idrives.com*), the $85 SmartFDD (Microtech, *www.microtech-pc.com*), or the $90 USB Floppy Drive (VST, *www.vsttech.com*).

None of these devices require a power cord; they get electricity from the iMac itself. (The uDrive comes with a power cord, though, if you'd prefer that the drive not sip juice from the computer itself.)

SuperDisk drives — A SuperDisk drive looks just like an external floppy drive — many are made of iMac-colored translucent plastic — but it's a two-in-one disk drive. It accepts *both* floppy disks (from Macs or Windows machines) *and* SuperDisks, which look like floppies but hold 83 times more (120 megs). Those bigger-capacity disks are $65 for a five-pack.

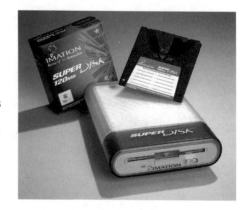

SuperDisk drives (pictured here) are sold by Imation ($140, *www. imation.com*), Winstation ($150, *www.winstation.com/ssdspec.html*), or Global Village ($170, *www.globalvillage.com*).

USB Zip Drive — A Zip drive is another kind of external disk drive. It doesn't accept standard floppy disks, but it does accept Zip disks that hold 100 or 250 megabytes, depending on the model you buy, just like the millions found in Macs and PCs worldwide. You can get, for example, the Anaconda Zip 250 (from EZQUest, *www.ezq.com/z250.html*), the regular Zip drive from the maker, Iomega (about $130 for the 100MB version, more for the 250MB, *www.iomega.com*), or the extremely sleek, small Mil Zip 100 ($200, *www.microtech-pc.com/products_imac.shtml*). Zip disks cost about $12 each.

Rewriteable CD-ROM drives — Using one of these gadgets, you can actually make your *own* CDs, filled with either music (for your stereo) or information (for your iMac). Note, however, that actually figuring out how to use them is not a task for the weak of stomach (or the new to computing). They're sold by LaCie ($300, *www.lacie.com*), Mitsumi ($380, *www.mitsumi.com*), and QPS ($275, *www.qps-inc.com*).

Additional hard drives — Your iMac's hard drive is immense by 1995 standards, but not so huge by today's. If you're heavily into graphics, digital sound, or digital movies, your 3.2 gigabytes will fill up quickly.

Most people solve the "out of space" problem by buying a Zip or SuperDisk drive, as described in the previous paragraphs. A few, however, prefer to add *another* hard drive. An external USB hard drive is about the size of a deck of cards, and could not be more convenient — it requires no power cord, and its cable pops right into your USB port. VST, for example, makes sleek, attractive hard drives in capacities of 4 and 6 gigabytes ($330 and $400, *www.vsttech.com*), and with both tangerine and blueberry cases. If you need even more space than that, and don't care so much about looks, visit *www.fantomdrives.com*, where you'll find hard drives from 4.3 gigs ($260) all the way up to a mind-blowing *25* gigs ($530).

If you have an iMac DV, moreover, you can attach a *FireWire* hard drive. The term FireWire refers to the way these hard drives attach to your iMac. (See Appendix A for a diagram that shows your FireWire jacks.) These amazing hard drives are extremely small and extremely fast, don't require external power, and don't require you to turn off the computer before plugging them in. They make an ideal means, therefore, of transferring lots of stuff back and forth between two FireWire-equipped Macs. The VST FireWire drives, shown above, are the most popular such drives (*www.vsttech.com*).

Joysticks and Game Pads

As far as its circuitry is concerned, the iMac is a great gadget for games. What's lousy, however, is the experience of trying to fly a Falcon fighter jet by dragging a *mouse.* Flying your plane/spaceship/laser destroyer is far more enjoyable with a joystick or gamepad instead.

You can choose from dozens of these USB devices — if I tried to describe them all here, I'd waste enough paper to tear down half the Brazilian rain forest. Begin your quest, therefore, at one of the Web sites listed at the beginning of this chapter — *www.imacintouch.com* or *http://guide.apple.com/ uscategories/usb.html.* Each has a special category listing for joysticks, game pads, and other gaming gadgets.

Keyboard and Mouse Replacements

What's great about the iMac's mouse and keyboard is that they're see-through and included in the price of the computer. What's not so great is that some people find the keyboard a little cheap and the mouse too round and too small. Thus is a market opportunity born . . .

Mice

Most iMac mice are made of translucent blue plastic. Some have two or three "mouse" buttons on top — they all, oddly enough, do exactly the same thing as the button on a one-button mouse. You can choose from the Podiki mouse, which is transparent right down to its power cord (Ariston, $25, *www.ariston.com);* the translucent blueberry Compucable USB mouse (*www.compucable.com*); the smoothly sculpted, see-through iMaccessories mouse ($20, *www.imaccessories.com*); MacAlly's iSweet mouse, which comes with five translucent snap-on fruit-colored shells ($40, *www.macally.com*); and many others. (MacAlly's iMouse is pictured here, at right.)

You might be particularly intrigued by Microsoft's $75 IntelliMouse USB, which is an *optical mouse.* It doesn't have a ball underneath to detect motion (a magnet for lint, cat hair, and other crud); instead, it detects motion using a tiny electronic eyeball underneath. You can program its two mouse buttons to perform different functions — and the smoothly turnable fingerwheel between the buttons lets you scroll down Web pages or word processor documents without having to use the actual scroll bar.

Trackballs

A *trackball* is another alternative to a mouse or mouse. It looks like an 8-ball in a pedestal; you control the mouse pointer by rolling the ball with your hand. The buttons are on either side.

Some people adore trackballs because they sit in one place and don't require a lot of desk space (the trackballs, that is), as a mouse does. Others find trackballs difficult to control. If you're a trackball kind of person, however, here are some to consider: The offering by Mousetrak has six big, programmable buttons around the ball, which you can set to click, double-click, or drag, for example (*www.mousetrak.com*). The one from iMaccessories ($40*www.imaccessories.com)* actually lights up. And the MacAlly iBall, pictured in the previous figure, at left, is made of cool see-through blue plastic ($30, *www.macally.com*).

Keyboards

The world teems with great USB add-on keyboards, like those from MacAlly (*www.macally.com*), iMaccessories (*www.imaccessories.com*), and Cherry(*www.cherrycorp.com*). Each has its own charms and features — for example, the Cherry keyboard is both a keyboard *and* a USB hub! Get this clever keyboard, and you also get four empty USB jacks, suitable for plugging in all the other gadgetry in this chapter. (Read about USB hubs at the end of this chapter.)

Scanners

As described in Chapter 11, a scanner is eyeballs for your iMac: It captures a flat image (usually a photo) and turns it into a graphics file (or even text file) on your computer. Once it's on the iMac, you can edit it, mail it to friends, and so on.

You'll find a complete line of USB scanners, starting at about $120, from Umax (*www.umax.com),* Agfa *(www.agfa.com),* Microtek (*www.microtek*.com), Epson (*www.epson.com*), and others.

You might even be intrigued by the NEC PetiScan (*www.petiscan.com*). It's a tiny little thing, 8.5 by 5.5 inches (and 1.4 inches tall), weighing only 1.3 pounds, and it doesn't need a power cord. It's too small to scan full-sized pages — the max scanning size is 5.8 by 3.9 inches — but as a portable photo scanner, there's nothing like it.

Speakers

If you've got one of the recent iMac models (the ones with the CD slot), you're already in sonic heaven, thanks to the built-in Harmon Kardon sound system. But if you've got one of the 2,000,000 iMacs sold before the end of 1999, your speakers are nowhere close to being able to shake the rafters. That's why you might consider plugging a pair of these into the speaker jack on the left side of your computer. You can find deliciously designed, translucent blueberry- or tangerine-encased speakers from, for example, Pele ($50, *www.pelezone.com*) or Ushischiba ($90, *www.cozo.com*).

If you're willing to forgo translucent fruit colors, you might also want to consider flat-panel speakers ($90, *www.benwin.com/fpmain.htm*) or 3D-spatially enhanced ones ($40, *www.ariston.com*). (Your local computer store stocks many other brands of computer speakers that aren't necessarily iMac-ish in design.)

USB Hubs

Once you've read this chapter, you'll no doubt be salivating, shouting: "All — I want 'em *all!*"

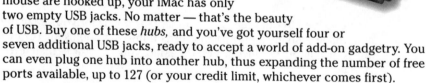

Assuming your credit line can, in fact, handle such extravagance, only one more obstacle stands in your way: Once the keyboard and mouse are hooked up, your iMac has only two empty USB jacks. No matter — that's the beauty of USB. Buy one of these *hubs,* and you've got yourself four or seven additional USB jacks, ready to accept a world of add-on gadgetry. You can even plug one hub into another hub, thus expanding the number of free ports available, up to 127 (or your credit limit, whichever comes first).

There are close to 34 trillion different USB hubs for sale; even USB hubs *not* designed for the iMac work with the iMac. Many of them, like the Interex model (*www.interex.com*) model pictured here, plus those made by Entrega, MacAlly, and iMaccessories, are made of translucent fruit-colored plastic, like the iMac.

Expect to pay about $50 for four USB jacks, and $80 for seven. Note, incidentally, that a few USB gadgets described in this chapter — especially scanners, CD-ROM makers, and SCSI adapters — require a lot of power. They work only when they're plugged *directly* into the iMac's USB jack or into a *powered* USB hub. Shop accordingly.

Index

Discover Dummies Online!

The Dummies Web Site is your fun and friendly online resource for the latest information about ...*For Dummies®* books and your favorite topics. The Web site is the place to communicate with us, exchange ideas with other ...*For Dummies* readers, chat with authors, and have fun!

Ten Fun and Useful Things You Can Do at www.dummies.com

1. Win free ...*For Dummies* books and more!
2. Register your book and be entered in a prize drawing.
3. Meet your favorite authors through the IDG Books Author Chat Series.
4. Exchange helpful information with other ...*For Dummies* readers.
5. Discover other great ...*For Dummies* books you must have!
6. Purchase Dummieswear™ exclusively from our Web site.
7. Buy ...*For Dummies* books online.
8. Talk to us. Make comments, ask questions, get answers!
9. Download free software.
10. Find additional useful resources from authors.

Link directly to these ten fun and useful things at
http://www.dummies.com/10useful

For other technology titles from IDG Books Worldwide, go to
www.idgbooks.com

Not on the Web yet? It's easy to get started with *Dummies 101®: The Internet For Windows® 98* or *The Internet For Dummies®*, 6th Edition, at local retailers everywhere.

Find other ...*For Dummies* books on these topics:
Business • Career • Databases • Food & Beverage • Games • Gardening • Graphics • Hardware
Health & Fitness • Internet and the World Wide Web • Networking • Office Suites
Operating Systems • Personal Finance • Pets • Programming • Recreation • Sports
Spreadsheets • Teacher Resources • Test Prep • Word Processing

IDG BOOKS WORLDWIDE
BOOK REGISTRATION

Register
This Book
and Win!

We want to hear from you!

Visit **http://my2cents.dummies.com** to register this book and tell us how you liked it!

- ✔ Get entered in our monthly prize giveaway.

- ✔ Give us feedback about this book — tell us what you like best, what you like least, or maybe what you'd like to ask the author and us to change!

- ✔ Let us know any other ...*For Dummies*® topics that interest you.

Your feedback helps us determine what books to publish, tells us what coverage to add as we revise our books, and lets us know whether we're meeting your needs as a ...*For Dummies* reader. You're our most valuable resource, and what you have to say is important to us!

Not on the Web yet? It's easy to get started with *Dummies 101*®: *The Internet For Windows*® *98* or *The Internet For Dummies*®, 6th Edition, at local retailers everywhere.

Or let us know what you think by sending us a letter at the following address:

...*For Dummies* Book Registration
Dummies Press
10475 Crosspoint Blvd.
Indianapolis, IN 46256

™

BESTSELLING
BOOK SERIES